History HL
FOR THE IB DIPLOMA
Europe

Sam Olofsson

PEAK

Published by:
Peak Study Resources Ltd
1 & 3 Kings Meadow
Oxford OX2 0DP
UK

www.peakib.com

History HL: Europe
Study & Revision Guide for the IB Diploma

ISBN 978-1-913433-42-0

© Sam Olofsson 2017–22

Sam Olofsson has asserted his right under the Copyright, Design and Patents Act 1988 to be identified as the author of this work.

All rights reserved. No part of this publication may be reproduced, stored in a retrieval system, or transmitted in any form or by any means, without the prior permission of the publishers.

PHOTOCOPYING ANY PAGES FROM THIS PUBLICATION,
EXCEPT UNDER LICENCE, IS PROHIBITED

Peak Study & Revision Guides for the IB Diploma have been developed independently of the International Baccalaureate Organization (IBO). 'International Baccalaureate' and 'IB' are registered trademarks of the IBO.

Books may be ordered directly from the publisher (see www.peakib.com) and through online or local booksellers. For enquiries regarding titles, availability or retailers, please email books@peakib.com or use the form at www.peakib.com/contact.

Printed and bound in the UK by CPI Group (UK) Ltd, Croydon, CR0 4YY

www.cpibooks.co.uk

Cover image: Map of Europe (Adobe Stock)

To write a guide covering Europe is difficult due to the fact that the History syllabus is extensive. No school covers all the topics in the syllabus and you will not find any textbook which covers all the topics in depth.

Consequently this guide is an attempt to show examples of topics that appear frequently on IB exams. The guide does not cover every bullet point in every related topic in the syllabus, it is more an attempt to focus on key topics.

While the book is titled "History HL", and is a natural fit with the History of Europe option that HL students may follow for Paper 3, there is also overlap with some of the World history options that are examined in Paper 2. I have included a table in the introduction showing the sections of the book and the parts of the syllabus to which they relate.

In the introduction I have also set out the way I think you can make best use of this guide with the time you have available to study and prepare for exams. Note that at the start of each topic I have made an attempt to identify issues worth considering when reading the text – try to keep them in mind.

This is material that I have compiled after more than 25 years of IB teaching at Malmö Borgarskola, and revision courses in Oxford, Cambridge and Boston. Today, I divide my time between teaching at Malmö Borgarskola – it is a passion – and working as Secretary General for Star for Life, an educational organisation reaching over 100,000 pupils in schools in Southern Africa.

I hope that this guide will provide you with historical knowledge and also encourage you to write outlines for essays – I strongly recommend that you prepare in this way.

Good luck!

Sam Olofsson

HISTORY HL: EUROPE

Acknowledgements

I am very grateful for the support and the advice that was given to me by one of the History Teachers at the OSC courses, Anders Arnberg. When writing a guide like this, it is invaluable to have other experienced teachers offer their perspectives and details to refine further my work.

List of figures

Figure 1.1: Engraving of Voltaire, 1889. H. Rousseau (Graphic Designer), E.Thomas (Engraver) Augustin Challamel, Desire Lacroix [Public domain], via Wikimedia Commons

Figure 1.2: Estates-General of 1789. Isidore-Stanislaus Helman (1743-1806) and Charles Monnet (1732-1808) (Bibliothèque nationale de France) [Public domain], via Wikimedia Commons

Figure 1.3: Declaration of the Rights of Man and of the Citizen in 1789. Jean-Jacques-François Le Barbier (1738 - 1826) (Musée Carnavalet) [Public domain] via Wikimedia Commons

Figure 1.4: The Third Estate (commoners) carrying the First (clergy) and Second Estate (nobility) on his back. Creator: M. P, Source: Bibliothèque nationale de France, [Public domain], via Wikimedia Commons

Figure 2.1: Map of the Unification of Italy. Rickard Lundquist (Own work)

Figure 2.2: Statue of Giuseppe Mazzini in Pisa. Sculpted by Orazio Andreoni (1883) — Creator: Harlock81 (Own work) [CC BY-SA 3.0 or GFDL], via Wikimedia Commons

Figure 2.3: Camillo Benso, Conte di Cavour by Francesco Hayez. Source: "10,000 Masterpieces of Painting", Collection: Pinacoteca di Brera, Milano, [Public domain], via Wikimedia Commons

Figure 2.4: Portrait of Giuseppe Garibaldi, Musée Masséna Nice. Dalbera (Flickr: Giuseppe Garibaldi (musée Masséna, Nice)) [CC BY 2.0], via Wikimedia Commons

Figure 3.1: German Zollverein, 1834-1919. Source: IEG-Maps project by Andreas Kunz, B. Johnen and Joachim Robert Moeschl: University of Mainz, User: 52 Pickup at the English language Wikipedia [GFDL, CC-BY-SA-3.0 or CC BY-SA 2.5], via Wikimedia Commons

Figure 3.2: Otto von Bismarck. Source: Kabinett-Photo, Creator: AD.BRAUN & Cie Dornach [Public domain], via Wikimedia Commons

Figure 3.3: The Province of Schleswig-Holstein (red), within the Kingdom of Prussia, within the German Empire, 1866-1920. Source: IEG-Maps project by Andreas Kunz, B. Johnen and Joachim Robert Moeschl: University of Mainz, User: 52 Pickup [CC BY-SA 2.5], via Wikimedia Commons

Figure 4.1: The Treaty of Frankfurt that endend the Franco-Prussian War. Author: Sendker, Source: Bismarck Foundation and Archives in Friedrichsruh (Schleswig-Holstein), [Public domain], via Wikimedia Commons

Figure 4.2: 'Between Berlin and Rome', with Bismarck on the left and the Pope on the right, from the German satirical magazine *Kladderadatsch*, 1875. Creator: Wilhelm Scholz (1824-1893), Source: *Kladderadatsch* May 16, 1875; again in Bismarck album of *Kladderadatsch*. With three hundred drawings by Wilhelm Scholz and four facsimilierten letters of the Chancellor. Berlin 91890, p.86, [Public domain], via Wikimedia Commons

Figure 4.3: A barricade on Rue Voltaire, after its capture by the regular army during the Bloody Week. Creator: Bruno Braquehais (1823-1875), Source: BHVP/Roger-Viollet, [Public domain], via Wikimedia Commons

Figure 5.1: Alexander II of Russia. Creator: Neizvsten, Source: Runivers cultural and historical project, [Public domain], via Wikimedia Commons

Figure 5.2: A peasant leaving his landlord on Yuriev Day (a feast day of St. George in autumn to celebrate the end of the harvesting season). Creator: Sergey Vasilyevich Ivanov, [Public domain], via Wikimedia Commons/Ghirlandajo

Figure 6.1: Coronation of Nicholas the II by Valentin Serov. Creator: Valentin Alexandrowitsch Serow [Public domain], via Wikimedia Commons/Alex Bakharev

Figure 6.2: Russian wheat field where USDA plant explorers found wheat varieties from which they later bred the disease-resistant wheat that saved the wheat-growing industry in the West, ca. 1910. Department of Agriculture. Office of the Secretary. Office of Information. 1925-ca. 1981 (https://catalog.archives.gov/id/5729275)

Figure 6.3: A locomotive overturned by striking workers at the main railway depot in Tiflis in 1905. Source: Jones, Stephen F. (2005), Socialism in Georgian Colors: The European Road to Social Democracy, 1883-1917. Harvard University Press, ISBN 0674019024, Creator: Unknown, [Public domain], via Wikimedia Commons

Figure 6.4: Pyotr Stolypin, Third Chairman of Council of Ministers of the Russian Empire. From the George Grantham Bain collection at the Library of Congress. According to the library, there are no known copyright restrictions on the use of this work, via Wikimedia Commons

Figure 7.1: Patrol of the October Revolution. Source: The magazine "Our Heritage", 1988; The original is kept in the Central State Archive of Film and Photo Documents of St. Petersburg, storing the code D 14594., Author: J. Steinberg, [Public domain], via Wikimedia Commons

Figure 7.2: Petrograd, July 4, 1917. Street demonstration on Nevsky Prospekt just after troops of the Provisional Government have opened fire with machine guns. Source: Sergey Morozov. Creative Photography. MM:. Publishing house "Planeta", 3rd edition, 1989, ISBN 5-85250-029-1, Author: Viktor Bulla (1883-1938), [Public domain], via Wikimedia Commons

Figure 7.3: Anti-Bolshevik Volunteer Army in South Russia, January 1918. Source: "La guerre en Russie et en Sibérie" by Grondijs, Lodewijk Hermen, [Public domain], via Wikimedia Commons

Figure 8.1: Vladimir Lenin. Source: United States Library of Congress's Prints and Photographs division under the digital ID cph.3c01877, Author: Soyuzfoto, [Public domain], via Wikimedia Commons

Figure 8.2: Photocopy of the first two pages of Brest-Litovsk Peace Treaty between Soviet Russia and Germany, Austria-Hungary, Bulgaria and Turkey, March 1918. German photograph, [Public domain, copyright expired], via Wikimedia Commons/Andros64

Figure 9.1: The first page of the edition of the *Domenica del Corriere*, an Italian paper, with a drawing of Achille Beltrame depicting Gavrilo Princip killing Archduke Francis Ferdinand of Austria in Sarajevo. Creator: Achille Beltrame, [Public domain], via Wikimedia Commons

Figure 10.1: The Paris Peace Conference: signing of the Treaty of Versailles in the Hall of Mirrors. Source: US National Archives, [Public domain], via Wikimedia Commons

Figure 12.1: Benito Mussolini dressed in the Fascist uniform. Source: German Federal Archives, Aktuelle-Bilder-Centrale, Georg Pahl (Bild 102), Creator: Unknown, [CC BY-SA 3.0 DE], via Wikimedia Commons

Figure 12.2: The March on Rome: Mussolini surrounded by Black-Shirts. Original author of photograph unknown, [Public domain], via Wikimedia Commons/R-41

Figure 12.3: A 20 lire coin from 1928. [GFDL or CC BY-SA 3.0], via Wikimedia Commons/Sailko

Figure 13.1: German states during the Weimar Republic period. Source: Putzger – Historischer Weltatlas, 89. Auflage, 1965, [GFDL, CC-BY-SA-3.0 or CC BY 2.5], via Wikimedia Commons/Kgberger

Figure 13.2: Barricade in Berlin during the uprising, January 1919. Source: Scan from the original - Bernd Schwabe in Hannover, Creator: Alfred Grohs, [CC BY 3.0], via Wikimedia Commons

Figure 13.3: Franz von Papen. Bundesarchiv, Bild 183-S00017 / CC-BY-SA 3.0 [CC BY-SA 3.0 DE], via Wikimedia Commons

Figure 14.1: Adolf Hitler and Ernst Röhm inspecting the SA in Nuremberg in 1933. Bundesarchiv, Bild 146-1982-159-21A / CC-BY-SA 3.0 [CC BY-SA 3.0 DE], via Wikimedia Commons

Figure 14.2: Adolf Hitler at the Nuremberg Rally, September 1935. Source: Charles Russell Collection, NARA, [Public domain], via Wikimedia Commons

Figure 15.1: Soviet dictator Joseph Stalin. By Ephraim Stillberg (Own work) [CC BY-SA 3.0 or GFDL], via Wikimedia Commons

Figure 16.1: Anachronistic world map showing member states of the League of Nations from 1920 to 1945. User: Reallyjoel (Own work), [CC BY-SA 3.0], via Wikimedia Commons

Figure 16.2: The Gap in the Bridge: cartoon about the absence of the USA from the League of Nations. Source: *Punch* Magazine 10 December 1919 Raffo, P. (1974), Creator: Leonard Raven- Hill, [Public domain], via Wikimedia Commons

Figure 17.1: Benito Mussolini and Adolf Hitler in 1938. Bundesarchiv, Bild 146-1969-065-24/ [CC BY-SA 3.0 DE], via Wikimedia Commons

Figure 17.2: Molotov-Ribbentrop Pact—political map of Central Europe in 1939-40. Creator: Peter Hanula (Own work - Based on File:Ribbentrop-Molotov.PNG.) [GFDL or CC-BY-SA-3.0], via Wikimedia Commons

Figure 18.1: Atomic bomb mushroom clouds over Hiroshima (left) and Nagasaki (right). Source: National Archives and Records Administration, User: Binksternet, Creator: Charles Levy from one of the B-29 Superfortresses used in the attack (Nagasaki Bomb), Creator: Personel aboard Necessary Evil (Hiroshima Bomb), [CC BY-SA 3.0], via Wikimedia Commons

Figure 18.2: Cold War map of Eastern and Western Blocs in Europe. [Public domain], via Wikimedia Commons/Goldsztajn

Figure 18.3: The Iron Curtain depicted as a black line. Sources: Image - Blank_map_of_Europe_cropped.svg by Revolus under licence CC-BY-SA 2.5; itself from Image - Europe countries.svg by Júlio Reis alias Tintazul, under licence CC-BY-SA 2.5; Image - Cold war europe military alliances map.png by San Jose under licence GFDL; Image - Iron Curtain Final.svg by Vernes Seferovic alias Kseferovic under licence GFDL & CC-BY-SA, User: Sémhur/Wikimedia Commons

Figure 18.4: Occupation zone borders in Germany, 1947. Source: IEG-Maps project by Andreas Kunz, B. Johnen and Joachim Robert Moeschl: University of Mainz, User: 52 Pickup, [CC BY-SA 2.5], via Wikimedia Commons

For information about licensing terms, see:

CC BY 2.0	https://creativecommons.org/licenses/by/2.0)
CC BY-SA 3.0	https://creativecommons.org/licenses/by-sa/3.0
CC BY-SA 3.0 DE	https://creativecommons.org/ licenses/by-sa/3.0/de/deed.en
GFDL	https://www.gnu.org/licenses/fdl-1.3.html

Contents

Chapter 1: The origins of the French Revolution 1
- 1.1 Long-term causes — 1
- 1.2 Short-term causes — 2
- 1.3 Historiography and analysis — 4

Chapter 2: The unification of Italy 9

Chapter 3: The unification of Germany 16
- 3.1 Long-term causes — 16
- 3.2 Short-term causes — 18
- 3.3 Importance of the wars and Bismarck — 18
  - 3.3.1 The Schleswig-Holstein question 1863–65 — 18
  - 3.3.2 The Franco-Prussian War 1870–71 — 20
  - 3.3.3 Historiography and analysis — 20

Chapter 4: Bismarck's Germany 1871–90 24
- 4.1 The Liberal era — 25
- 4.2 The Kulturkampf — 25
- 4.3 Bismarck and the growth of socialism — 26
- 4.4 Economic development — 27
- 4.5 Foreign policy — 27

Chapter 5: Alexander II and Alexander III 30
- 5.1 Reforms — 32
- 5.2 Opposition — 33
- 5.3 Economic development — 34
- 5.4 Foreign policy — 34
- 5.5 Historiography and analysis — 34
- 5.6 Alexander III and the return to reaction 1881–94 — 36

Chapter 6: Russia 1894–1917 39
- 6.1 Russia at the turn of the century — 39
- 6.2 Agriculture — 40
- 6.3 Social life — 41
- 6.4 The industrial sector — 41
- 6.5 Political life — 41
- 6.6 The army — 42
- 6.7 The 1905 revolution — 42
- 6.8 The Duma experiment – a lost opportunity? — 43
- 6.9 Russia and WWI — 44

Chapter 7: The October Revolution 50
- 7.1 The causes of the October Revolution — 50
- 7.2 Historiography — 53
- 7.3 Weaknesses of the Provisional Government — 53
- 7.4 Strengths of the Bolsheviks — 53
- 7.5 Other factors — 54

Chapter 8: Lenin 57

- 8.1 How the war was ended — 57
- 8.2 How should they establish political control? — 58
- 8.3 How was a planned economy introduced? — 60
  - 8.3.1 State Capitalism October 1917 to June 1918 — 60
  - 8.3.2 War Communism 1918–21 — 60
  - 8.3.3 The New Economic Policy (NEP), 1921–28 — 61
- 8.4 Marxism-Leninism — 61

Chapter 9: The Causes of WWI 65

- 9.1 Long-term causes — 65
- 9.2 Short-term causes — 66
- 9.3 What can different countries be blamed for? — 67
- 9.4 Historiography — 68

Chapter 10: The Peace Settlements 72

- 10.1 Background to the Peace Conference — 73
- 10.2 Terms of the Treaty of Versailles — 74
- 10.3 The Treaty of Saint-Germain-en-Laye — 74
- 10.4 The Treaty of Trianon — 75
- 10.5 The Treaty of Neuilly — 75
- 10.6 The Treaty of Sèvres and Lausanne — 75
- 10.7 The Treaty of Brest-Litovsk, March 1918 — 75

Chapter 11: Spain 1918–39 78

- 11.1 Long-term causes of the Spanish Civil War — 78
- 11.2 Short-term causes of the Spanish Civil War — 79
- 11.3 The course of the Civil War — 82
- 11.4 Analysis — 82
- 11.5 Historiography — 83

Chapter 12: Mussolini and Italy 1918–39 86

- 12.1 Why was Mussolini appointed Prime Minister in 1922? — 87
- 12.2 The Fascist seizure of power — 87
- 12.3 How did the Fascists establish dictatorial power? — 89
- 12.4 The Fascist state – Mussolini: "I want to make Italy great again" — 90
- 12.5 Mussolini and the Catholic Church — 91
- 12.6 Control of media and education — 92
- 12.7 Fascism and women — 92
- 12.8 Fascism and the use of terror — 93
- 12.9 Historiography and analysis — 93
- 12.10 Mussolini's foreign policy — 94

Chapter 13: The Weimar Republic 1919–33 98

- 13.1 The foundation of the Republic — 98
- 13.2 The first crisis of the Republic 1919–23 — 99
- 13.3 The Stresemann years 1923–29, years of recovery — 101
- 13.4 The second crisis of the Weimar Republic 1929–33 — 102
  - 13.4.1 Brüning, March 1930–May 1932 — 102
  - 13.4.2 Von Papen, May 1932–December 1932 — 103
  - 13.4.3 Von Schleicher, December 1932–January 1933 — 103
  - 13.4.4 Hitler, Chancellor in January 1933 — 103
- 13.5 The strengths of the Nazis — 103
- 13.6 Historiography — 104

Chapter 14: The Third Reich 108

- 14.1 How did Hitler succeed in establishing dictatorial power? — 108
- 14.2 The pattern of dualism in the Nazi state — 111
- 14.3 The economy — 111
  - 14.3.1 Nazism and 'big business' — 112
  - 14.3.2 Nazism and small businesses — 112
  - 14.3.3 Farmers — 112
  - 14.3.4 Workers — 112
- 14.4 Social life in Nazi Germany — 113
- 14.5 Nazism and education — 113
- 14.6 Indoctrination and propaganda — 114
- 14.7 Relationship with the churches — 114
- 14.8 The legal system/apparatus of coercion and terror — 114
- 14.9 Antisemitism — 115

Chapter 15: Stalin 117

- 15.1 The power struggle — 117
- 15.2 Stalin's economic policy — 119
- 15.3 Impact of agricultural policies — 120
- 15.4 Industrialisation — 121
  - 15.4.1 Reasons for industrialisation — 121
  - 15.4.2 Impact of industrialisation — 121
  - 15.4.3 Living standards — 121
- 15.5 The purges — 122
- 15.6 Society and culture — 124
  - 15.6.1 Social changes — 124
  - 15.6.2 Education — 124
- 15.7 Bolshevik/Stalin's foreign policy — 124
  - 15.7.1 Stage I: Early development — 124
  - 15.7.2 Stage II: 1933 Hitler becomes Chancellor: a turning point — 124
  - 15.7.3 Stage III — 125

HISTORY HL: EUROPE

Chapter 16: The League of Nations ... 129

16.1 Foundation of the League of Nations 129
    16.1.1 The aims of the League 130
    16.1.2 The organisation of the League 130
16.2 Early successes – the 1920s 130
16.3 Failing major tests – the 1930s 131

Chapter 17: The origins of WWII ... 136

17.1 The origins of the Second World War in Europe 136
17.2 Effects of Munich 139
17.3 Why appeasement? 140
17.4 Summary of possible reasons for WWII 141

Chapter 18: The origins of the Cold War 1945–49 ... 146

18.1 Possible explanations for the Cold War 147
    18.1.1 The Cold War as a result of two different ideologies 147
    18.1.2 The Cold War as a result of WWII 148
18.2 Key developments following WWII 150

Chapter 19: Khrushchev ... 157

19.1 The transition from Stalin to Khrushchev 157
19.2 Khrushchev's Secret Speech 157
19.3 Economic policies 159
19.4 Trouble spots in foreign policy 159

Chapter 20: The fall of communism in the USSR ... 165

20.1 Soviet problems in the early 1980s 165
20.2 Gorbachev and the fall of communism 166
20.3 Why did Soviet communism collapse? 168

Introduction

Overview of curriculum relevance

This guide provides valuable summaries of 20 key areas from the syllabus as well as essay outlines related to these topics. While primarily aimed at helping prepare HL students who are studying Europe for Paper 3, the guide will also be useful for both SL and HL students preparing for selected topics studied for Paper 2.

Below you can find an overview of this book's chapters and how they link to the history curriculum for the IB Diploma. *Please bear in mind that the chapters do not cover every bullet point in every topic on the syllabus*, but they have been carefully written to offer you good examples of topics frequently appearing on IB exams.

Book chapter	Paper 2 topics	Paper 3 sections
1: The origins of the French Revolution		Section 8
2: The unification of Italy		Section 11
3: The unification of Germany		Section 11
4: Bismarck's Germany 1871–90		Section 11
5: Alexander II and Alexander III		Section 12
6: Russia 1894–1917	Topic 10	Section 12
7: The October Revolution	Topic 10	Section 12
8: Lenin	Topic 10	Section 12
9: The Causes of WW I	Topic 11	Section 13
10: The Peace Settlements	Topic 11	Section 15
11: Spain 1918–39	Topics 10+11	Section 14
12: Mussolini and Italy 1918–39	Topic 10	Section 14
13: The Weimar Republic 1919–33	Topic 10	Section 14
14: The Third Reich	Topic 10	Section 14
15: Stalin	Topic 10	Section 16
16: The League of Nations	Topic 11	Section 15
17: The origins of WW II	Topic 11	Section 15
18: The origins of the Cold War 1945–49	Topic 12	Section 17
19: Khrushchev	Topic 10	Section 16
20: The fall of communism in the USSR	Topic 12	Section 16

Key to Paper 2 World history topics:

Topic 10: Authoritarian states (20th century); Topic 11: Causes and effects of 20th century wars; Topic 12: The Cold War: Superpower tensions and rivalries (20th century)

Key to Paper 3 option 4: History of Europe sections:

Section 8: The French Revolution and Napoleon; Section 11: The Unification of Italy and Germany; Section 12: Imperial Russia, Revolution and the Establishment of The Soviet Union; Section 13: Europe and the First World War (1871–1918); Section 14: European States in the Inter-War Years (1918–1939); Section 15: Versailles to Berlin: Diplomacy in Europe (1919–1945); Section 16: The Soviet Union and Post-Soviet Russia (1924–2000); Section 17: Post-War Western and Northern Europe (1945–2000).

xi

HISTORY HL: EUROPE

How to use this guide

There is a method behind the writing, which I, from my experience, feel is very important to explain. I therefore recommend you use the guide in the following way:

1. **Read** the text covering the topic (but not the essay outline which follows after).
2. Use an **essay template** and try to answer the practice question by **writing down your main points** (not the details).
3. **Compare** your answer to the outline in the guide and assess the answers.
4. To read a guide and to write outlines does not prepare you fully for the exam. But when you think you know the main points of a topic, read your **text book** which is much more **in-depth**.

An essay outline can, in many ways, be seen as an 'open document'. *There are always different interpretations and views and ways of structuring a question*. The aim of this guide is to show you possible 'yes' and 'no' arguments and topics to discuss.

My candidates have been trained to use this approach, i.e. first to study the topic in depth and then put a lot of effort into trying to outline answers for essays. My experience is that the first five minutes used for an essay is of major importance. You need to:

- read the question thoroughly and identify the command terms so that you understand what is required;
- avoid the question if there are any terms you are unfamiliar with;
- use some minutes to outline your essay before starting to write.

This guide is structured to enable you to study efficiently:

- key terms are highlighted in bold,
- discrete sections of text such as timelines and historical perspectives are clearly marked,
- cross references link topics spanning more than one part of the guide, and
- practice questions follow the relevant sections of text.

To access the higher marks on Paper 2 and Paper 3, examiners expect candidates to show an awareness of and to evaluate differing historical perspectives.

Key to icons used in this study guide

	Study notes and exam tips	A combination of suggestions for revising specific topics, guidance on what helps you prepare for exams, and tips to guard against common errors or misconceptions.
	Timeline	Sequences that help to visualise and contextualise important events.
	Historical perspectives	An overview of differing historical views of events.
	Practice question	Questions to help you self-test your understanding. Essay outlines provided allow you to assess progress.
	Example/case study	Helpful worked illustrations to explain a concept or problem type.
	Key concept/information	Recurring or significant ideas/information that are particularly important to understanding the subject.
	Key term	Selected words and phrases whose definitions you should be familiar with.
	Cross-reference	Links between connected content in the guide.
	More information	Pointers to resources outside this guide that will boost your understanding of the topic.

Guidance on answering essay questions

Since 2017 exams, essay questions have used five command terms:

'Discuss'

'Examine'

'Evaluate'

'To what extent'

'Compare and contrast'

In Paper 2, the questions are '**open**', i.e. they do not refer to a specific topic.

Examples of two questions asking the same thing:

Paper 2 (an 'open' question): "A successful economic policy was essential for the maintenance of power by authoritarian leaders". With reference to one authoritarian leader, say to what extent you agree with this statement?

Paper 3: To what extent was a successful economic policy essential for Hitler to maintain his power?

It is of major importance to be aware of what structure is required in each question. The following explains this in more detail.

1. **List questions, i.e. 'discuss', 'examine', and 'evaluate', you list the points you want to discuss.**

Examples:

Discuss the reasons for the Cold War.

Go through the reasons for the Cold War and support each point with appropriate evidence. ('Discuss' could also be linked to a 'yes or no' question—see the text in point 2).

Examine the reasons for the Nationalists' victory in the Spanish Civil War.

Account for, and examine critically, the strengths and weaknesses of each point, explaining the reasons for the Nationalist party victory. You examine both the strengths of the Nationalists and the weaknesses of the Republicans.

Evaluate the success of Lenin's economic policies.

You are to weigh the strengths and the weaknesses of each point when explaining Lenin's economic policies.

The questions ask you to examine and evaluate, i.e. to discuss critically all relevant points. It is not only a question of making a list of all the arguments. What you do additionally is assess each point in the question more critically, presenting both support and counterarguments to each point.

2. **'To what extent' and 'discuss' questions.**

These questions require the same type of answer: You need to show arguments for "to what extent it was" and arguments showing "to what extent it was not".

Let me give you some examples:

"*To what extent* was the Cold War a result of WW II?"

You must find arguments to show how the Cold War reasons can be seen as a result of WW II, but also arguments showing that the Cold War resulted from other reasons than just the effects of WW II. The arguments can be presented in two parts.

HISTORY HL: EUROPE

"The Cold War was a result of WW II." *Discuss* the validity of this claim concerning the emergence of the Cold War.

Show and analyse critically the importance of WW II, and show all other reasons in the second part of the essay.

3. **'Compare and contrast' questions.**

Example:

"*Compare and contrast* the aims and the policies of the two superpowers between 1945 and 1949."

The question asks you to show (a) the **similarities**, and (b) the **differences** between the two superpowers: a **comparison**. In many questions where you are asked to compare and contrast, the question is so extensive that you can *only* compare and contrast.

If the question is "Compare and contrast the reasons for WWI and WWII", it would be impossible to write with the approach of explaining the reason for WWI and WWII, and then compare and contrast the reasons: you don't have enough time. Go *immediately* to the similarities and after that to the differences, written in two parts of your essay. When you show the differences, *refer to both conflicts* throughout your presentation.

Personally, I often advise students to write two lists. One describing 'yes' arguments, and one describing 'no' arguments. While some teachers may think this is too simplistic, my aim is to help students in preparing each answer in the best way possible. It doesn't mean they have to slavishly follow the advice. But the guide and the outlines will show you possible arguments to use.

List of essay practice outlines in this guide

I have included more than forty essay outlines to help you consolidate your understanding of the topics and provide practice for the exam. Use these in conjunction with copies of the blank essay outline structure that I have included at the end of the book for you to cut out and photocopy, or which can be downloaded from the Peak Study Resources website.

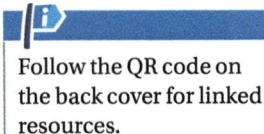
Follow the QR code on the back cover for linked resources.

1. *Discuss* the reasons for the French Revolution. — p. 6
2. "Economic reasons played a key role in making the French Revolution." *To what extent* do you agree with this statement? — p. 7
3. *To what extent* was the Italian unification a result of Cavour's policies? — p. 13
4. *To what extent* were foreign powers important in the unification process in Italy? — p. 15
5. "The German empire was built more truly on coal and iron than on blood and iron." *To what extent* do you agree with this statement? — p. 21
6. *Discuss* the importance of diplomacy and wars in the process of German unification between 1862 and 1871. — p. 22
7. *Compare and contrast* the unifications of Italy and Germany. — p. 23
8. *To what extent* did Bismarck's rule 1871–90 strengthen Germany? — p. 28
9. *Discuss* the reasons for Alexander II's reforms and *evaluate* their success. — p. 37
10. *Discuss to what extent* Russia was a backward state at the end of the 19th century. — p. 45
11. *Discuss* the reasons why Tsardom survived the revolution of 1905 and not the revolution of 1917 — p. 47
12. *To what extent* did WW I cause the fall of Tsardom? — p. 48
13. *Discuss* the reasons for the October Revolution. — p. 54
14. *Evaluate* the importance of Lenin in the Bolshevik seizure of power. — p. 56

15. *To what extent* was Lenin a successful politician? —p. 63
16. *Discuss to what extent* Lenin followed his ideology. —p. 64
17. *To what extent* was Germany responsible for the outbreak of WWI? —p. 69
18. *Discuss* whether WWI was a result of miscalculations and misunderstandings. —p. 70
19. *To what extent* is it possible to defend the way in which the Treaty of Versailles dealt with Germany? —p. 76
20. *Discuss* the reasons for the Civil War in Spain in 1936. —p. 84
21. *Discuss* the reasons for the Nationalist's victory in the Civil War. —p. 85
22. *Examine* the reasons for the Fascist seizure of power in 1922. —p. 95
23. *Evaluate* the successes and failures of Mussolini's domestic policies. —p. 97
24. *To what extent* did the Treaty of Versailles cause the fall of the Weimar Republic? —p. 105
25. "The constitution of the Weimar Republic played a major role in the fall of the Republic." *To what extent* do you agree with this statement? —p. 106
26. *To what extent* did the Wall Street Crash cause the fall of the Weimar Republic? —p. 107
27. *Discuss* how Hitler achieved dictatorial power? —p. 115
28. *Discuss* why there was so little resistance against the Nazi regime? —p. 116
29. *Discuss* why it was Stalin, and not Trotsky, who succeeded Lenin. —p. 126
30. *Evaluate* whether Stalin's domestic policies strengthened the USSR. —p. 127
31. *Discuss* why the League of Nations was set up in 1920 and what the results were. —p. 132
32. "The League of Nations failed due to its own weaknesses." *To what extent* do you agree with this statement? —p. 134
33. *To what extent* was the failure of the League of Nations responsible for the outbreak of WWII? —p. 135
34. "Hitler planned and was responsible for WWII." *To what extent* do you agree with this statement? —p. 142
35. *Discuss* why Britain and France followed a policy of appeasement in the 1930s —p. 143
36. *Compare and contrast* the reasons for WWI and WWII. —p. 144
37. *To what extent* was the Cold War a result of WWII? —p. 153
38. "The Cold War was a clash between two irreconcilable ideologies." *To what extent* do you agree with this statement? —p. 154
39. By referring to events from the period 1945–49, *discuss* how historians have explained who was responsible for the Cold War. —p. 155
40. "With the possible exceptions of Khrushchev and Gorbachev, no Russian ruler brought so much relief to so many of his people as did Alexander II, autocratic and conservative." *To what extent* do you agree with this statement concerning Khrushchev made by the historian J N Westwood? —p. 162
41. "It is unjustified to see Khrushchev as a 'Cold Warrior'." *To what extent* do you agree with this statement? —p. 163
42. *To what extent* did external pressure lead to the collapse of the Soviet system? —p. 172
43. *Examine* whether Gorbachev was responsible for the collapse of the Soviet system? —p. 173

Chapter 1: The origins of the French Revolution

Issues

Was the revolution inevitable, i.e. how much attention should be given to long-term or short-term causes? How shall we describe the French revolution? The Marxist interpretation, which has dominated for a long period, describes the revolution as a class struggle between the aristocracy and a new class of capitalists. How valid is it?

1.1 Long-term causes

1. **The tax system and feudal rights.** France in the 18th century was the richest country in Europe with a population (24 million) nearly triple that of England. The French language was the language of the educated classes throughout Europe at the time. Society was organised along **feudal** lines where every person belonged to an '**estate**'. The first estate was made up by the clergy, the second by the nobility and the third included everyone else. Status, civil rights, and privileges were to a major extent determined by the estate to which you belonged. France's major problem was that while the country was quite prosperous the state was constantly poor due to an inadequate tax system. The nobility and the clergy, who owned approximately one third of the land but only made up 3% of the population, were **exempted from most taxes**. Members of the bourgeoisie could buy tax exemption. The burden of paying taxes fell mostly upon the peasantry who made up 80% of the population.

2. **Support to the American colonies.** France had given support to the American colonies in their War of Independence (1775-83) against England. France had also fought in the War of the Austrian Succession 1740-48 and the Seven Years War in 1756-63. Defence costs made up a quarter of the state budget by 1780 and in 1788 half of the expenditure was devoted to paying debts caused by the wars.

3. **The philosophers.** Throughout the 18th century the third estate or, more correctly, the bourgeoisie, had been affected by the writings of a number of philosophers. Montesquieu, Voltaire, and Rousseau were highly influential in their writings and had challenged the authority of the king, the nobility and the church. The fact that the nobility had exclusive rights to the best positions in the bureaucracy,

Figure 1.1: **Engraving of Voltaire, 1889.**

army and the church, was greatly resented by the bourgeoisie. The combination of the injustices of the tax system and that this emerging class of professional and educated people and businessmen were excluded from public office united them in their struggle against **the Old Regime**. These thoughts were eloquently expressed by the philosophers in their writings.

4. **Problems with the economy.** France not only suffered from a financial crisis in terms of lack of revenue, since 1778 there had been an agricultural depression. The French textile industry also suffered from competition from England. The economic situation became acute in 1787–89 when there were harvest failures resulting in food shortages. There were thousands of unemployed workers in Paris alone and there were many poor peasants in the countryside living under terrible conditions. A worker in Paris could use 75% of his salary just to buy bread due the effects of the harvest failure.

5. **The aristocracy blocked reforms.** Formally, Louis XVI was an absolute monarch. But the aristocracy had been able to increase their power in the 18th century and could block or delay legislation or reforms through the *parlements*, i.e. regional law courts. The king is normally described as a rather weak leader but in an attempt to break the deadlock caused by an obstructive aristocracy and to find a possible solution to a severe economic crisis, he agreed to convene the Estates-General.

1.2 Short-term causes

The king, Louis XVI, had made some attempts to reform the tax system but did not support his officials, first Necker and later Calonne, when facing opposition from the nobility.

1. **The bourgeoisie revolted when the Estates-General met in 1789.** When the king couldn't collect taxes or borrow money and faced bankruptcy, he was forced to call for a meeting of the Estates-General in 1789. They had not met since 1614, some 175 years previously. **The Nobility claimed that it was only the Estates-General that could approve new taxes. They also thought that this body could reduce the king's power**. Therefore, **the aristocracy forced the king to summon the Estates-General**. Until now, the bourgeoisie had mostly supported the nobility against the king and his ministers but when the Estates-General finally met in 1789 and the nobility insisted that they should meet as they had done in 1614, **the bourgeoisie revolted against the aristocracy and the revolution started**.

Figure 1.2: **Estates-General of 1789**

1. THE ORIGINS OF THE FRENCH REVOLUTION

The decision to convene the Estates-General had been met by great expectations from different groups.

- The king hoped to find a solution to **the financial crisis** through a tax reform. It was the only way to solve the financial crisis when all other attempts had failed due to opposition from the aristocracy.
- The representatives from the nobility/aristocracy saw the meeting of the Estates-General as a way to **block the king's plans** for far-reaching reforms. Previously, they had compelled the king to abandon plans to reform and in the Estates-General the old system of voting meant that each estate had one vote. So the aristocracy and the clergy could control the assembly and outvote the commoners or the third estate.
- Many representatives from the bourgeoisie saw it as a golden opportunity to **end the privileges of the two other estates** (the nobility and the clergy). The third estate was made up by all people who did not belong to the nobility or the clergy and amounted to 97% of the population. Most of them were poor peasants and workers but these had no representatives in the Estates-General. The representation of the third estate was made up by lawyers (25%), doctors, businessmen and bankers, many of whom had become very wealthy from the flourishing international trade during the 18th century. The composition of the Estates-General did not in any way reflect the social or economic situation in France at the time.

When the Estates-General finally met in June 1789 they could not agree on voting procedures. The third estate refused to participate unless the estates met as one body. The king had made attempts to compromise and had allowed the third estate to double their number of representatives (to 600), as many as the other two estates. But the nobility and the clergy refused to give up the system of each estate having one vote. On 17 June, the third estate declared themselves the **National Assembly** and invited the two other estates to join them. They were excluded from their normal hall and on 20 June they met on a nearby tennis court. They swore to never dissolve until they had produced a new constitution, which would limit the power of **the Old Regime**. This was a revolutionary act but the king reluctantly recognised the new Assembly.

2. **Workers revolted and stormed the Bastille.** The king ordered the clergy and the nobility to join the third estate in the new National Assembly, but the situation was very tense. Groups of small workshop masters and workers – **sans-culottes** – were destroying customs barriers and had seized weapons. These groups were suffering from the economic recession and the failed harvest. Radical political agitation at the time forewarned the workers of the potential for some sort of royal or aristocratic counter revolution. When the king plotted against the Assembly and ordered troops to surround Versailles and Paris, the people became apprehensive. The regime could not control subsequent developments. On the evening of 14 July, a group consisting mainly of sans-culottes (workers) stormed the **Bastille**. The fortress was a symbol of royal power and the assault set off a wave of popular violence, which soon spread throughout the country. In provincial towns the breakdown of law and order continued.

3. **The peasant revolution.** In the countryside, the peasantry, suffering from the bad harvest and feudal obligations, soon took action. Food convoys were attacked, peasants refused to pay taxes and attacked the manor houses of the nobles and destroyed the records of feudal dues.

The National Assembly now set up a constitutional monarchy. On 4 August the new National Assembly decided to abolish all privileges of the nobility and the clergy (the Saint Bartholomew of privilege) in an attempt to prevent the spread of violence. On 26 August the **Declaration of the Rights of Man** was adopted. The document reflects the writings or ideas of the philosophers and in the first article we can read: *"Men are born and remain free and equal in rights"*.

Figure 1.3: **Declaration of the Rights of Man and of the Citizen in 1789**

1.3 Historiography and analysis

Some historians see the French Revolution as inevitable. It was a result of an emerging middle class and capitalists with growing economic power who demanded political rights. The nobility, who were also suffering from the economic recession, stubbornly refused to give up their privileges and this refusal finally led to the revolution in which the bourgeoisie, the working class, and the peasantry all took part. It would finally lead to the abolition of the monarchy (1792) and the bourgeoisie emerging as a new leading group replacing the landed aristocracy. But there was no talk of economic equality or 'one man, one vote' in spite of the leading principle of **liberty, equality, and fraternity.** It would also be wrong to see this development as unique to France. In the American Declaration of Independence from 1776, i.e. before the French Revolution, Thomas Jefferson wrote: "*all men are created equal*" (compare the Declarations of Rights of Man from France 1789, Figure 1.3). Both these declarations clearly reflect the ideas of the philosophers and a breakthrough for a new era.

Some historians would, however, emphasise more short-term causes. It was the recession in combination with the harvest failure which was the driving force behind the revolution. By emphasising these short-term causes the revolution must be seen as less inevitable.

1. THE ORIGINS OF THE FRENCH REVOLUTION

The **Marxist or leftist interpretation** dominated the debate until the 1960s. The revolution was a result of economic activity with increased international trade and industry, which created a new economy and a new group of capitalists who now finally seized power through the revolution. Between 1715 and 1789 France had increased its international trade by 440%. It was a **class struggle between two social classes**, the land-owning aristocracy and the capitalist bourgeoisie. The bourgeoisie overthrew and replaced the aristocracy simply because they now had the economic power. According to Marxist terminology it was a classic revolution where one emerging class outmanoeuvred another class due to their economic strength. Marxist historians compare the French Revolution to the February revolution in Russia in 1917, where the middle class represented in the Duma, finally seized power from the Tsar and the landed aristocracy who supported him.

George Lefebvre, probably the most prominent French historian, is also a Marxist. To him the revolution was a bourgeois revolution, a class struggle between the aristocracy and the bourgeoisie. However, as a background factor, he emphasises the importance of economic support to the Americans in their war against England: *"The government crisis went back to the American war* [It]*...may in fact be considered as the principal direct cause to the French revolution [...] it stirred up great excitement in France, and because Louis XVI in supporting it got his finances into very bad conditions"*. Lefebvre's contribution to the debate is subdividing the revolution into four revolutions:

- The **first** revolution had already started earlier in the 18th century, many years before when the **aristocracy** had revolted against the king and his absolute power. They had advanced their position and could block the king's power mainly through the regional *parlements*. They also hoped to block the king's plans for economic reforms in the Estates-General, when it finally met in 1789. By doing that they unknowingly opened the door to the revolution.

- The **second** revolution took place when the third estate, i.e. the **bourgeoisie**, refused to accept the old voting system in the Estates-General in June–July 1789 and declared themselves to be the new National Assembly.

- When the king made threatening moves against the new Assembly it triggered off a **third** revolution when a group consisting mainly of **workers** turned to violence by storming the Bastille.

- Finally, the **fourth** revolution was triggered when **peasants** turned to violence throughout the country by storming the manor houses of the nobility and destroying the records of feudal dues.

Figure 1.4: **The Third Estate (commoners) carrying the First (clergy) and Second Estate (nobility) on his back**

Lefebvre concludes that the outcome was that the bourgeoisie finally seized control of France, but the single most important contribution to the success of the revolution was actually made by the peasantry. He writes:

> "*We realize today that without their* [the peasantry] *adherence the Revolution could with difficulty have succeeded. Their grievances had been disregarded [...]. Their complaints were by no means uppermost among the interests of the National Assembly, in which there were no peasant member. Then suddenly they too revolted [...] delivering a death blow to what was left of the feudal system. The peasant uprising is one of the most distinctive features of the Revolution in France".*

In the 1960s, the Marxist interpretation was challenged by revisionist or non-Marxist historians. The English historian Alfred Cobben showed that the revolutionary bourgeoisie were not rich capitalists but rather lawyers and other professional groups. The richer capitalists did not lead the third estate and did not gain from the process. **Hence, the Marxist**

interpretation of class struggle has to be discarded. Other revisionist historians have emphasised that land, tax exemption, and privileges could be bought. The bourgeoisie did not want to get rid of the aristocracy, they wanted to be a part of it. The richest people in France by the time of the revolution were still noblemen.

In conclusion, the revisionists have shown that it is a **simplification to describe the French revolution as a class war** between richer groups of emerging capitalists and a declining aristocracy. But it cannot be denied that the French revolution was led by the **bourgeoisie** and that these groups of **educated middle-class people** were ultimately the **chief beneficiaries** of the revolution.

> Now, when you have read the text:
> 1. Study the questions that follow (but not the answers!)
> 2. Copy a template and outline your answer.
> 3. Compare the two answers and analyse any possible difference.

1. Discuss the reasons for the French Revolution.

(This is a 'list-question', i.e. it asks you to list all the reasons for the French Revolution. Show a range of arguments, factors and hypothesis.)

Long-term causes:

1. The expansion of international trade and industry **created a new and wealthy middle class**. Due to a system of **privileges**, this class was denied political power and access to the best jobs in the army, the church, and in the bureaucracy. Many historians, not only Marxists, would emphasise this point. Revisionist historians have, however, shown that the revolution was not led by wealthy capitalists but rather by educated groups from the bourgeoisie. The classic Marxist interpretation of a class struggle can be questioned.
2. The **tax system** in France was ineffective and didn't bring revenues to the state. The nobility and the clergy owned one third of the land, but made up only 3% of the population, and paid virtually no taxes. The bourgeoisie could buy tax exemption.
3. The wars had a disastrous effect on the state's economy and in 1788 50% of the state expenditure was used to pay debts. Lefebvre describes **the support to the American colonies** as *"the principal direct cause to the French revolution".*
4. The **writings of the philosophers were widely read** and expressed eloquently the ideas of the new emerging middle class.
5. The French textile industry suffered from **competition especially from England**. This led to unemployment.
6. The problem of taxation was not new and both the **king and the nobility** must bear responsibility for not being able to solve this critical problem.

Short-term causes:

1. There were **harvest failures** 1787–89. This led to increasing bread prices and a worker could use 75% of his salary just to buy bread.
2. The **policies of the king** must be scrutinised. He had fully supported a tax reform and he did not give full support to the third estate over the voting system and when tension rose he called in troops and probably plotted with the nobility, planning a counter revolution. Attempts to reform were far too late and only serve to support the view of the French philosopher Alexis de Tocqueville who wrote in *L'ancien régime et la revolution*: *"The most dangerous moment for a bad government is when it begins to reform".*

1. THE ORIGINS OF THE FRENCH REVOLUTION

3. The nobility and the clergy were not prepared to compromise over the voting procedure in the Estates-General which led to the **second revolution**, according to Lefebvre in July 1789.

Conclusion: Historians are divided in their explanation to the French revolution. It can be argued that it was a combination of long-term and short-term causes. Lefebvre describes it as four different revolutions, which indicate different causes, i.e. a combination. Revisionist historians have concluded that it is a simplification to see the revolution as a class war between an emerging capitalist group and the old landed aristocracy.

2. "Economic reasons played a key role in making the French Revolution." To what extent do you agree with this statement?

(List all reasons where the economy was of importance and then discuss all other reasons that cannot be classed as economic reasons. This is a question which invites you to discuss different historiographical views.)

Yes, the economy played an important role:

1. The **growth of a capitalist middle class** which challenged the old elite can be seen as a very important long-term cause of the revolution. The industrial part of national production increased throughout the century at the expense of agricultural production. The combination of the economic strength of this new emerging middle class and their lack of power and exclusion from employment in the army, church and bureaucracy etc., made the situation very tense. This view has been the dominant explanation amongst Marxists and many other historians. But **notice the revisionist view** that the revolution was led by **educated groups from the middle class**, and not the richer capitalists.

2. The **system of taxation did not bring revenues** to the state and was the reason why the Estates General met in 1789 and why the old system of **privileges** was under attack.

3. The **support for the American colonies** in their war of independence had a major impact on France's national debt. It is described by the historian Lefebvre as *"the principal direct cause to the French revolution"*.

4. The whole **system of privileges** was of course in many ways an economic issue. Job opportunities and taxation were affected by this system and this was the main reason for the political development in France which led to the revolution.

5. The **recession** and **problems with the harvest** created a very explosive situation not only in 1789. Bread riots and peasant unrest were not new in France.

There were other reasons that had nothing to do with the economy:

6. It can be argued that the system of ruling the country by **the king** with divine rights and privileges, reflected an **ideology** more than an expression for economic interests. Jean Jacques Rousseau had been very influential and in his *Social Contract* (1762); he argued that the kings must rule with a two-way contract in mind where there were obligations and consultations between the monarch and the population. Rulers like Catherine II of Russia, Frederick the Great of Prussia ruled as **enlightened despots** and had no visions of sharing power as constitutional monarchs.

7. The **writings of the philosophers reflected new ideas** and new ideologies that were driven by other factors than purely economic considerations. Liberty, equality and fraternity etc. might of course reflect economic relations but also other values. Their writing was a very important contribution to the revolution. An interesting aspect to discuss concerning the philosophers is whether interest for their ideas was a result of economic development. Would writers like Voltaire and Montesquieu have had a

reading public if it hadn't been for the economic development which created this new middle class who consumed their writing?

8. The **French support for the American colonies was not only an economic consideration**. There were other reasons which made the French support the Americans, for instance a French desire to play a leading political role.

9. The **policies of the king** might be emphasised as another reason for the revolution. By calling in troops, plotting against the Assembly, etc, he can be held partly responsible for starting the revolution. His actions were not primarily driven by economic considerations. The stubbornness of the two first estates when the Estates-General met led to the bourgeois revolution which set the whole process in motion.

Conclusion: Even though some other elements affected the process towards revolution, it must be concluded that economic reasons had a major impact on the development and the background to the French revolution. It is, however, a simplification to describe the revolution as mainly a class struggle between new groups of capitalists and the landed aristocracy.

Chapter 2: The unification of Italy

Issues

There are a number of factors explaining this event and historians emphasise different reasons.

The Vienna Settlement was concluded after the Napoleonic Wars in 1815 with the aim that Europe should return to peace and stability. It was a **return to conservatism** and old rulers were restored on the basis of the principle of legitimacy. In Italy, it was applied to Piedmont, Tuscany, Modena, and the Papal States. The Austrian chancellor Prince Metternich was the driving force of the Quadruple Alliance between Austria, Russia, Prussia and Britain. Its aim was to:

- prevent and control French radicalism and prevent the Bonaparte dynasty returning to power;
- prevent and **combat revolution** anywhere in Europe.

Figure 2.1: **Map of the Unification of Italy**

With the exception of a few tiny principalities, Italy was made up of nine sovereign territories or duchies. Lombardy and Venetia belonged to Austria and the duchies of Parma, Modena, Tuscany, and Lucca were ruled by branches of the **Habsburg dynasty**. It was only the Papal States and Piedmont which had non-Austrian or native Italian rulers.

Conservative rulers who had been restored by the Vienna Settlement were opposed by liberals. **Liberals** demanded constitutions which would limit the power of the ruler. In Italy, this went **hand-in-hand** with a desire for free and independent states, in other words **nationalism**. This was due to the fact that these conservative rulers who opposed the liberals both had a foreign background and support i.e. Austrian.

2.1 Long-term causes

1. **Nationalism.** The 19th century was the era of nationalism. Nationalism in this context means that a group of people, a nation, with a common sense of belonging to the same national identity, should also form a state. This sense of identity could be based on culture, religion, language, ethnic background and traditions. This belief could both unite a country (Italy and Germany) and divide a country (Austria). To form a new state

was to redraw the map of Europe which was a violation of the Vienna Settlement. The 'Italian school' of historians has emphasised that Italian nationalism was a driving force behind the unification. **Denis Mack Smith, refutes this claim**. That Cavour and others believed in one unified Italy is described by Mack Smith as a '**cover-up**'. He believes that economic interests were the driving force, and that Cavour was forced to take action in the south due to a need to stop Garibaldi, who was Republican. There was no national identity or a wish to create it. Fewer than 3% of the people on the Italian peninsula spoke the Italian language, according to Mack Smith.

There was a constitutionalist revolt in Naples in 1820–21, which was crushed by Austrian troops. New revolts followed in 1831. By this time five out of six rulers in northern Italy, Piedmont being the exception, had called on Austrian troops for support in times of revolt. The early revolts were caused by **Carbonaris**, groups who used conspiracy and revolts to provoke general uprisings. But there were no real plans for a unified Italy among the Carbonaris.

2. **Mazzini's influence**. The promotion of the idea of unification was to some extent the work of one man with a Carbonari background, Giuseppe Mazzini. He founded the 'Young Italy' movement and even if he failed in many aspects when organising revolts in the 1830s and 1840s he, more than anyone else, was able to arouse enthusiasm among Italians for unification. Mazzini has been referred to as the **soul** of the unification. Mazzini was also able to establish a reputation among liberals in many European countries.

Figure 2.2: **Statue of Giuseppe Mazzini in Pisa**

1848 represents the year of revolution in Europe. There were a number of national rebellions where liberals and nationalists challenged the conservative system with its roots in the Vienna Settlement. Piedmont seized the opportunity and declared war on the disintegrating Austrian empire (**The First War of Independence**) but when stability returned to Europe, Austria defeated Piedmont twice, at Custozza in 1848 and Novara in 1849. Even if Prince Metternich of Austria, the symbol of conservatism and maintenance of status quo, was forced to resign, it must be concluded that in many cases the existing power structures remained. *"The royal war is over, the war of the people begins"* declared Mazzini and paved the way for a second struggle. In Rome a republic was proclaimed and Garibaldi was responsible for the military defence. Church land was distributed to poor peasants and this radical policy was brought down by France and Austria in June 1849. **A French garrison was now stationed in Rome**.

Italian freedom had failed but Settembrini (an Italian patriot) claimed that 1848 was *"the point at which we became Italians and felt ourselves united and gathered together under a single standard"*.

3. **The importance of Piedmont and Cavour**. After 1848, the return to the old order in the duchies of Italy resulted in foreign military occupations and repression. There was only one exception, which still retained its territorial integrity and freedom from Austrian occupation and that was Piedmont. It was ruled by King Victor Emmanuel II from 1849

and in 1852 Camillo Count of Cavour became Prime Minister. Cavour admired Britain and realised the importance of industrialism hence he encouraged industrial and commercial development. Traditionally, the policies in Piedmont had been very liberal. Laws, which curtailed the rights of the church, had been introduced in 1850. When the Archbishop of Piedmont ordered his clergy to ignore these laws he was imprisoned. A number of economic reforms and policies ensured that Piedmont became a leading state in Italy. Its trade trebled in value in the 1850s, and of Italy's 1798 km of rail track in 1859, Piedmont had 819 km. By the late 1850s Piedmont had the most liberal constitution, the most modern army, and the strongest economy in Italy. But Piedmont, standing alone was not strong enough to be a driving force in a unification process challenging Austria. If we compare Italy to Germany, Prussia alone was strong enough to outmanoeuvre great powers by its own strength.

Figure 2.3: **Camillo Benso, Conte di Cavour by Francesco Hayez**

It must be emphasised that Cavour's aim from the beginning was an enlarged Piedmont. One piece of evidence for this is the discussion at Plombières, where the plan was for four Italian kingdoms. Mack Smith writes: *"Cavour had never been south of Florence [and] he showed little interest in the idea of Italian unification."*

2.2 Short-term causes

1. **Participation in the Crimean War and the war in 1859.** The first significant step was taken when Piedmont joined Britain and France in the Crimean War in 1854. 18,000 men from Piedmont were sent to Crimea and this contribution entitled Piedmont and Cavour to participate in the Paris Peace Conference together with the great powers of Europe. Even if nothing was achieved it is normally considered that the Italian question was now placed firmly in the context of European diplomacy. In 1858, Cavour and Napoleon III made an agreement at **Plombières** to cooperate to oust the Austrians from northern Italy. It must be noted that when they planned for a future Italy, **they planned for four kingdoms**: Upper Italy, a kingdom in central Italy, Rome, and Naples. It was to be a confederation under the presidency of the Pope, i.e. no 'Italy'. As a result of the meeting a military alliance was formed in January 1859 and a **war started in May 1859 – The Second War of Independence**. The allies were victorious but Napoleon soon realised that it would be wise to end the Italian campaign. Prussia was mobilising in the Rhineland so French troops could be needed elsewhere.

   France signed an armistice with Austria at **Villafranca** in July 1859, without the presence of Piedmont, and Lombardy was surrendered to France. The rulers of Tuscany and Modena, who had fled their duchies during the war, were to be restored. It also meant that Venetia was still controlled by Austria. The outcome was unacceptable to Cavour who wanted to continue the war without France. When the king said no, Cavour resigned.

2. **Tuscany, Parma and Modena join Piedmont after the war.** Now the course of events took an unexpected turn. Encouraged by Cavour, Provisional Governments in Tuscany, Parma, and Modena were not prepared to accept the return of the old rulers. Instead, they declared that they wanted to be a part of an Italian kingdom led by Victor Emmanuel. When Napoleon III made it clear that he refused to use military power against the duchies, a plebiscite was organised. The result was that an overwhelming majority wanted to be a part of Piedmont. The result was a first step towards an Italian unification and Piedmont now doubled in size and population.

3. **Garibaldi's importance.** In 1860 a **revolt in Sicily** by republican Mazzinians broke out. They revolted against the king, Francis II. Sicily was a part of Naples. The year before, republicans in Sicily had refused to support the monarchy in Piedmont in the war against Austria. The result was that **Cavour**, who had now returned to power, **refused to**

support the Sicilian revolt. It was now time for another main character in the unification of Italy to enter the scene: Giuseppe Garibaldi. In May 1860, without any **support from the government** of Piedmont, he left Genoa with a thousand volunteers, protected by the British navy and with support from Sicily. The troops from Naples were defeated and soon left for the Italian mainland. To Garibaldi, this legendary victory opened up new opportunities. If the troops from Naples had been defeated in Sicily they could be defeated again and Naples would be conquered. And if Naples were conquered the next step could be its northern neighbour: the Papal States. That would, however, most likely lead to international implications – a French intervention.

To Piedmont, Garibaldi's success was problematic. Cavour wrote in a letter: *"If Garibaldi passes over to the mainland and seizes the kingdom of Naples […] as he has done with Sicily and Palermo […] King Victor Emmanuel loses more or less all his prestige […] and he is no more than Garibaldi's friend"*. Garibaldi was also a **Republican** and success in the South could be very dangerous to the king. When Garibaldi crossed the straits and successfully entered his campaign and occupied Naples, Cavour went into action. He sent troops to the Papal States and informed the European powers that the aim was to restore order. After the fall of Naples, on 26 October, a **dramatic meeting** took place at Teano where Garibaldi was forced to make a **choice** between handing over his conquests to Victor Emmanuel or to fight him. Garibaldi accepted the ultimatum and after a new plebiscite the kingdom of Naples and the Papal territories of Umbria and the Marches became parts of the new kingdom of Italy, which was officially announced in March 1861. These conquests were the exceptions in the unification process since they were accomplished mainly without foreign involvement.

Figure 2.4: **Portrait of Giuseppe Garibaldi, Musée Masséna Nice**

The English poet George Meredith summed up the situation when he wrote *"Cavour, Mazzini, Garibaldi […] her brain, her soul, her sword"*.

4. **The Austro-Prussian war 1866** (the Third War of Independence). There were still two pieces missing in making a unified Italy, i.e. Venetia and Rome. When Prussia's and Austria-Hungary's relation deteriorated due to disagreements over Schleswig-Holstein, new opportunities opened for Italy. In June 1866, Prussia attacked Austria. Before doing so it secured Italian support in the conflict. This time it was agreed that none of the parties could conclude a separate peace with Austria, meaning a new Villafranca should not be repeated. The war was a military disaster to Italy but **the Prussian war-machine crushed Austria** at the battle of Sadowa in July 1866. The outcome from an Italian point of view was that **Italy gained Venetia**.

5. **The Franco-Prussian war 1870**. The only remaining part in the unification process was the Papal territories which had not been taken in 1860, when Umbria and the Marches became a part of the new Italian kingdom. From an Italian point of view the main problem was that the Pope was protected by French troops, hence to conquer it would

have international implications. This made Italy, but not Garibaldi, act cautiously. He made two attempts to conquer the territory but without government support he was too weak. In 1864 Italy made an agreement with France to remove its troops from the Papal territories if the Italian state guaranteed to protect the Papal territory from external attacks and in 1866 the **French troops started the withdrawal**.

In 1870 the Franco-Prussian war resulted in the defeat of France and the unification of Germany. After the defeat Italy sought international support from Spain, Austria and the Catholic states in Germany, to annex the Papal territories. When this was agreed the **Italian army occupied Rome in September 1870**. The Pope, **Pius IX**, was offered the right to the Vatican and a number of other rights but he **refused to recognise the Italian state**. This problem was only solved when Mussolini concluded the Lateran Treaty with the Papacy in 1929, but the final step in the unification process of 1870 was accomplished due to favourable international relations, i.e. the defeat of France in the Franco-Prussian war.

2.3 Historiography

The unification of Italy has been described differently by different historians. The Italian **'nationalist' school** tended to emphasise the importance of the Piedmont king and A. Oriano describes Victor Emmanuel as *"the grandest and most glorious sovereign in the history of Christian Europe"*. The **'liberal'** school emphasises and defends the actions of Cavour in the light of his success. The unification was part of a broader process in Europe at the time, where liberalism outmanoeuvred the conservative restoration from the Vienna Settlement. In this school Cavour's importance has been emphasised.

Left-wing historians are less sympathetic to the unification. Antonio Gramsci describes the unification as a 'failed revolution' where right-wing politicians like Cavour created a state riddled by class conflicts, which would ultimately lead to the rise of Fascism in Italy in the 1920s.

Denis Mack Smith must be seen as the most dominant non-Italian historian to discuss the unification in recent years. He is not sympathetic to Cavour and sees him as a cunning politician representing Piedmont's interests more than a unified Italy. He also refutes the 'nationalist' school and its admiration for the king. Mack Smith is more sympathetic to Mazzini and sees him as a man of integrity and honour contrasting both Cavour and Victor Emmanuel.

Now, when you have read the text:
1. Study the questions that follow (but not the answers!)
2. Copy a template and outline your answer.
3. Compare your answer with the one given and analyse any possible differences.

3. To what extent was the Italian unification a result of Cavour's policies?

(Show in what way Cavour was of importance and all other reasons as well.)

Yes:

1. He became Prime Minister in 1852. He was very important in modernising the state. **Trade trebled** in the 1850s.

2. Failure in 1848 led Cavour to conclude that **foreign help was necessary** to exclude Austria from northern Italy. But Cavour's early aim was to strengthen Piedmont's position in northern Italy, and not to unify Italy
3. The **Crimean War**: a diplomatic master-stroke to place the Italian question firmly into the general context of European diplomacy. Cavour was however more reluctant to join than the king who wanted to divert attention from domestic problems.
4. Cavour played a very important role in the **Plombières Agreement**, but note that he planned for four Italian kingdoms when the Austrians had been defeated. Cavour resigned after the armistice at Villafranca which indicates that he had no master-plan or wish for an Italian unification. He was able to take advantage of the risings in the duchies of the North and the final result was a greatly enlarged kingdom of Piedmont. This development was probably very important for the unification.
5. The process of unification in southern and central Italy was very much the work of Garibaldi. By entering the Papal States and **preventing Garibaldi** from reaching Rome, Cavour was able to control the situation and avoid foreign intervention. Cavour: *"If Garibaldi passes over to the mainland [...] king Victor Emmanuel loses more or less all his prestige...he is no more than Garibaldi's friend".*
6. Cavour had no master plan for unification but he was a great opportunist who could move with the events and use them to his advantage. The liberal school emphasises the importance of Cavour and he has been described as the **brain** behind the unification.

There were other factors as well:

1. **Nationalism/liberalism.** Groups like the Carbonari viewed revolts as the best means to provoke a general rebellion against absolutism in the 1820s and 1930s. Liberalism was closely related to nationalism in the early development. This kind of radicalism was opposed especially by the **Austrians** and Metternich who controlled much of northern Italy.
2. **Mazzini**, and his Young Italy, was the **soul** behind the unification. Denis Mack Smith emphasises the importance of Mazzini.
3. **The importance of King Victor Emmanuel**, is often underestimated. He had a main role in the decision to join the French in the Crimean War and was very important in the process which led to the Plombières Agreement. Again we must be aware that from the beginning his plan was an enlarged Piedmont and four Italian kingdoms. Denis Mack Smith emphasises the role of the king at the expense of Cavour. He held back Piedmont after Villafranca when Cavour instead resigned
4. **Garibaldi** is of course important in the extension of the unification process to southern and central Italy.
5. **Rivalry between the great powers.** This frequently helped Italy and sometimes hindered it: French support against Austria after Crimea, France defeated Austria in 1859, Prussia defeating first Austria (Venetia to Italy) and then France (Papal State incorporated). The support of the great powers was very important in the unification process.
6. **Cavour passed away in 1861**, before Venetia and Rome became parts of the Italian Kingdom.

Conclusion: Yes, Cavour was of importance but there were many other reasons as well, and it is important to be aware that initially he had no plan for one Italy. It was Garibaldi who forced him to take action in the south.

4. To what extent were foreign powers important in the unification process in Italy?

(Show their importance and show other factors as well.)

Yes, the actions of foreign powers had an impact on the unification process.

1. The implementation of the Vienna Settlement in Italy and domination, repression and military actions by **Austria in suppressing revolts** naturally spurred Italian nationalism.
2. Piedmont was **defeated by Austrian troops** in 1848/49. Both Cavour and Victor Emmanuel now realised the importance of the support of great foreign powers.
3. Piedmont's participation in the **Crimean War** in the mid-1850s was very successful in placing the Italian question firmly into the context of European diplomacy. It led to the **Plombières** Agreement between France and Piedmont in 1858 and the war against Austria the next year. The outcome of this conflict led to three Italian duchies becoming a part of Piedmont. **France** made it clear that it would **not intervene** over this issue. Piedmont doubled its size and population.
4. **Prussia's defeat of Austria** in 1866 led to Venetia becoming a part of the Italian kingdom.
5. **Prussia's defeat of France** in 1870 led to that the Papal territories in 1870 became a part of the Italian Kingdom. The annexation was supported by Spain and Austria.

However, there were other factors that were not due to other great powers.

1. The idea of **nationalism**.
2. **Mazzini**'s influence.
3. The traditions and growth of **Piedmont**.
4. **Cavour and Victor Emmanuel's** policies.
5. **Garibaldi's** actions. His expedition to Sicily and Naples where the only conquests made cannot be seen in the light of a great power conflict.

Conclusion: It must be concluded that even if there were other factors which were important in the unification process, actions by other great powers had a major impact on the unification. It is difficult to see how the Italian duchies could have succeeded without support from France and Prussia in ousting Austria from the Italian peninsula.

HISTORY HL: EUROPE

Chapter 3: The unification of Germany

Issues

How important was Bismarck in the unification process, or was it the strong economy of Prussia which made the unification possible?

3.1 Long-term causes

1. **The Congress of Vienna 1815.** It was decided that 39 German states (including Austria) should make up a new German Confederation. **Prussia was given the Rhineland with all its natural resources.** The area was, however, separated from Prussia and if it wanted to consolidate its territories, the greater part of Germany would be unified. Prussia had strengthened its position step by step during the 18th century and with the defeat of Napoleon it was a leading great power in Europe. The Quadruple Alliance between Austria, Russia, Prussia and Britain aimed to control France and it opposed political changes within states, such as demands from constitutionalists and liberals. **Austria and Metternich** were eager to maintain influence in German affairs and could do so because Austria was the leading power of the Confederation and its assembly, the *Diet*.

2. **The rise of nationalism.** The 19th century was the era of nationalism. Nationalism in this context means that a group of people, a nation, with a common sense of belonging to the same national identity should also form a state. This sense of identity could be based on culture, religion, language, ethnic background or traditions. This belief could both unite a country (Italy and Germany) and split a country (Austria). To form a new state was to redraw the map of Europe, which was a violation of the Vienna Settlement. In the **Carlsbad Decrees** of 1819, following the murder of a reactionary propagandist, Metternich persuaded the Diet to introduce closer supervision of universities and increased censorship. There was political tension between liberals/nationalists who opposed conservatives/Austria.

3. **The Zollverein and the growth of the Prussian economy.** Prussia was blessed with natural resources in the **Rhineland** including **coal** and **iron**. The state also introduced many reforms to improve the economy such as **reforming the tax system, building roads,** introducing an **effective banking system,** and **technical education.**

   In Prussia alone, there were 67 different tariffs making trade very difficult. The idea behind the Zollverein was that these internal customs barriers had to be removed if trade was to develop. A **customs union** between a number of German states, the Zollverein, was formed in 1834. The **Zollverein** area included 23 million people and Prussian tariffs were recognised as the norm for all states who participated. It led to a dramatic rise in custom revenues: 14.4 million thalers in 1834 to 27 million thalers in 1845. **Prussia had the right to negotiate on behalf of the Zollverein. Austria was excluded** from the Zollverein and a number of favourable trade agreements were concluded with states like Piedmont, France, Belgium, and Holland. The very fact that Austria was excluded had a major impact on the balance of power in central Europe. The historian Geoff Ley has concluded "[...] *Austria's defeat in 1866 is less decisive than its exclusion from the Zollverein*".

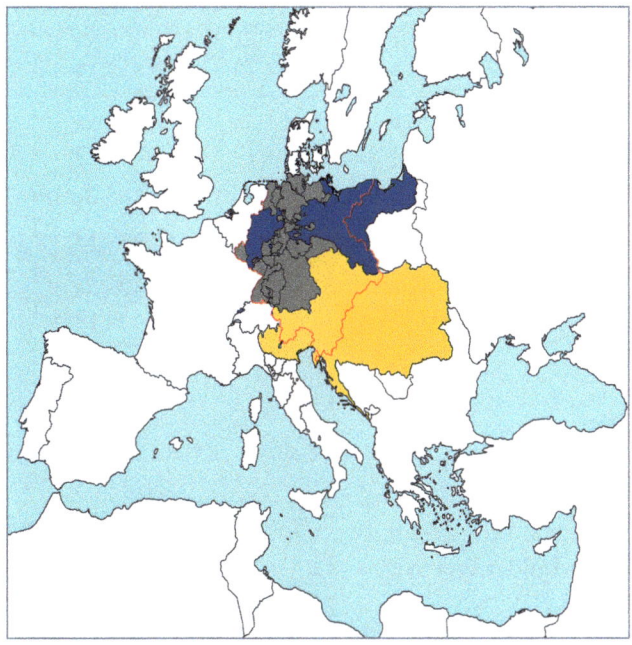

Key:

Blue: Prussia in 1834

Grey: Areas included until 1866

Yellow: Austrian possessions outside the Zollverein

Red: Borders of the 1828 German Confederation

Figure 3.1: **German Zollverein, 1834–1919**

There was a tremendous **growth of the Prussian economy**. The number of steam engines in Prussia increased from 419 in 1837 to 1,444 in 1848. Between 1841 and 1849, 24 new deep-level mines were opened in the Ruhr. In the 1840s, the Prussian state took a very active role in building railways, which had significance not only economically but also militarily. The famous British economist John Maynard Keynes has concluded: *"The German empire was built more truly on coal and iron than on blood and iron"*.

4. **Army reforms**. It is worth noting that as late as 1859 the Prussian army was not the effective war machine with which we are familiar from the 1860s. W. McElwee writes: *"to the outward eye the Prussian army in 1859 was as clumsy and antiquated an instrument as any of the others"*. In 1857, Helmut von Moltke was appointed Chief of Staff. A program of reform was introduced which gave Prussia a standing army of 180,000 soldiers and a reserve of 175,000 putting the army on a par with Austria's. Prussia could also take advantage of an effective **railway system** and in the Austro-Prussian War in 1866 the army could be mobilised in five days, something which took 45 days for Austria.

In Europe, 1848 was the year of revolutions: from Sicily to Denmark, and from France to Hungary. Europe suffered bad harvests, reduced demands for manufactured goods, and unemployment. The revolts were led by liberals and one of the major outcomes was that the symbol of repression and conservatism, Prince Metternich in Austria resigned and fled the country. In German states liberals were able to arrange elections for a German National Parliament. Liberalism went hand-in-hand with nationalism since conservative control was to some extent maintained through foreign powers, i.e. Austria. But this **Frankfurt parliament** failed in its aim to create a unified Germany including Austria (the *Grossedeutsch* solution) mainly since it lacked any real power. A second attempt in 1850 to form a union of North German states (*Kleindeutsch* solution), the **Erfurt Union**, also failed due to the fact that a number of smaller states feared Prussian domination and finally even the king of Prussia, the leader of this new state, decided to abandon this 'dangerous' innovation. Conservatism and the German Confederation were revived and Prussia had to wait another fifteen years to take up the leadership of Germany.

The late 1850s witnessed the revival of Prussian liberalism and German nationalism. In the 1862 elections to the Landtag (the representative assembly of the Kingdom of Prussia) the liberals won 83 seats and the conservatives only 16. In 1859, the War Minister Albrecht von Roon proposed to create 53 new army regiments and an army which would be dominated by officers from the nobility. It was opposed by the Landtag. It led to long-lasting political controversy between the new king Wilhelm I and the parliament. It culminated in 1862 with the Landtag refusing to approve the national budget.

3.2 Short-term causes

1. **The role of Bismarck**. In 1862 the king decided to appoint Otto von Bismarck as the new Minister President (Prime Minister) of Prussia. He was a conservative Prussian Junker (rich landowner and member of the nobility) and monarchist without any visions about a German unification. Bismarck's policies were:

    Figure 3.2: **Otto von Bismarck**

    - to secure the **army reform**;
    - to **illegally collect taxes** to finance them ('gap theory' – the budget was a joint responsibility of the Landtag and the Monarch, when these could not reach an agreement power would revert to the king according to Bismarck).
    - **resisting the opposition,** i.e. the **liberals** and **nationalists**;
    - ruling Prussia for four years in defiance of the majority in the Assembly.

2. In 1863, Prussia supported Russia during the Polish revolt. If Prussia should later attempt to change the balance of power in Central Europe i.e. to attack Austria, it would be more likely that it would have support from Russia.

Bismarck pushed through the army reform without the support of the Landtag and for four years he ruled the country without an approved budget. Most taxes were indirect, from customs, and Bismarck could use the money for the army.

3.3 Importance of the wars and Bismarck

The importance of Bismarck has been debated. Some would argue that it was the Prussian economy which enabled Bismarck and Prussia to take actions. Others would emphasise the importance of Bismarck and his role in implementing army reform, his diplomacy, his leadership and his being the planner behind the wars.

But it must be concluded that even if the Prussian economy and army were very strong, Bismarck's leadership cannot be ignored. The very result of the unification, a Germany also including the Southern German states, was not an inevitable outcome from the beginning. These states, which were mainly Catholic, could just as well have turned to Austria.

3.3.1 The Schleswig-Holstein question 1863–65

The two duchies belonged formally to Denmark but enjoyed a large degree of independence. In 1863, the new Danish king, Christian IX, tried to annex the areas. **Bismarck asked Austria to form an alliance in order to defeat Denmark,** probably because he wanted to avoid action by the Confederation which would give Austria more influence. Bismarck was now able to show the strength and the need of the army. After the war in 1864 Denmark had to renounce both Schleswig and Holstein. Otto Pflanze writes: *"almost overnight the **Bismarck cult** was*

>
> In his first speech to the Landtag, Bismarck claimed: *"the greatest questions of the day will not be decided by speeches and the resolutions of majorities – that was the great mistake of 1848 and 1849 – but by iron and blood".*

3. THE UNIFICATION OF GERMANY

born" in Prussia. Many liberals, i.e. nationalists, in Prussia now started to support Bismarck. Had he had a 'hidden purpose' when he violated the constitution with the army reform?

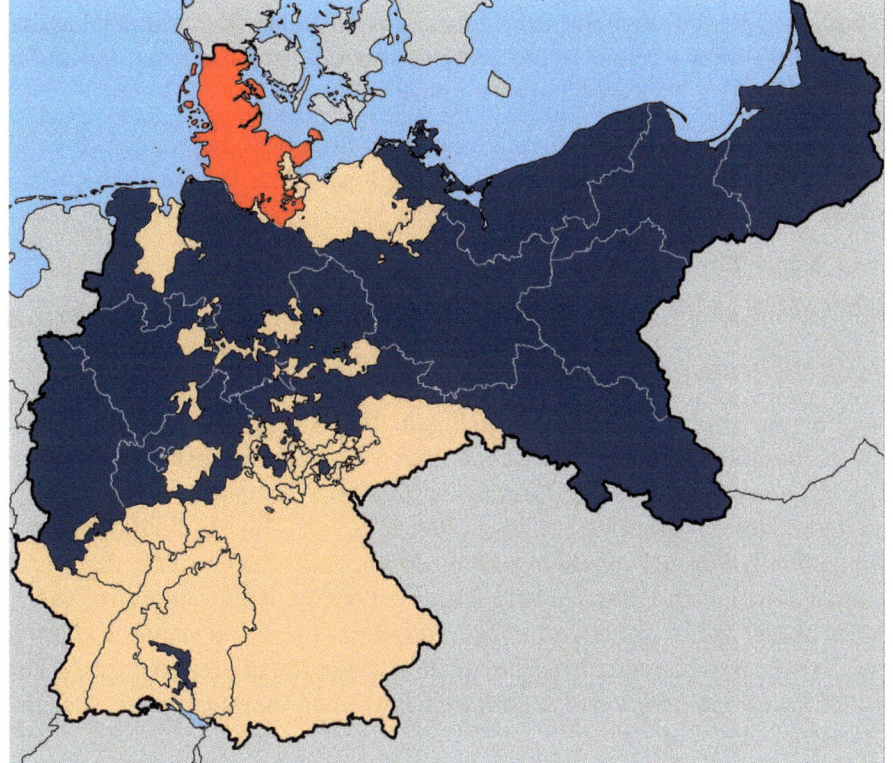

Figure 3.3: **The Province of Schleswig–Holstein (red), within the Kingdom of Prussia, within the German Empire, 1866-1920.**

Did Bismarck have a master plan for unification, or was an aggressive foreign policy a means to contain liberals and their demands for reforms within Prussia? Bismarck realised, step by step, that foreign policy could be used for domestic reasons.

The **Austro-Prussian War of 1866** started with disputes over the administration of the Danish duchies. eight German states supported Austria. Bismarck was able to get a guarantee from France (Biarritz) that it would remain neutral and that Italy would join Prussia attacking Austria on two fronts. Russia remained neutral partly as a result of Prussian support during the Polish revolt in 1863. **A swift Prussian mobilisation and superior Prussian infantry, tactics, and armament ensured Austrian defeats in this 'Seven Weeks' War'**.

In the peace which followed the war Bismarck acted as a skilled diplomat. He had to use all his abilities to convince the king and the generals that Austria should not be punished or humiliated. The **Treaty of Prague** of 1866 is probably the most important diplomatic agreement in Europe since the Vienna Settlement.

- All German territories north of the River Main now belonged to a new North German Confederation controlled by Prussia i.e. the death of the old German Confederation. Prussia made up 5/6 of the population.

- Austria lost no territories (apart from Venetia); *"we need Austria's strength in the future for ourselves"* said Bismarck. But Austria was now banished from influence in both Germany and Italy (which resulted in that it turned to the Balkans). It also led to the compromise with Hungary, or the creation of the Dual Monarchy in 1867.

German liberals now surrendered to Bismarck's success: *"I bow before the genius of Bismarck"* one of his critics wrote. Bismarck seized the opportunity and turned to the Landtag with an 'act of indemnity' in which he sought admission for having acted illegally over the past four years (no budget approved when the army reform was carried out). The liberal Landtag supported him with 230 votes against 75. The army reform had been implemented and he now had a compliant Landtag. Two wars had accomplished it.

After the North German Confederation had been created there was one danger: the four German states in the South who stood outside. They feared Prussian absolutism and militarism and could:

- inspire liberalism in the North; and
- turn to either Austria or France as many were Catholic.

3.3.2 The Franco-Prussian War 1870–71

In 1868 a revolution overthrew the monarchy in Spain. After a number of candidates had rejected the offer to the Spanish throne, Prince Leopold von Hohenzollern of Prussia accepted the **candidature. France was alarmed** by the growing strength of Prussia/the North German Confederation and could not accept a Prussian ruler in Spain. The candidature led to a political crisis and finally Prince Leopold turned down the offer. The day after, the French ambassador was sent to meet the Prussian king at Ems to demand that Prussia and the king would never again accept such a candidature. This request was turned down by the king and Bismarck released to the press an edited version, the **Ems telegram**, of a report from the king to Bismarck, which gave an impression of **a blunt exchange of diplomatic insults**. The crisis led to France declaring war in July 1870.

Recent research has revealed Bismarck's close links to the candidature (Georges Bonnin and Erich Eyck).

Bismarck had concluded some military treaties with the **Southern states** in 1866. When the war started they fulfilled their obligation and joined the Northern states. Nationalism ran high in the South when the war started and Bismarck also used bribes and promises that the states would **retain some independence if they joined the North** in the war and also formed one German state.

The war was a brief conflict and again a swift German mobilisation was of importance. France was defeated and the Second Empire collapsed and Napoleon III had to abdicate. The Unification of Germany was declared at Versailles and Wilhelm I, the Prussian king, was proclaimed German Emperor.

3.3.3 Historiography and analysis

- **The orthodox view**, endorsed by **Bismarck** himself in his memoirs written in the 1890s, claims that Bismarck was the driving force behind the unification and that he was driven by a master plan to accomplish this aim. He had been able to implement the army reform and through a number of diplomatic manoeuvres and through three different wars, he finally accomplished his **master plan**. Without Bismarck's actions nationalism in Germany could have taken other directions. One example is that the Southern states could have remained independent or joined Austria. The British statesman Disraeli recounted a conversation he had with Bismarck in 1862 when he came to power. Bismarck told Disraeli. *"As soon as the army shall be brought into such a condition as to inspire respect, I shall seize the first best pretext to declare war on Austria, dissolve the German Diet and give national unity to Germany under Prussian leadership"*.

- **Others** have seen Bismarck as an opportunist who, step by step, **changed his aims** and finally supported the national dream. Bismarck can be seen as a Prussian monarchist who was fighting liberalism and nationalism in the Landtag and who, over time, **came**

3. THE UNIFICATION OF GERMANY

- **to realise** that nationalism could be used to accomplish his aims. As late as in 1866 after the Austro-Prussian War, he wrote to his wife *"there is nothing more to do in our lifetime"* hence showing that he had **no master plan** for a unification.
- A **revisionist group of historians led by Helmut Böhme** have claimed that the driving force behind the unification was **the strong economy and the social forces** created by this development. Bismarck's opportunities and course was driven by these forces and this view is to some extent supported by Keynes: *"The German empire was built more truly on coal and iron than on blood and iron"* – and not by one individual or wars. Geoff Ley supports the view that the economy, and not wars and Bismarck's diplomacy, was of major importance: *"Austria's defeat in 1866 is less decisive than its exclusion from the Zollverein"*.

> Now, when you have read the text:
> 1. Study the following questions (but not the answers!)
> 2. Copy a template and outline your answer
> 3. Compare the two answers and analyse any possible difference.

5. "The German empire was built more truly on coal and iron than on blood and iron." To what extent do you agree with this statement?

(Introduction: show that you understand the question: a strong economy was more important than the wars. Show 'yes' and 'no' arguments.)

Yes, I do agree:

1. The Rhineland a part of Prussia in the Vienna Settlement.
2. The creation of the Zollverein in 1834. Account for the growth of the economy, industrialisation, railway building etc. Prussia controlled the Zollverein and Austria was excluded from it in 1864. Ley concludes: *"Austria's defeat in 1866 is less decisive than its exclusion from the Zollverein"*.
3. Prussia had a lot of natural resources especially in the Rhineland.
4. Successful state intervention in economic life: education, banking, roads, taxes. The Prussian economy made it possible to build railways and a strong army.

No, I don't agree e.g. 'blood and iron' decisive

1. Albrecht von Roon, War Minister responsible for army reforms who created 53 new regiments from 1859. Without the strength of the army, Austria and France could not have been defeated.
2. Chief of Staff Helmuth von Moltke reorganised the army organisation and technique.
3. The 3 different wars were very important in: a) creating a national mood for unification; b) excluding Austria; and c) strengthening Bismarck's image: *"I bow before the genius of Bismarck"*. Write about the wars and how they affected Bismarck's and Austria's positions.
4. Bismarck supported the importance of military strength in his famous speech from 1862: *"the greatest questions of the day will not be decided by speeches and the resolutions of majorities – that was the great mistake of 1848 and 1849 – but by iron and blood"*. To Bismarck, ***real power*** was the same as military and political power.

Finally, write one paragraph where you partly question the assumption made in the question: economic factors and wars are not sufficient in explaining the unification. The idea of nationalism and the importance of Bismarck cannot be ignored.

Conclusion: The unification was accomplished through: a strong economy, wars, growth of nationalism and Bismarck as an individual. It is difficult to ignore that a strong industrial base was very important for success in war. But unification doesn't necessarily always require a strong economy.

6. Discuss the importance of diplomacy and wars in the process of German unification between 1862 and 1871.

(Structure: Try to show a balanced view where these two factors are covered. See points to discuss below.)

Part I: diplomacy

1. Prussia's support for Russia during the Polish revolt of 1863. This would later partly lead to Russian neutrality in the Austro-Prussian War of 1866.
2. It was an act of diplomacy by Bismarck to make Prussia and Austria, and not the Confederation, attack Denmark in the war of 1863–64.
3. Bismarck met Napoleon III in 1865 (Biarritz) and was promised French neutrality in the event of an Austro-Prussian War. Very important move.
4. In December, the same year, Prussia signed an alliance with Italy where Italy promised to fight with Prussia in a war against Austria, making it into a two-front war.
5. Russia remained neutral in the war in 1866 in alleged support for Bismarck's support during the rising in Poland 1863.
6. By deliberately not humiliating Austria after the victory in 1866, Bismarck prevented a campaign of revenge later.
7. Negotiations/bribes/secret treaties made the Southern German states support the North German Confederation in the war against France in 1870 and a unification under Prussian leadership.
8. Bismarck stood behind the Hohenzollern candidature in Spain and the Ems telegram which finally led to the war against France.

Part II: wars were important

1. The war against Denmark led to Bismarck gaining lots of support in Prussia which made it easier to later attack Austria later; *"...overnight the Bismarck cult was born"*.
2. The Austro-Prussian War finally excluded Austria from the German states, created the North German Confederation when Prussia annexed Hanover, Hesse-Cassel, Nassau, Frankfurt and Schleswig-Holstein. In Prussia critics declared: *"I bow before the genius of Bismarck"*.
3. The war of 1870 finally led the Southern German states, and the King of Prussia, to fully accept a unification of Germany. Bismarck: *"the greatest questions of the day will not be decided by speeches and the resolutions of majorities – that was the great mistake of 1848 and 1849 – but by iron and blood"*.

Part III: other factors

There were also other factors that cannot be linked to war and diplomacy, which were decisive such as the growth of the **Prussian economy**, **nationalism**, and **Bismarck** as an individual.

Conclusion: the wars played a decisive role but the importance of the economy and the idea of nationalism, and Bismarck's diplomacy, should not be ignored.

3. THE UNIFICATION OF GERMANY

7. Compare and contrast the unifications of Italy and Germany.
(Show the similarities and the differences.)

Similarities:

1. **Nationalism**: The 19th century was the era of nationalism. Nationalism in this context means that a group of people, a nation, with a common sense of belonging to the same national identity, should also form a state. This sense of identity could be based on culture, religion, language, ethnic background or traditions.
2. **Diplomacy** played an important role in both Italy and Germany. Piedmont's involvement in the Crimean War, the cooperation with Prussia in 1866, international support to invade the Papal states were crucial. Prussia supported Russia during the Polish revolt. France promised to remain neutral in the Austro-Prussian War while Italy was an ally. Austria was not punished after the war in the Treaty of Prague. The states in Southern Germany were convinced to take part in the unification.
3. **Wars** were very important in both of the countries. The Crimean War, the war against Austria in 1859, the Austro-Prussian War in 1866 and the Franco-Prussian War in 1870, were very important in **Italian** unification. The war against Denmark in 1863, the Austro-Prussian War in 1866 and finally the Franco-Prussian War in 1870, were very important to **German** unification.
4. **Prussia and Piedmont** were both driving forces in the unification of each country. Both were the strongest states in each country partly due to an ambitious reform programme where the government in each country played a very important role.
5. Austria was the main enemy of both Prussia and Piedmont.

Differences:

1. The main difference was probably that **foreign powers** were so important in Italy. Piedmont was too weak to oust the Austrians and without help from France and Prussia it had been difficult. So support was needed in Italy while Prussia needed to defeat its enemies to establish power.
2. There was **no Bismarck in Italy**. To some extent Cavour might be compared to him but in Italy politicians like Mazzini and Garibaldi made their contributions.
3. **Garibaldi** played a very important role in Italy and note that he in many cases acted against the will of Cavour. There was no 'Garibaldi' in Germany and no Mazzini.
4. The **Prussian war machine** was decisive in Germany while the army of Italy was not so important.

Conclusion: summarise the similarities and the differences.

Chapter 4: Bismarck's Germany 1871–90

Issues

One of the main debates over Bismarck's rule is whether he, by crippling the development of true democratic institutions, indirectly paved the way for Nazism, that is what is later referred to as the 'continuity school'.

> See the text about the Weimar Republic from page 98 for more about the 'continuity school'.

In the **Treaty of Frankfurt**, signed in May 1871, France was punished for the war. They had to pay an **indemnity** of 5 billion francs over a period of three years. **Alsace-Lorraine** was also handed over to Germany. After this Bismarck knew that Germany must have Russia as an ally, which would be a cornerstone in his foreign policy – France would always be the enemy.

The new empire was a **federal state:** each state had substantial autonomy and their own domestic administration. The federation was dominated by Prussia, which comprised over 60% of the area. **The political system was not a true parliamentary system**. Neither the Chancellor (Prime Minister) nor the ministers were responding to the parliament, and it agreed in 1874 to approve the budget for a period of seven years. The power to approve the budget was normally a key tool for the parliament to exercise control over

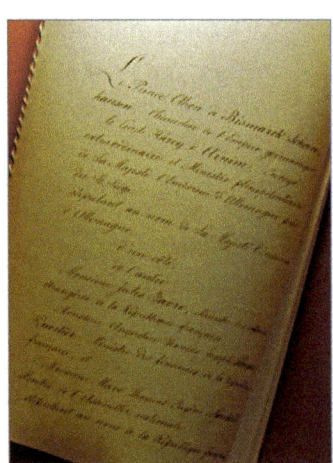

Figure 4.1: **The Treaty of Frankfurt that endend the Franco-Prussian War**

Figure 4.2: **'Between Berlin and Rome'**, with Bismarck on the left and the Pope on the right, from the German satirical magazine **Kladderadatsch, 1875.**

the government. Real power lay in the hands of the **King of Prussia/the Kaiser,** and the ministers he had appointed.

4.1 The Liberal era

The years 1871-78 represent Bismarck's '**liberal era**'. In 1862, the Liberals had been his political enemies, but had become his enthusiastic supporters due to:

- Bismarck had been the architect behind the Liberals main aim: the **unification**;
- the Liberals also supported his economic policy: **free trade**;
- they also supported Bismarck in the **Kulturkampf**, the clash with the Catholic Church;
- after 1871 Bismarck's policies were aiming at consolidation of **national unity** and centralisation of the administration. The National Liberal Party supported this.

Examples of this were that one **national currency** was introduced, all **internal tariffs** were abolished, a new **commercial law** was introduced, a **Reichsbank** was formed and a **national legal system** established. The German language were to be used in schools and administration (important in regions like Alsace-Lorraine). The Liberals, who also were nationalists, supported this policy. But no major political concessions were made to the Liberals creating a true parliamentary system.

4.2 The Kulturkampf

The first decade of the Second Reich was also dominated by Bismarck's clash with the Catholic Church in the South – **The Kulturkampf**. The Liberals supported the Chancellor in this struggle. Why was there a clash and what happened?

- Firstly, it had deep roots with previous church and schools laws. Secondly, the four Catholic states had once stood outside the North German Confederation. Liberal policies of curtailing church power had been met with the publication of Pope Pius IX's **Syllabus of Error** in 1864. To the Pope this signalled a moral warfare against liberalism and anti-clericalism.
- To Bismarck it was a struggle between the King/state versus the church/clergy.
- In 1872 diplomatic relations with the Vatican were severed and the Jesuit order was banned in Germany.
- The May Laws 1873 brought the inspection of schools. Clerical appointments and education of clergy were brought under state control.

This led to a major clash with the church in the South 1874-75. **Eight of the 12 bishops were deprived their offices and more than 1,000 priests were suspended.** It had no effect politically and the Centre Party in the Reichstag increased their support substantially from 61 to 91 seats. Instead it can probably be argued that they gained from 'martyrdom'. The policy also met resistance from conservatives in Protestant areas who saw this policy as too liberal (liberals were supporters of freedom of worship). It was also dangerous taking into account that Austria was a Catholic state.

When Pius IX passed away in 1878 Bismarck saw an opportunity to bring the Kulturkampf to an end. He dismissed the Minister for Religious Affairs and repealed some of the May Laws. Many consider that Bismarck lost the Kulturkampf and without any doubt it gave him many enemies in the South and did not contribute to the national unification he endeavoured.

The '**Great Depression**' in the 1870s brought the co-operation with the liberals to an end. As the country was going through economic hardship, industrialists wanted protective tariffs. When the agricultural sector, with **Junker** landowners, was facing competition, especially from the US, they also wanted tariffs. They formed strong pressure groups. These old and new elites formed **the Alliance of Rye and Steel**.

The result was **a dramatic switch by Bismarck** to economic and political conservatism. Why?

- Industrialists and Junkers were together a very **powerful opposition**.
- With cheap grains coming from the US, the **Junkers** (rich landowners) were clearly under pressure.
- **France**, **Russia** and **Austria/Hungary** had all introduced protective tariffs.
- Tariff incomes would give the government valuable **incomes**.
- It can also be seen as an attempt to seek support against the **socialists**.

In **1879 new tariff laws** were enacted and with this **the Liberal era had come to an end**.

4.3 Bismarck and the growth of socialism

Figure 4.3: **A barricade on Rue Voltaire, after its capture by the regular army during the Bloody Week**

Conservative politicians feared the socialists. When there were **two attempts to kill the German Kaiser** in 1878, Bismarck saw the opportunity to call for new elections, 'the Fatherland was in danger'. The National Liberals lost support, from 141 to 109 seats, while the Conservatives went from 40 to 59 seats (Social Democrats from 12 to 9). In October, anti-socialist laws were enacted:

- **meetings with the aim to spread socialist ideas were banned**;
- **trade unions were outlawed**;
- **45 newspapers were closed**.

But Bismarck did not only use oppression. In a policy from 1883, referred to as **'state socialism'**:

- **medical insurance** was introduced;
- **sick pay was introduced**;
- **insurance** of industrial injuries; and
- **old age pension** (1889) was also introduced.

But the growth of the support of the Social Democratic Party could not be prevented, as can be seen by their seats in the Reichstag:

1871	1874	1877	1878	1881	1884	1887	1890
2	9	12	9	12	24	11	35

4. BISMARCK'S GERMANY 1871–90

4.4 Economic development

The economic development during the Second Reich is impressive. With the incorporation of Alsace-Lorraine, Germany got access to the largest deposits of iron ore in Europe. If we add to this the Rhineland with its natural resources, especially coal, the economic potential was enormous. With the legislation from 1870, a single currency and no custom barriers, the Great Depression in the 1870s had no major significance in a longer perspective. We can clearly see the tremendous growth of Bismarck's Germany compared to France:

	1870	1890
Population (millions)		
France	36	38
Germany	41	49
Coal (million tons)		
France	13	26
Germany	38	89
Steel (million tons)		
France	0.08	0.6
Germany	0.3	2.2
Iron ore (million tons)		
France	2.6	3.5
Germany	2.9	8

4.5 Foreign policy

With the victory in the **Franco-Prussian War** in 1870–71 and the unification under Prussian leadership, Bismarck had achieved what he wanted. After this, '**status quo**' and good relations with **Russia** were the primary aims in his foreign policy. **Austria** was also a key country if we take into account that France was the enemy.

The League of the Three Emperors, was first established in 1872. Germany, Russia, and Austria-Hungary promised each other support in the event of one of them was attacked by a fourth power. Bismarck had three aims:

- it was a **union of conservative countries** which could co-operate against dangerous forces like **nationalism and socialism**;
- neither Austria nor Russia would support the **French** in an attack;
- A J P Taylor has argued that it would also **prevent Russia and Austria-Hungary coming into conflict over problems in Eastern Europe**.

In 1875, a revolt of South Slav peoples started against the Ottomans in the Balkans. As an outcome of the **Russo-Turkish War of 1877** and the Treaty of San Stefano in 1878, Bulgaria, Serbia, Montenegro, and Rumania gained independence or territories from the Ottomans. The states have been described as '**client states**' to Russia, an outcome that was **unacceptable to Austria-Hungary**. Austria had first lost its power and influence in northern Italy in 1859 and finally in the German Confederation with the defeat against Prussia in the Austro-Prussian War in 1866 (where it also lost Venetia).

If Russia were to gain considerable influence in the Balkans, it would be a disaster to Austria. This may affect the relations in the League of the Three Emperors and could destroy Bismarck's security system against the French.

At the **Congress of Berlin** in 1878 under the leadership of Bismarck, Russia was forced to accept the loss of Slav territories from the war i.e. some of the gains of San Stefano. It put a lot of strain to German-Russian relations and Alexander II saw it as *"a European coalition against Russia under the leadership of prince Bismarck"*.

As a result of this development Bismarck felt that he had to secure stronger bonds with Austria-Hungary. He could not risk isolation and some have even argued that this was intended to frighten Russia into co-operation. In this **Dual Alliance from 1879** the two countries pledged to support each other in case of the event of a Russian attack. They also promised neutrality if one was attacked by a third state – presumably France. The alliance was seen as rather surprising taking into account the war in 1866.

Russia was, however, still of vital interest in making Germany secure. In 1887 Germany and Russia signed the **Reinsurance Treaty**. In the treaty each power promised neutrality in the event of one of them being attacked by a third power. There could be no two-front war if France attacked.

It must be noted that Bismarck did not take part in the 'scramble for Africa' or attempts to gain colonies in any other part of the world. In 1881 he declared, *"As long as I am Chancellor we shall pursue no colonial policy"*. There was one smaller exception in 1884, when Germany involved herself in what is today known as Namibia.

> Now, when you have read the text:
> 1. Study the question that follows (but not the answer!)
> 2. Copy a template and outline your answer.
> 3. Compare your answer with the one given and analyse any possible differences.

8. To what extent did Bismarck's rule 1871–90 strengthen Germany?

(Give the 'yes' and the 'no' arguments.)

Yes, it strengthened Germany:

1. Bismarck's followed a policy of consolidation of **national unity** and centralisation of administration after 1871. Examples of this were that one **national currency** was introduced, all **internal tariffs** were abolished, a new **commercial law** was introduced, a **Reichsbank** was formed and a **national legal system** established. He created a 'common German market'.

2. Taking into account that there were three wars 1864–1871, it must be noted that during the period 1871–90 Germany enjoyed peace. To some extent it can be argued that Bismarck's foreign policy is part of the explanation to this. He was satisfied with the unification and formed alliances, which would avoid a new war.

3. It must be concluded that his social policies were very advanced for this period: medical insurance, sick pay, insurance for industrial injuries and old age pension.

4. Finally, the growth of the economy is by far the most important point. It can of course be argued that it's wrong to claim that one individual shall be credited for this, but Bismarck was to a major extent involved in creation of this 'market', i.e. Germany, with one currency and no internal tariffs.

If we look at these figures, it must be concluded that Germany was an enormous economic success:

	1870	1890
Population (millions)		
France	36	38
Germany	41	49
Coal (million tons)		
France	13	26
Germany	38	89
Steel (million tons)		
France	0.08	0.6
Germany	0.3	2.2
Iron ore (million tons)		
France	2.6	3.5
Germany	2.9	8

No, it did not strengthen Germany:

1. In many ways it can be argued that he did not bring national unity – he brought confrontation to Germany domestically and ruled the country with shrewdness. Examples of this is the Kulturkampf and the anti-socialist laws.
2. His social legislation should not be exaggerated. One example is that old age pensions were paid from the age of 70, an age few workers reached in the 1870s.
3. Bismarck did not allow a true parliamentary system to develop. By obstructing such a development he contributed to tension and troubles to come. Some even argue that this legacy is a part of the explanation for the Nazi seizure of power in the 1930s. Germany never enjoyed a true democratic tradition. Max Weber writes: *"Bismarck left behind him as a political heritage a nation without any political education […] a nation without any political will, accustomed to allow the great statesman and its head to look after its policy for it".*

Conclusion: It is a valid point to conclude that politically he left a legacy of an uneducated nation, which would cause problems in the future. It is debatable whether or not this argument should be used to explain the rise of Nazism, but he is partly responsible for the lack of a democratic tradition.

On the other hand, Bismarck must to some extent be credited for the formation of a Germany as one economic market. The growth of Germany economically after 1871 must to some extent be credited to Bismarck.

Chapter 5: Alexander II and Alexander III

Issues

There are two major issues that you need to be able to discuss: why did Alexander II reform, and how successful were his reforms?

Alexander II became Tsar of Russia during the Crimean War in March 1855. Russia had been defeated by Britain and France (Turkey and Piedmont had also joined the coalition to fight Russia) in a war fought in Russia; the war had shown that the vast military power of Russia was an illusion. As a response Alexander introduced a reform programme where the most well-known reform was the **Emancipation of the Serfs**.

A **serf** was someone who was owned by the nobility or the crown and could be bought and sold and forced to work when the owner wished, and who had virtually no legal rights. They worked the land that belonged to the nobleman. But when they fulfilled their duties to the nobleman, they could use their time as they wished to cultivate the land of

Figure 5.1: **Alexander II of Russia**

the serfs and retain any profit from their work (if there was any). So from that point of view they can't be compared to an American slave. In the census of 1816, half of the population were serfs owned by the nobility and 32% were serfs who used land owned by the crown.

RUSSIA'S DEFEAT IN THE CRIMEAN WAR

Russia was defeated in the Crimean War because of its backwardness:

- it lacked a modern system of communications, i.e. an effective **railway system**. Even though the war was fought in Russia it could only mobilise 60,000 of its one million soldiers.
- its industry couldn't equip the soldiers properly with modern **long-range rifles**. Only 4 per cent of the Russian troops had these rifles while 50 per cent of the British troops used them.
- Russians soldiers served for 25 years. One result was that the soldiers were **older** than the enemy soldiers. After 25 years in the army you returned as a free man. Russia had a standing army of one million men but no reserve. It was ineffective and expensive.

So in total, the peasant population made up more than 80% of the population, showing that this was a key area if Russia were to be reformed.

After the war, Alexander introduced a reform programme. Why?

Historians emphasise different reasons:

1. Alexander realised the need of modernisation. There is no doubt that one aim was to **strengthen the autocracy and Russia**. The justification for Tsardom was the strength of Russia. A humiliation like the Crimean War had of course undermined and affected the autocracy and Russia as a country.

2. **Economic arguments**: some argue that the emancipation of the serfs was a necessary precondition for industrialisation. The industry needed free labour. **But there is little evidence that the government at this time had any strong desire to encourage industrialisation**, except for building railways, which can be clearly linked to military needs.

   Marxist and Soviet historians emphasise that serfdom and exploitation had ceased to be profitable for the nobility, and hence a new mode of production which was more profitable for the nobility had to be introduced. It was seen as a crisis for the feudal system and this is the main reason for the reforms.

   Even if the Marxist interpretation has been refuted by many, it must be concluded that the Russian economy was increasingly lagging behind the economies of Western Europe and that this problem could be one reason for introducing an economic reform programme.

3. **Fear of revolution from below**: this argument was emphasised by the Tsar in his famous emancipation speech of 1856: *"it is better to abolish serfdom from above than to wait for the time when it will begin to abolish itself from below"*. Some historians argue that Alexander tailored his argument to convince his audience, the nobility. It was the nobility who had to give up land and jurisdiction so he needed to convince them about the need for reform. Many other historians argue that there was actually a genuine fear of peasant revolts. The outbreak of peasant revolts and disobedience was rising steadily. Between 1826–34 there were 148 outbreaks and between 1845–54 there were 348 such outbreaks.

4. **'The power of ideas'**: In the mid-19th century, few influential figures could be found who could provide a principal defence of the institution of serfdom. There were actually spokesmen for emancipation both among liberals and noblemen. The problem was to find an acceptable solution especially one which would satisfy the nobility who had to give up land. This view was reflected by Nicholas I, Alexander's father, when he said in 1842: *"Serfdom is an evil, palpable and obvious to all, but to touch it now would be even more disastrous"*.

5. **Military arguments**: Most historians agree that the timing of the reform, after defeat in war, shows us that military arguments were important. The government wanted to reduce the period of service. It was reduced from 25 to 15 years in 1859 and finally to six years in 1872. Why was a long time of service a disadvantage?

   - The system with soldiers serving for longer periods resulted in that Russian soldiers were older than the enemy soldiers.
   - You had to serve for 25 years and then you left the army as a free man. This resulted in Russia having no military reserve to use in case of war. The size of the army's active force was the same in peace as in war time. This was a very expensive system. If you only served for 6 years you could be used in the reserve after your military

service and consequently the size and the cost for the army in peace time could be reduced.

If the army were to be reformed by reducing the period of service there were two alternatives:

(a) to return the serfs without an emancipation. However, sending back men with military training and to force them to go back to serfdom when the tradition was to give them free, could be dangerous and had to be avoided;

(b) to continue to let ex-soldiers be free men. With a reduced time of service, most men would survive their time in the army. In a longer perspective it would result in two social classes in the countryside, which would destabilise the social situation. **Conclusion**: if you wanted to reduce the time of service you had to emancipate the serfs! The abolition of serfdom was a pre-condition for reforms in the army. General Miliutin summarised: *"Serfdom doesn't permit us to shorten the term of service"*.

Conclusion: Alexander's attempt to modernise Russia was intended to both strengthen Russia and the institution of Tsardom. To do that you had to reform the army → then you had to emancipate the serfs → then you had to introduce other reforms (explained in the next section) like introducing *zemstva* and legal reforms. To some extent Alexander's reforms can be seen as a **chain reaction**.

Key question to understand: Why did you have to emancipate the serfs if you wanted to reduce the time of service?

5.1 Reforms

1. **Some initial reforms**: censorship was relaxed, prisoners released, tax arrears were cancelled, and some liberties were restored to Poland and the Catholic Church.

2. **The emancipation of the serfs 1861**: land was taken from the nobility and the state but serfs had to pay **redemption dues** for 49 years. Land was not given to the individual but to the *Mir*, the local peasant council. Land was then distributed to each family annually according to the size of the family (led to population growth). But the peasants had the right to their personal belongings and were now formally free men. They couldn't be forced to work for the noble man like as in the old system.

3. The main weakness of the reform was that areas granted to the serfs were too small compared to redemption payments, i.e. the price they had to pay for the land was set **too high**. This of course led to an increase in poverty. The redemption dues in combination

Figure 5.2: **A peasant leaving his landlord on Yuriev Day (a feast day of St. George in autumn to celebrate the end of the harvesting season).**

with the highest natural **population growth** in Europe are key points in explaining Russian rural development in the late 19th century.

Population growth =
number of births
− number of deaths
+ immigration
− emigration

The size of the Russian population was approximately:

1800	1860	1900
30 million	60 million	120 million

With a growing population, the size of the average peasant land holding went down. In 1877 it was 35 acres and in 1905 it was 28 acres (a reduction of 20%). There were of course other reasons for the growth of the population than just the fact that land was given to each family according to its size.

From a long-term perspective, once Russia started to industrialise, peasants could more easily move to industrialised areas. From a shorter perspective, the *Mir* which was responsible for collecting taxes, started to restrict free travel in order to ensure an available for force.

4. The **zemstva** (singular *zemstvo*): local administrative power of the nobility was broken and *zemstva* were created to deal with local administration such as: primary education, public health, poor relief, local industry and the maintenance of the highways. These bodies were dominated by the nobility but both peasants and the nobility were represented. However, when asked to form a 'national *zemstvo*' (i.e. a *Duma*), the Tsar refused to do this.

5. **Legal reforms**: There were substantial reforms of the Russian legal system: proceedings were conducted in public, they were uniform to all classes of society, jury system and independent judges were introduced.

   According to Seton-Watson: *"the court room was the one place in Russia where real freedom of speech prevailed"*. These reforms are normally considered to be the most successful of Alexander's reforms.

6. **Military reforms**: the term of service was reduced from 25 to 6 years, universal military service was introduced, brutal forms of punishment were abolished as was the system of military 'colonies.'

7. **Education**: the number of university students was allowed to rise, lectures on 'European government' and philosophy were permitted and finally universities were given more autonomy. Women were allowed to study at universities. In the *Press Law* issued in 1865 *"all publications of academics, universities"* were freed from preliminary censorship. In the *University Regulations* from 1863 it was stated in §130: *"Books [...] that the universities receive from foreign countries are not subject to examinations by the censorships"*. Seen in a Russian context at this time it was a drastic change.

5.2 Opposition

It is interesting to notice that even though Alexander to some extent reformed Russia he was **met by opposition from most groups in the society**. Seton-Watson concludes that he tried to seek an unrealistic compromise between autocracy and liberal reforms. It can be seen as a good example of what the French philosopher Alexis de Tocqueville wrote in *L'ancien Régime et la Revolution*: *"The most dangerous moment for a bad government is when it begins to reform"*.

Opposition from within the ruling classes and the peasantry:

- **Conservatives** resented their loss of influence and privilege.
- **Liberals** became frustrated at the Tsar's refusal to create a national assembly.
- **The peasantry** had worked the land given to them, for generations. Many of them couldn't accept that they had to pay for land they thought belonged to them.

Radical opposition:

Nihilism, populism emerged (the 'Going to the People' movement tried to re-educate the peasantry). The People's Will advocated the use of terrorism and finally killed the Tsar with a bomb in 1881.

Poland:

Poland had been controlled by Russia since the Congress of Vienna in 1815. In 1861, nationalist demonstrations broke out in Warsaw. They were mainly met by concessions: Jews were emancipated and the Warsaw University was re-opened. In 1863, 700,000 peasants were given freehold tenure without redemption payments. It didn't calm the situation and Polish nationalism remained strong. In 1863, an armed insurrection broke out which was crushed by the Russian army in 1863–64.

5.3 Economic development

There was a significant increase in railway building in the 1870s. Industrial output also increased but not as much as in Western Europe. The overall conclusion about the economic development is that even though the railway building spurred a general growth of the economy, the gap between Western Europe and Russia continued to grow.

5.4 Foreign policy

Russia defeated Turkey in the Russo-Turkish War in 1877–78. But the Western powers forced Russia (Congress of Berlin) to give back land to Muslim Turkey, because they opposed growing Russian influence in the Balkans. It was humiliating to Russia and Alexander. The outcome of the war led to the creation of independent Balkan states supported by Russia and this development increased the tension in the region due to the fact that Austria-Hungary also had a desire to control the Balkans.

Was the victory due to Alexander's military reforms? Probably not. It was *"a war between the one-eyed and the blind"* according to L. Kochan. Both Russia and the Ottomans were in decline.

5.5 Historiography and analysis

Historians are divided in their views about Alexander. This is perhaps one reason why this topic is so popular amongst examiners. Westwood writes: *"With the possible exception of Khrushchev and Gorbachev, no Russian ruler brought so much relief to so many [...] as did Alexander II"*. While Stevenson writes: *"Nothing Alexander did alter, was intended to alter the fundamental political fact of a God-created autocracy"*. A judgment about Alexander is therefore problematic.

Marxist historians: the emancipation reform was just another way of putting more money in the pockets of the nobility – serfdom was already on its way out! The reason for the reform programme was a crisis of the feudal economy and the emancipation was an attempt to continue to extract even more money from the masses.

Hugh Seton-Watson: Alexander tried to enjoy the best of two worlds: he didn't abandon autocracy and he finally failed because he sought to reach an unrealistic compromise between autocracy and modern reforms.

John Westwood, a representative of a pro-Alexander historian: the reforms must be ranked among the most successful achievements of the autocratic system in Russia. He writes: *"Despite the imperfections the Emancipation reform was an enormous step forward"*.

As can be seen in these views, there is no consensus amongst historians. There are various reasons why he introduced the reform programme. The very timing of the reforms, after defeat in war, indicates that military reforms were of major importance. To make Russia militarily stronger would also lead to a stronger Russia in general and the strengthening of Tsardom. Trotsky, the revolutionary leader in 1917, once wrote: *"War is the locomotive of history"*. Reforms and changes could be seen in Russia after the Crimean War, the Russo-Japanese War 1904–05 and finally after (or even during) WWI. This is a very valid point when discussing Russian history: Tsardom never reformed unless there was pressure from war.

To assess whether Alexander was a successful reformer or not, i.e. how the reforms affected Russia, is a more complicated issue. It is correct to say that Alexander's reforms affected the daily life of all Russians. Some reforms were important and some even survived the rule of his son Alexander III (the emancipation reform and legal and military reforms), but it is easy to criticise the reforms – the emancipation reform didn't solve the problem of poverty amongst the Russian peasantry. Economically the peasants were worse off and incomes halved due to the redemption payments, higher taxes and population growth. From an economic point of view the emancipation reform can be criticised from the following aspects:

- the redemptions dues were far too high compared to land output i.e. prices had been set too high;
- land was annually redistributed by the *Mir* according to the size of the family, which stimulated population growth;
- the land was given to the *Mir* and not to the individual. The fact that land was collectively owned did not promote innovation in farming techniques. One example is that the system of strip farming continued in Russia.

Richard Pipes concludes in *Russia under the Old Regime*: *"In fact, after 1861, the economic situation of the Russian peasant deteriorated, and in 1900 he was, by and large, **worse off than he had been in 1800**"*.

Alexander's refusal to allow the formation of a National Assembly, a Duma and a written constitution meant that autocracy remained and Russia would enter the 20th century without a political system designed to deal with the problems of a modern and industrialised society. In some aspects demands for reforms were met by repression. The autocracy (and Russia) was not strengthened, it lost support from almost all classes in Russia!

Was Alexander a clever and realistic politician who realised that he couldn't reform too fast? Was he a pragmatic leader who believed in reforms but realised that you couldn't go from autocracy, serfdom and illiteracy to parliamentarism in a couple of years? Well, he is not described in that way. A contemporary noted *"when the Emperor talks to an intellectual he has the appearance of someone with rheumatism standing in a draught"*. One historian, Saunders, writes *"the laws which freed the serfs emerged from a process that the Tsar barely understood and over which he had partial control"*.

On the other hand there are historians who describe Alexander's reforms as *"probably the greatest single piece of state-directed social engineering in modern European history prior to the 20th century"*! After all Alexander had succeeded in emancipating the serfs and it may be noticed that it took the American president four years of civil war to achieve the same thing in the US in the 1860s. Russian citizens were now legally free citizens. The number of peasant revolts also went down. David Christian writes *"The peasant disturbances which had continued for so long, like approaching thunder, died away to a distant rumble for 40 years after 1862"*. This was a gigantic first step and could have been followed by others if a terrorist bomb had not killed him in 1881. 'Rome wasn't built in a day'!

The fact that historians are so divided shows that there is no simple 'right or wrong' answer to the question if he was a successful reformer. Make sure that you know the arguments and try to take your own stand and that you know how to argue in the best possible way to defend that argument.

5.6 Alexander III and the return to reaction 1881–94

This first part of the text is intended to provide you with some material to answer the question: *Was Russia a backward state by the end of the 19th century* (see practice question 10 on page 45).

To Alexander III, it was clear that the assassination of his father was a result of Alexander II's own liberal experiments. Consequently, he returned to conservatism, or as Hugh Seton-Watson writes: *"Alexander III was a true Russian. He knew his people. He would not sacrifice the true Russian principle of autocracy"*. As a result:

- **All liberal ministers were replaced**.
- Russia returned to **pan-Slavism,** that is the idea that Russia did not belong to western Europe because Russia and Slavism had its own history and culture. Some would describe it as an aggressive, autocratic form of Russian nationalism.
- **Konstantin Pobedonostev** became the most trusted advisor. He claimed that parliamentarism was the *"triumph of egoism"*, that the sovereignty of the people was *"among the falsest of political principles"* and that the freedom of the press was one of the *"falsest institutions of our time"*. He was also the tutor to the coming Tsar, Nicholas, which made his influence stretch well beyond his time in power.
- The new office of **Land Commandant** was given the power to override the *zemstva*.
- The **franchise was revised** so that the nobility was given more power in the *zemstva*.
- **Education was brought back under firm control** and the autonomy of the universities was restricted. Fees were raised to prevent children from lower classes going on to higher education.
- A policy of **Russification** in non-Russian territories was introduced. Alexander believed that all cultures and nationalities within the empire should be wiped out (but not physically) and that all the people within the empire should become 'Great Russians'. Examples were that the property of the Polish Roman Catholic church was seized, Warsaw University was closed, and the Russian language was to be the only administrative language. Religion was closely supervised and 100,000 Tartars were converted to the Russian Orthodox Church. Finland had enjoyed their own constitution, which was ended. It's possible to give a number of examples from other parts of the empire, showing how the regime Russified the country.
- **Jews were subjected to a ruthless policy** where religious antisemitism was combined with a more crude popular antisemitism. The government permitted and even encouraged pogroms (when Jews were attacked and violence exercised). In one pogrom in Odessa in 1905 nearly 500 Jews were killed. 215 such disturbances were recorded between 1881 to 1905. Quotas for Jews were set in schools and universities. Many Jews emigrated from Russia.
- The *Okhrana* was formed by Alexander III after the assassination of his father. This secret police grew in importance during the last decades of the century. It was known for multiple methods, including covert operations, undercover agents, and agent provocateurs.

When Alexander passed away in 1894, the 29-year-old Nicholas ascended to the throne. His dominant and determined father had not had the capability of preparing Nicholas in a proper way. This was perhaps Alexander III's most important legacy.

5. ALEXANDER II AND ALEXANDER III

> Now, when you have read the text:
> 1. Study the following question on the next page (but not the answer!)
> 2. Copy a template and outline your answer.
> 3. Compare your answer with the one given and analyse any possible differences.

9. Discuss the reasons for Alexander II's reforms and evaluate their success.

(List the reasons for the reforms and assess, i.e. show strengths and weaknesses of their success.)

Why:

1. There is no doubt that one reason was to **strengthen Russia** and thereby to **strengthen Tsardom**.
2. **Fear of revolution from below**. The number of peasant revolts increased. Alexander also referred to this in his Moscow speech in 1856. Some have argued that he tailored his argument to convince the nobility who had to give up land. But it is realistic to believe that there was a genuine concern over this matter.
3. **Economic arguments**. Soviet historians/Marxist historians have argued that the feudal economy was in crisis and that the reform was an attempt to introduce a new system of production which would bring more money to the landowners.
4. Others have argued that to emancipate the serfs was a precondition for industrialisation. But there is little evidence that Alexander had a genuine desire to industrialise, except for building railways and that the industries that existed had any problems finding workers.
5. Few people at the time could support or defend the system hence '**the power of ideas**' was of some importance. The problem was the way in which serfdom should be replaced.
6. **Military arguments**. The very timing of the reform, after the Crimean War, indicates that military reasons were of importance. To make the army more effective would strengthen both Russia and the Tsar. The time of service in the army had to be reduced and this led to the emancipation reform which then led to many of the other reforms.

With what success?

The emancipation of the serfs was Alexander's main reform. The serfs were given their **legal freedom**. Land was taken from the nobility and given to the serfs. The nobility was compensated with government bonds. The emancipation reform had three main weaknesses:

1. The peasants had to pay redemption dues for the land for 49 years and it is normally considered that these dues were far too high compared to the land output, i.e. **the price of the land was too high**.
2. Land was not given to the individual but to the local peasant council, which redistributed land annually according to the size of the family. This is one explanation for the population growth. The result was that the average size of landholding went down. The outcome of the emancipation reform in combination with the **population growth**, led to the peasants being **worse off economically** (supported by Pipes).
3. The fact that land was collectively owned didn't promote innovations in farming techniques.

But it had also positive effects:

1. It was a major step to give the majority of the population their **legal freedom** without any major revolts. A similar reform in the US led to a four-year civil war.
2. The number of **peasant revolts** went down after the reform. Christian writes: *"The peasant disturbances [...] died away"*.
3. The *zemstva* system led to an establishment of political bodies with both noble and peasant representation. The Tsar, however, refused to allow a Duma.
4. The **legal reforms** are often seen as Alexander's most successful reform and they survived the repressive policies of his son Alexander III.
5. The **education reforms** were far reaching. The number of students at universities was allowed to increase and censorship relaxed. Women were allowed to attend university. But it also led to a growth of a radical *intelligentsia* and these radicals finally killed the Tsar in 1881.
6. The **army** was also reformed and the term of service was finally lowered to six years and brutal forms of punishment were abolished. But it cannot be concluded that the army gained in strength in any substantial way.

Conclusion: Alexander's aim was primarily conservative. He wanted to strengthen Russia and the institution of Tsardom. To do that an army reform was necessary which led to the emancipation reform, *zemstva*, and legal reforms. Another possible reason was probably fear of revolution from below. As has been clearly shown in the text you will find historians supporting either the 'failure' or the 'success' view – the reforms were insufficient, or a first but significant step forward. *Make sure that you can explain both views and that you can support your own conclusion.*

It can be discussed whether his reforms strengthened Russia. What is clear is that they did not strengthen Tsardom. He was faced with opposition from most groups and was finally assassinated in 1881.

Chapter 6: Russia 1894–1917

Issues

When you are studying this period in Russian history, it is clear that the main issue is: *Why was there a revolution in February 1917?* However, it is also possible to focus on the background or to assess whether Russia was a 'backward state by the turn of the century' or not.

Let's identify some key questions that will be expanded later:

1. Was Russia a backward state by the end of the 19th century?
2. Why did Tsardom survive the revolution of 1905 and not the revolution of 1917?
3. Were the reforms and the development in Russia by 1914 sufficient for the survival of Tsardom?
4. To what extent did WWI cause the fall of Tsardom?

6.1 Russia at the turn of the century

How would Russia be described as the 19th century came to a close? In 1894, Tsar Nicholas II ascended the imperial throne of Russia. The **census** of 1897 gives us valuable information about the situation and the status of the country:

- peasants – 82%
- upper class (nobility, clergy, officers) – 12%
- commercial class – 1.5%
- working class – 4%

From this we can conclude that this is an agricultural country with a small commercial and working class, i.e. a weak industrial sector.

Figure 6.1: **Coronation of Nicholas the II by Valentin Serov**

The weakness of Russian industry is also clear if we compare figures from other European states.

	Britain	Germany	Austria	Russia
% of national production coming from industry in 1910	75%	70%	47%	30%

In 1910, Russia was still lagging behind. Notice that this is *after* Witte's industrialisation in the 1890s which is normally considered an industrial breakthrough (read more about this in section 6.4).

6.2 Agriculture

If you want to understand the problems in Russia before the revolution, the **agricultural sector** in combination with the **population growth** is an absolutely **key factor**.

Serfdom had been abolished by Alexander II in 1861. In many aspects this was a very important step forward, but land was not individually owned and the peasants had to pay redemption dues which in most cases were far too high compared to the land output. Economically

Figure 6.2: **Russian wheat field where USDA plant explorers found wheat varieties from which they later bred the disease-resistant wheat that saved the wheat-growing industry in the West, ca. 1910**

the peasants were worse off due to the emancipation reform. It was the local commune, the *Mir*, which controlled the land, i.e. it was not individually owned. Land was periodically redistributed within the commune according to the size of the family. This is probably one, but of course not the only, explanation for the population growth in Russia.

	1800	1860	1900
Size of the population (million)	30	60	120

It would have been possible to compensate the population growth with migration or increased productivity, but Russian peasants did not emigrate and the productivity within the agricultural sector was not enough to equal the population growth:

	Britain	US	Russia
1 acre of land produced (bushels)	35	14	9

There were famines in Russia in 1891, 1892, 1898 and 1901. If 82% of the population in a country is struggling for their survival it is a major problem:

- no money will be created for financial investments within the agricultural sector i.e. productivity will remain low.
- this will also affect the resources for the industrial sector since no money will be created to support investments in the industrial sector and there will be no demand from the peasants for industrial products.

Due to the population growth the size of an average peasant holding shrank from 35 to 28 acres between 1877 and 1905 (-20%). It resulted in a '**land hunger**'. The combination of low productivity and population growth is dangerous and explains the poverty of the peasantry.

6.3 Social life

As late as 1917, there was no compulsory primary education in Russia. It is worth noting that as late as 1897, 79% of the population were illiterate. In other words, virtually all peasants were illiterate. Remember, this is in a country with an elite including such figures as the musician Tchaikovsky, the scientist Pavlov and writers like Tolstoy and Gorky.

6.4 The industrial sector

We have already noticed that the industrial sector of Russia was small in 1910, if we compare it to other Western powers. But there had been substantial growth in this sector since the 1890s. **Sergei Witte** realised in the 1890s that if Russia were to remain a great power, it had to be industrialised. By putting the rouble on the gold standard, by introducing protective tariffs and by attracting foreign investments, substantial growth took place. Railway building was also an important part of the modernisation. The growth of the industrial sector in the **1890s was 126%** and even taking into account that it started from a low base, the size of the industrial sector was now substantial. We tend to compare Russia with other Great Powers and countries in Europe. Be aware that these states were the strongest states at the time. **In 1914, Russia had the fifth largest economy in the world!** This was the industrial breakthrough for Russia.

Industrial development led to a very rapid growth of the urban population. In 1890, Moscow had 1 million inhabitants; in 1914 it was 1.7 million. Due to the population growth and the 'land hunger', many peasants left the countryside for the cities. It has been estimated that by the turn of the century 67% of the inhabitants of Moscow were peasants (and hence not legally registered as residents). Families were left behind, employment and living conditions were terrible. Workers employed in the growing industries also had terrible working conditions. These groups were now concentrated in key cities of Russia and were soon radicalised politically, formed political parties, and a working class consciousness developed. In 1914, the urban proletariat made up 12% of the population and politically they were normally not loyal to the Tsar.

6.5 Political life

Russia entered the 20th century with Tsar Nicholas II as an absolute ruler. The Fundamental Law from 1832 stated that *"The Emperor of all the Russians is an autocratic and unlimited monarch. God himself ordains that all must bow to his supreme power"*.

There were official bodies like the Imperial Council, the Cabinet of Ministers and the Senate, but they were all appointed by the Tsar and had a purely advisory and administrative role. All legislative power belonged to the Tsar. No Duma (parliament) existed.

Consequently, there was **no constitution**, the **press was censured** and **political parties were not tolerated**. It was a criminal offence to oppose the Tsar and his government. The result was that the political opposition had to go underground and these groups had by now been very radical for decades. Alexander II had for instance been assassinated by radicals as early as 1881. The role of controlling the opposition was given to the Tsar's secret police, the Okhrana. In many aspects, Russia at the beginning of the 20th century, can be described as a police state.

6.6 The army

Russia had the largest standing army in the world (2.6 million men), but for various reasons it was not the strongest army.

- The industrial sector of Russia was, compared to potential enemies like Germany, unable to provide the army with adequate and sufficient equipment. Industrial backwardness obviously affects military strength. It had been evident already during the Crimean War when only 4% of the Russian soldiers had long-range rifles compared to 50% of the British troops. When WWI started the infantry only had one rifle for every three soldiers.
- Russia was slow to mobilise which of course was partly due to the distances within the Empire. But it was also due to an inadequate railway system. Again we can see the importance of the industrial sector.
- Russian rulers always feared internal revolts and had to keep troops prepared, even in times of external conflict, to crush internal revolts. It was evident during the Russo-Japanese War in 1904, and this of course weakened the army.

6.7 The 1905 revolution

The Russo-Japanese War was a result of two imperialist states trying to expand into the same power vacuum: old imperial China. Military disasters and impact of the war, soon resulted in a revolutionary situation in Russia. In January 1905 a demonstration in St Petersburg led to a massacre. **Bloody Sunday** turned a tense political situation into a general revolt. In February 1905, 400,000 workers were on strike and in November the same year this number had escalated to 2.7 million. There were signs of mutiny in the army and peasants started to occupy land belonging to the aristocracy. Nicholas now faced a real threat to his power and the question was: how would he survive politically?

The first step was to bring the war to an end. In 1905 Witte was able to sign the Treaty of Portsmouth, which let the Russians off lightly. What was more important was that the army could now be brought back from Asia and that pressure from war lessened. One key to survival was the attitude of the army.

The revolution had encouraged the opposition and the formation of political groups. *Zemstvo* politicians had formed different liberal groups and the Russian political left now started to form Soviets. Witte persuaded Nicholas to accept far-reaching concessions. In October the Tsar finally issued the **October Manifesto** in which he promised full civil rights and the formation of a parliament, a Duma.

In the **November Manifesto** the Tsar cancelled the redemption dues that the peasants had to pay for the land given to them in the Emancipation Reform. In November he also promised better pay and fairer treatment to the soldiers.

Figure 6.3: **A locomotive overturned by striking workers at the main railway depot in Tiflis in 1905**

With the concessions made in the October Manifesto, **liberals** had been satisfied. The November Manifesto and the promises made to the army, gave him support from **peasants** and **soldiers**. **Conservatives**, i.e. the church, the nobility, and army generals, had supported the Tsar throughout the conflict. What was left of the revolution was only the radical political left. In December 1905, the Tsar could use a loyal army to arrest the St Petersburg Soviet and to crush the revolutionaries in the Moscow Uprising when 1,000 radicals were killed after a five-day siege. At the beginning of 1906 the Tsar was able to get a loan from France, the largest loan contracted so far by any country. It made the Tsar financially much stronger domestically and French support must be seen in light of the alliance system. The Tsar now quickly recovered his political confidence and this was the beginning of a new period.

6.8 The Duma experiment – a lost opportunity?

In April 1906, only a week before the two chambers of the Duma were to meet, the Tsar issued the **Fundamental Law**. In this law the Tsar made it clear that the ministers were dependent upon the Tsar for their appointment and dismissal, that legislative power belonged to the Tsar and that he had the right to govern by decree. This of course **deprived the Duma** all real political power. However, the importance of the Duma must not be underestimated. As a forum for discussion and criticism towards the Tsar, it attracted attention. The Tsar realised this and **dissolved** it after only 73 days. The second Duma continued to criticise the regime and was dissolved after three and a half months. The new president of the Council of Ministers, Stolypin, now altered the **Electoral Law**. The new law gave much more power to the propertied classes. Only one in six of the male population had the right to vote and peasants and workers were excluded. The richer landowners now controlled more than 50% of the seats in the Duma and the third Duma (1907-12) was far more loyal to the regime. In 1912 a fourth Duma was elected. This period was affected by public disorder and the advent of WWI and the relation between the Tsar and the Duma soon deteriorated.

Historians are divided in their opinions about the Duma. It is clear that it had no genuine power and that it never became a true representative body for the masses of Russia. But on the other hand, Russia now had a 'semi-parliament' and political parties could express their views in this parliament and in the press.

Stolypin was, alongside Witte, the most outstanding politician during this period. He was Chairman of the Council of Ministers from 1906-11, when he was assassinated. In 1906-07 he started a reign of terror against violent political opposition. In 1907, 1,231 officials and 1,768 private citizens were assassinated in terrorist attacks. Stolypin now set up his 'field court martial' and 1,144 death sentences were carried out in only six months.

Figure 6.4: **Pyotr Stolypin, Third Chairman of Council of Ministers of the Russian Empire**

Stolypin is, however, best known for his **agricultural reforms**. He realised that reform of Russia's most dominant sector, agriculture, was essential. Peasants made up the army and were, compared to workers in the cities, traditionally more conservative and loyal to the Tsar. A conservative class of richer peasants would be a strong support for the regime. In 1907, redemption payment was abolished.

Stolypin made it possible to buy the land from the *Mir*. The Land Bank offered low interest rates and state land was transferred to the bank.

In 1905, before Stolypin introduced his reform programme, some 20% of the Russian peasantry enjoyed hereditary ownership of their land. **It had risen to 50% by 1915**. Stolypin claimed: *"Give the state twenty years of domestic and foreign peace and you will not recognise present day Russia"*.

However, after an initial success with hundreds of thousands of households buying out their land the process slowed down and WWI almost brought it to a halt. Another problem with his reforms was that the other 50% of the peasantry were left out. This group made up an extremely poor agricultural proletariat. A group that was potentially dangerous to the regime. Another weakness of the reform, or the main weakness, was that even if 50% had now bought their land, they didn't consolidate it to single holdings. 90% remained in the commune system and continued with strip farming.

Many of these poorer peasants moved to the cities. The political situation in Russia must be, even before the outbreak of WWI, described as revolutionary. The best way of showing this is to account for the number of strikes in Russia:

1910	222
1911	466
1912	2,032
1913	2,404
1914 (from Jan. to July)	4,098 – a 20-fold increase in 4 years!

Even if it is not evident how many individuals were involved in each strike, we can conclude that this shows that public disorder had reached a critical point in 1914.

6.9 Russia and WWI

When WWI started in August 1914, Russia's regime and the Tsar enjoyed more support than at any other point of its rule. But the war did not go well for Russia. By early 1917, 1.6 million were dead, 3.9 million wounded, and 2.4 million had been taken prisoners (in total this is 7.9 million). It was a disaster.

In 1915 the Tsar had made himself **Commander-in-Chief**. This had two major **consequences**:

1. Defeats in the war were now directly linked to the Tsar.
2. With the Tsar at the front, the Tsarina and her trusted advisor Rasputin obtained much more influence. The rise of Rasputin was disastrous for the reputation of the Tsar and the Tsarina. The nobility strongly disliked the influence of this monk and it eroded the support from the ruling elite. Many saw his influence as the main explanation to the 'ministerial leapfrogging' that began in 1915. Rasputin was killed by a nobleman in late 1916 but the damage was irreparable. Robert Massie writes: *"Thus, the next sixteen months saw a sad parade of dismissals…and intrigues. In that time Russia had four different prime ministers, five ministers of interior, four ministers of agriculture and three ministers of war…It was an amazing, extravagant, and pitiful spectacle, and one without parallel in the history of civilised nations"*.

The war also resulted in domestic problems. The regime created 'military zones' where civil administration was subjected to the army. Both Duma and *Zemstvo* politicians wanted to influence the decision-making. In 1915, a union of Kadets, Octobrists and Progressists, formed the '**Progressive Bloc**', demanding a government which possessed 'the confidence of the public'. In September the Tsar responded by dismissing the Duma. In 1916, Miliukov asked, in the Duma, if the government's policy was 'stupidity or treason' and said *"we have lost faith in the ability of this government to achieve victory"*.

In December 1916 Rasputin was killed. By the beginning of 1917 inflation was out of control and the railway system was unable to transport enough food to the cities. In January, on the anniversary of Bloody Sunday, 150,000 exhausted people demonstrated against the regime. In February, on International Women's Day, 250,000 people demonstrated and soon it led to violence. After some 40 demonstrators had been killed, the soldiers sided with the population.

Nicholas, who was 500 miles away at the western front and isolated from his wife, did not fully understand the situation. First, he planned to use the army in an assault upon the capital. Demands for reform from Rodzianko, a leading Duma politician, were rejected as *"some nonsense from that fatty Rodzianko"*. Unable to compromise and without support from even his generals, Tsar Nicholas II abdicated in March 1917.

This time he did not have the support from the army and the elite. The 1917 February revolution is, however, normally described as a spontaneous, leaderless revolution from below. The historiography of this revolution will be further developed in the outlines.

Finally, some useful quotes which will enrich an essay:

"I know nothing": Nicholas when he ascended the throne.

"The key to Russia's future greatness lay in industrialisation": Witte.

"Curse the Duma": Nicholas II and his attitude to the Duma.

"The war was a mighty accelerator": Lenin on the impact of war.

"War is the locomotive of history": Trotsky, having learnt from 1855, 1905 and 1917.

"A constitution has been given, autocracy remains": Trotsky about the October manifesto.

" A dress rehearsal": Trotsky about the 1905 revolution.

> Now, when you have read the text:
> 1. Study the questions that follow (but not the answers!)
> 2. Copy a template and outline your answer.
> 3. Compare your answer with the one given and analyse any possible differences.

10. Discuss to what extent Russia was a backward state at the end of the 19th century.

(This question may occur on Paper III. It is difficult to find many arguments against that it was a backward state.)

Introduction: Indicate in your introduction that backwardness will be analysed from a political, economic, military and social perspective.

Analysis/backwardness

1. **Agriculture:** It is a key argument that some 80% of the population were still peasants by the turn of the century. Many of them were illiterate (79%) and due to the population growth, with a constant 'land hunger', they lived in poverty. The *Mir*, the local commune, which controlled the land after the emancipation reform in 1861, distributed land according to the size of the family. Russia had the highest population growth in Europe. The average peasant land holding actually went down from 35 acres in 1877 to 28 acres in 1905 (-20%), increasing poverty. The great majority didn't own their land, which was a result of Alexander II's emancipation reform. They also had to pay redemption dues to the state for the land they received in the reform. From such a class it was impossible to create a real demand for industrial products and a profit which could provide money for industrialisation and, which naturally was also important, to produce a surplus available

for investments in the agricultural sector. Consequently, the most important sector of the economy, agriculture was very inefficient compared to the west: an average acre of Russian farmland produced 8.8 bushels, 13.9 in the US and 35.4 in Britain!

2. **Industry**: In 1910, only 30% of Russia's national production came from industry (***key argument***). It was 75% in Britain, 70% in Germany and 47% in Austria-Hungary (Austria is normally described as a state in decline). Consequently Russia was less industrialised than other Great Powers in Europe.

   Witte's programme for industrialisation modernised the Russian economy in some respects, but it was a state-controlled process and no real middle class of capitalists was created. Benefits of the industrialisation didn't trickle down to the lower segments of the population. Living conditions for the working class in the cities were terrible. Russian industry was protected by high tariffs. But remember that we tend to compare Russia with other Great Powers and countries in Europe. Be aware that these states were the strongest states at the time. In 1914 Russia had the fifth largest economy in the world! This was the industrial breakthrough for Russia and the growth of the industrial sector in the 1890s was 126%.

3. **Political life**: Russia had, by the turn of the century, no constitution, no legal political parties and no representative assembly. It was ruled by an autocrat who thought he had divine rights (***key arguments***). There was a 'Fundamental Law' from 1832 declaring *"The Emperor of all the Russians is an autocratic and unlimited monarch; God himself […]"* Consequently there were no elections or political parties. Civil rights like freedom of speech, press etc. didn't exist. The secret police, the Okhrana, developed a bunker mentality and controlled the citizens closely.

   There were three official bodies through which the tsar exercised his power, the Cabinet of Ministers, the Imperial Council and the Senate. They were all appointed by the Tsar and had purely advisory or administrative power.

4. **Social life**: By the turn of the century, more than 80% of the population were peasants. Some 79% of the population were illiterate, mainly peasant. Education was restricted to a few i.e. the nobility. Morris describes Russia by the end of the century as 'a bizarre educational paradox': The elite included some of the most famous figures of the century, writers, scientists, and musicians. But the great majority had no political rights, they had no education, and most of them were extremely poor. No real middle class, comparable to that of other western countries, had developed. There was a small number of urban workers, i.e. industrialisation had not gone far.

5. **The army**: Russia had the largest standing army in the world but it was far from the strongest. A weak industrial sector could not provide the soldiers with modern equipment and there was no railway system for efficient and quick transportation. The regime also had to keep troops in the western part of the empire as a reserve in case of internal revolts.

Note: apart for Witte's reforms, ***most sectors of Russia were 'backward'*** – there is no real 'no' part here.

Conclusion: Russian economy was dominated by the agricultural sector. Alexander's reforms had not solved the problems in this sector. It can even be argued that it contributed to the population growth and the land hunger. The dominant sector could not create a surplus available for investments in the industrial sector. No educational reforms were carried out. Witte's industrialisation was successful but it was a revolution from above and no middle class of small-scale capitalists developed. The elite and the Tsar supported autocracy. Russia was definitely a backward state

> *Or why not quote Alexandra (Nicholas II's wife) "Russia needs and loves the feel of the whip!"*

11. Discuss the reasons why Tsardom survived the revolution of 1905 and not the revolution of 1917

(This is a 'list-question'. Consequently shows a range of arguments explaining the events.)

A. Why did Tsardom survive the revolution of 1905?

1. The war ended in the summer of 1905/**peace** in September. The soldiers came home i.e. pressure from war lessened.
2. **Concessions**: The October Manifesto promised a Duma and individual and religious rights. In the November manifesto redemption dues were cancelled for the peasants. The army was now also promised better salaries and fairer treatment.
3. Liberals, peasants and soldiers were satisfied with the concessions. The **army remained loyal** and could be used in December, to crush the left-wing revolutionaries.
4. The **revolutionary groups (Bolsheviks, Mensheviks) were divided** and were not prepared for this spontaneous revolt.
5. Foreign powers helped Russia. France and Britain gave **loans** – a strong Russia was a weaker Germany.
6. **Conservative** forces rallied to the help of the Tsar: church, nobility and generals.

B. What caused the fall of Tsardom in 1917?

Four long-term causes:

1. The **poverty of the peasantry**: write a few words about the effects of Alexander II's emancipation reform and that Stolypin's agricultural reforms excluded 50% of the peasants.
2. The **living conditions of the working class**: write about Witte's industrialisation and the creation of a working class which was soon radicalised and lived in key cities of Russia.
3. The rule of **Nicholas II**: write about his policies after the revolution of 1905, i.e. he promised full democratic rights but how he soon restricted the power of the Duma.
4. Europe's highest natural population growth contributed to the poverty of the peasantry. Pipes concludes that a Russian peasant was *"worse off (in 1900) than he had been in 1800"*.

Three short-term causes:

1. Write about the **impact of WW I**: how the Tsar made himself Commander-in-Chief in 1915 and the effects of this event. Write about how the war affected the civilian population and the army. 7.9 million soldiers had been killed, wounded or taken as war prisoners by 1917. Write about how the war affected the relation between the Duma and the Tsar.
2. The **Monk factor**: Rasputin discredited the reputation of the Tsar and the Tsarina. The elite did not remain loyal when the revolution from below started in February 1917. Was this due to the damaging impact that Rasputin had upon the reputation of the royal couple?
3. The Tsar's actions when the war had started. Write about the relation between the Tsar and the Duma after 1915 and how he acted in 1917 when the revolution had started.

Important differences between 1905 and 1917:

1. The army remained loyal in 1905 but not in 1917.
2. Pressure from war: there was much more pressure during WW I.

3. Conservative forces had rallied to the help of the Tsar in 1905: church, nobility and generals. But this did not happen in 1917. Why? Was it Rasputin who had destroyed the loyalty of the upper classes?

Historiography:

Marxists: Revolution was inevitable. It came from below i.e. the masses, but the first revolution in 1917 was a bourgeois revolution. The October Revolution 1917 was the Great proletarian revolution.

Stone (emphasis on impact of the war): The reforms (Duma, Stolypin) could have saved Russia if it wasn't for WWI.

Wood (emphasis on the Tsar's failures): Tsardom was throwing away its last chance when promises from 1905 were unfulfilled – expectations raised in 1905, but were dashed.

Pipes: Yes, there was a spontaneous uprising from below (common in Russian history). But this time it succeeded due to the fact that it had support from the ruling elite, which no longer supported the Tsar. If so, Rasputin is of great importance.

Conclusion: summarise your main points and emphasise what you consider decisive factors. Show also some important differences between 1905 and 1917 as a part of your analysis.

12. To what extent did WWI cause the fall of Tsardom?

(Show to what extent the fall of Tsardom was due to the war and then, in the second part of the essay, show what other reasons, that had nothing to do with the war, led to the fall of Nicholas II. In a question like this you are supposed to isolate one question and assess the importance of the factor by comparing it to other factors.)

Factors stemming from WWI:

1. The Tsar made himself **Commander-in-Chief** in 1915. This resulted in (a) more influence to the Tsarina and Rasputin (b) defeats in the war linked to the Tsar.

2. **Impact of War**: casualties, inflation, bread rations in cities. By early 1917 Russia had lost 1.6 million men, 3.9 million wounded, 2.4 million taken prisoners (in total 7.9 million). *This is a key point.*

3. The **Tsar's relation with the Duma** opposition deteriorated during the war. In 1915 the combination of Kadets, Octobrists and Progressists, formed a 'Progressive bloc' demanding a government 'possessing the confidence of the public'. In 1916 the Duma politician Miliukov questioned whether the incompetence of the government was 'stupidity or treason'! How much should we blame the war for this development? According to Lenin, the war was a 'mighty accelerator'!

No, it was not the war:

1. **Strikes:** There was a dramatic increase in the number of strikes before the war indicating that there would be a revolution even without WWI; 1910 = 222 strikes, 1911 = 466, 1912 = 2,032, 1913 = 2,404, **1914 in just six months = 4,098** (20-times increase).

2. **The Tsar** had neglected to fulfil his promises from 1905. By using the army against what was left of the opposition in December 1905, by issuing the Fundamental Law in April 1906, by appointing Stolypin who started a 'reign of terror', by changing the Electoral Law in 1907 (so that 1% of the population controlled 75% of the seats in the Duma) the Duma developed 'no roots amongst the people'. Trotsky said: *"a constitution has been given but autocracy remains"* and he described the revolution of 1905 as a *"dress rehearsal"*.

3. **The Tsar** couldn't compromise. He had a 'dogmatic devotion to autocracy'. When the revolution had started in February 1917 (but when he was still the Tsar) the Duma

opposition asked for last-ditch reforms. The Tsar described it as *"some nonsense from that fatty Rodzianko"* (Duma politician) and toyed with the idea of using the army upon his own capital. His generals now urged for constitutional reforms, but the Tsar was unable to do it, and abdicated.

4. **Rasputin**: destroyed the reputation of the Tsar and the Tsarina and alienated the upper classes (historiography: was it a revolution from below or from above? Well, when the revolution came in 1917 there was no longer any support from the elite. Why not? Was it Rasputin?)

5. **Poverty of the peasantry**: Alexander II's emancipation reform in 1861 had resulted in peasants paying redemption dues, which exceeded the land output. Land was not individually owned and was redistributed periodically by the *Mir* according to the size of the family. By the turn of the century Russia had the highest population growth in Europe. Stolypin made it possible to buy the land from the *Mir*. Stolypin's reforms excluded 50% of the peasants and they were extremely poor.

6. **The working class**: Witte and the consequences of 'forced industrialisation'.

Historiography:

Marxists: the Russian Revolution was inevitable.

Norman Stone: the reforms could have saved Russia if it hadn't been for WWI.

Wood: by undoing the promises from 1905, Tsardom was throwing away its last chances - expectations were raised but were dashed.

Conclusion: summarise your main points to support the answer. Impact of war was one very important factor for the revolution – but not the only one.

Chapter 7: The October Revolution

Issues

Was the October Revolution a *coup d'état* by Lenin's elite party or did it have the support of the masses?

In March 1917 Tsar Nicholas II abdicated. The combination of the inadequacy of Tsarist rule and impact of WWI had finally brought an end to his rule. The revolution brought the Provisional Government and local Soviets to power. Only seven months later there was a second revolution in Russia. The Bolshevik party, a small left-wing revolutionary party with a very narrow support in March, was able to seize power. This topic will shed light on why there was a second revolution in October 1917 and discuss the importance of Lenin in this second revolution. It will also discuss Bolshevik rule after October 1917. The following questions will be outlined:

1. What were the reasons for the October Revolution?
2. How important was Lenin in the Bolshevik seizure of power?

7.1 The causes of the October Revolution

Nicholas II abdicated in March 1917. The throne was offered to his brother Michael, who refused the crown and 304 years of Romanov rule had come to an end. The Provisional Committee of the Duma now formed a **Provisional Government** mainly made up by Kadets and Octobrists and it was led by Prince Lvov. The intention was that the new government should lead the country until elections could take place.

The government had to compete for power with local councils made up by workers and soldiers, **Soviets**. While the Provisional Government controlled national policies, local power

Figure 7.1: **Patrol of the October Revolution**

7. THE OCTOBER REVOLUTION

in major towns was controlled by the Soviets. These councils were dominated by left-wingers from the Menshevik and Social Revolutionary parties. This meant that no real authority and leadership was established. It is often referred to as a **'dual power'**. This 'dual power' can be clearly seen in the famous 'Order number I' from the Petrograd Soviet from March, where the Soviet orders officers to obey orders from the government as long as they don't contradict orders from the Soviet.

The new government was a coalition and had problems agreeing on a policy. When Russia needed a strong leadership it had a weak government. There are some notable mistakes, which contributed to the weakening of support for the government.

- The government decided to continue the war. They believed in a victorious war and needed Western capital, which was provided by its allies from Western Europe. The economic crisis was intensified as the war went on and there was hyperinflation.
- It put off a genuine land reform. Land was by far the most important question to poor peasants who made up the army. The government feared that starting a land reform, would make peasants desert the army. But the peasants were not willing to wait and started to take law into their own hands.
- Elections were also postponed.

In April, Lenin returned from Switzerland after years in exile. At this stage the Bolshevik Party had weak support. It numbered only 26,000 members and was in a minority in the Soviets. On the other hand they had not co-operated with the government and could not be linked to its failures i.e. they had '**clean hands**'. Today we know that they received substantial amounts of **German money** enabling them to spread their message. When Lenin returned he issued his '**April theses**'. He announced that there should be no co-operation with the Provisional Government and demanded that all power should be given to the Soviets. He also demanded 'bread, peace and land'. 'Bread' appealed to the workers in the cities, 'peace' to the soldiers and 'land' to the peasants. Trotsky remarked *"if the peasants had not read Lenin, he had clearly read the thoughts of the peasants"*.

Ideologically, Lenin rejected Marx's idea of a period of capitalism and a middle-class dominated parliamentary democracy, before a true socialist revolution. The Mensheviks and even some Bolsheviks argued that the 'madman' was ignoring the lessons of Marx, by ignoring this stage in Marxist terminology. But by the end of April his call for an immediate transfer of power to the Soviets, became the official Bolshevik policy.

At the beginning of June 1917 the Provisional Government decided to launch a major **war offensive** against the Germans in Galicia. It led to a major **collapse** of the Russian army. The offensive lasted only for three days but Russian casualties are estimated to have been hundreds of thousands. Whole regiments were now deserting and the economic situation deteriorated. Food didn't reach the towns. In July a revolt started, the **July Days**. 20,000 armed sailors from Kronstadt revolted. It has been widely discussed if it was a spontaneous uprising where the sailors picked up Bolshevik demands *or* if it was a first Bolshevik attempt to seize power. The Provisional Government was, however, able to restore order. The new Prime Minister Karensky accused Lenin of being a German spy and leading Bolsheviks were arrested. Lenin fled to Finland.

Figure 7.2: **Petrograd, July 4, 1917. Street demonstration on Nevsky Prospekt just after troops of the Provisional Government have opened fire with machine guns**

In May 1917 a new coalition had been formed made up by **five socialists** and a number of liberals from the Kadets. The liberals still dominated the government. Karensky, elected

Prime Minister in July, had a Social Revolutionary background. In the summer of 1917 when law and order collapsed, there was an increase of support for left-wing parties. The Bolsheviks were growing in strength. Karensky made an agreement with the new Commander-in-Chief, general Kornilov, to bring loyal troops to the capital in order to prevent new revolutionary activities. Kornilov exceeded their agreement when he saw an opportunity to march on the capital to end the influence of the Soviets and to cleanse the Provisional Government of socialist influence. Karensky now denounced Kornilov and called upon all loyal groups to protect the revolution. Trotsky, who had joined the party in the summer of 1917, and other Bolshevik leaders were released from prison and workers and soldiers were urged to stop a right-wing counter revolution. The Bolshevik Red Guards (the Bolshevik militia) were armed by the government and much of the defence was organised by the Bolsheviks. **The Kornilov revolt** failed and the Bolsheviks portrayed themselves as the saviours of the revolution.

The consequences were of major importance:

- It discredited the reputation of Karensky and the Provisional Government.
- This also affected the support of the Mensheviks and the Social Revolutionaries who had supported the government.
- The Bolsheviks could claim that they had saved the revolution and there was a dramatic increase of support for the Bolsheviks in elections to Soviets. In September the Bolsheviks held a majority of the Moscow Soviet. When all other parties disintegrated, the well-organised Bolshevik party grew in power and influence.

It is also interesting to study election results from the Moscow municipal elections in 1917:

	July	October
Social revolutionaries	58%	14%
Mensheviks	12%	4%
Bolsheviks	11%	51%

The support for the Bolshevik party in the autumn of 1917 has been questioned by some historians. Michael Lynch argues that attendance in the Soviets had gone down in the autumn, from which the well organised Bolsheviks gained. Lynch writes: *"The Bolshevik Party exerted an influence out of proportion to its number".* This view is supported by the fact that the Bolsheviks only gained 24% support in the elections to the new Constituent Assembly in November. The Social Revolutionaries got 53%.

In September Lenin secretly returned from Finland. On 12 September he wrote to the Central Committee: *"History will not forgive us if we don't seize power now".* He faced opposition because many leading Bolsheviks thought it was premature and that the party could not afford a second failed attempt (they had been blamed for the July Days). Lenin was, however, able to get support for the **October coup**. It was planned to take place on the day before the Second Congress of All-Russian Soviets should meet on 26 October. It was Trotsky who practically organised the seizure of power. Stalin wrote in *Pravda* on 10 November 1918: *"All practical work in connection with the organisation of the uprising was done under the immediate direction of comrade Trotsky".* Key position such as railway stations, telephone exchanges, banks and post offices were seized by Bolshevik Red Guards. On the night of 25–26 October the Bolsheviks remarkably easily seized control of the capital and the Winter Palace. When the Congress of Soviets met the next day Lenin announced that **the Soviets had seized power** and he read out a list with the members of the new government – containing only Bolsheviks. The Social Revolutionaries and the Mensheviks walked out in protest. Trotsky concluded *"You have played out your role. Go where you belong to the dust heap of history".*

7. THE OCTOBER REVOLUTION

7.2 Historiography

- To a **Marxist** and to most Russians before the fall of communism, the fall of the Provisional Government was inevitable and had the support of the masses. It was in line with Marxist terminology that a mode of production controlled by one oppressing class was doomed. After only a few months of bourgeois parliamentary rule, it can be argued that this was a premature revolution. But both Trotsky and Lenin supported it by arguing that a revolution could start in an underdeveloped country like Russia and spread to more advanced countries. WWI offered a unique opportunity.

- **The orthodox view** in the West after the revolution argues that the success of the Bolshevik party was due to the fact that the Bolsheviks were **well organised and disciplined**. Lenin had caused a split of the Social Democratic Party in London 1903, when he advocated an **elite party** of dedicated professional revolutionaries opposing the view of a broad mass-based party, an idea supported by the Mensheviks. The Bolshevik Party was seen as a tiny minority and seized power in a well-organised *coup d'état*. There was no majority support from the masses for the seizure of power.

- **Revisionist Western historians** argue that the Bolsheviks were well organised but the key explanation was that they just followed a 'popular trend' and that they *"rode to power on a wave of popular resentment"* (Lee) and just carried out the will of the masses. It had not been enough to be only well organised. After the Kornilov affair the masses wanted a change and the Bolsheviks could execute this will.

7.3 Weaknesses of the Provisional Government

1. The Government had no real authority i.e. the **Dual power**.
2. The PG had responsibility of government i.e. national issues.
3. Soviets controlled 'local practical' power.
4. This Dual power can be clearly seen in the famous Order Number 1 from March 1917.
5. They **continued the war**. Why? The PG had no money i.e. they needed Western capital. They also believed in a victorious war.
6. They **put off a land reform**. Land was by far the most important question to poor peasants who made up the army. The PG feared that starting a land reform, would make peasants desert the army.
7. **Elections were also postponed**.
8. The economic crisis was intensified as the war went on. There was hyperinflation.
9. The PG was a **coalition** and had problems agreeing on a policy. When Russia needed a strong leadership it had a weak government.

> When you analyse the reasons for the Bolshevik seizure of power, write a chronological account and conclude that the reason is a combination between 'weaknesses of the Provisional Government', 'strengths of the Bolsheviks' and 'other factors'.

7.4 Strengths of the Bolsheviks

1. **Lenin's undisputed leadership**.
   (a) He had created a **well-organised elite party**. This was crucial when everything collapsed in 1917. In 1903 there had been a split of the Social Democratic Party. Lenin strongly believed in organising an elite party while the Mensheviks wanted to organise a mass-based party.
   (b) Lenin **'timed' the revolution**. In September 1917 the Bolsheviks held a majority in the Soviets for the first time. Lenin realised that the party had a unique opportunity. Lenin now claimed: *"history will not forgive us if we don't seize power now"*.
   (c) Lenin **communicated well with the masses. April Theses**: Bread (to workers), Peace (soldiers), and Land (soldiers) and 'all power to the Soviets' (appealed to left-wingers)

2. **Bolshevik Red Guards** were important both during the Kornilov revolt and in the October Revolution. It was the only coherent and disciplined group in Russia when the army and political life disintegrated in 1917.

7.5 Other factors

It is clear that the Provisional Government didn't come to power in a **favourable situation**. The **impact of World War I** cannot be underestimated. The new government also suffered from old thorny questions like the land question, which was not easy to solve during a war.

Figure 7.3: **Anti-Bolshevik Volunteer Army in South Russia, January 1918**

Now, when you have read the text:

1. Study the questions that follow (but not the answer!)
2. Copy a template and outline your answer.
3. Compare your answer with the one given and analyse any possible differences.

---

13. Discuss the reasons for the October Revolution.

(Formally, this is a 'list' question. It means that you are supposed to just list all reasons you can find for the Bolshevik seizure of power and then analyse it.
Write a chronological account of the development between February and October 1917. Don't spend too much time on this part, because the analysis which will follow is very important.)

1. **The revolution** started spontaneously in February 1917.
2. The abdication of Nicholas in March and the formation of the Provisional Government and the Soviets. The **'dual power'** undermined the authority of the government.
3. There were some major **mistakes** made by the Provisional Government, i.e. to continue the **war**, to put off a **land reform** and to postpone **the elections**.
4. Lenin's return in April and his April Theses. From an ideological point of view it led to a dispute within the party.
5. The war offensive in June and the **July Days**.
6. **General Kornilov's revolt** in August and its significance.
7. The situation in September when the party discussed if they should make an attempt to overthrow the Government. Bolshevik **majority in the Soviets**.
8. The seizure of power in **October**. Explain how and why the Bolsheviks claimed that it was the Soviets which had seized power.

7. THE OCTOBER REVOLUTION

9. The main historiographical schools: the Marxist school, the orthodox view and the revisionist Western view.

In your analysis it is important to show that the reason for the Bolshevik success was a combination of weaknesses of the Provisional Government, strengths of the Bolsheviks and some other factors. Explain these factors.

A. Weaknesses of the Provisional Government

1. The Government had no real authority i.e. the **dual power**. The government was responsible for national questions while the Soviets controlled local power.
2. This dual power can be clearly seen in the famous Order Number 1 from March 1917.
3. They **continued the war**. Why? The PG had no money, they needed Western capital. They also believed in a victorious war.
4. They **put off a land reform**. Land was by far the most important question to poor peasants who made up the army. The PG feared that starting a land reform would make peasants desert the army
5. **Elections were also postponed**.
6. The economic crisis was intensified as the war went on. There was hyperinflation.
7. The PG was a **coalition** and had problems agreeing on a policy. When Russia needed a strong leadership it had a weak government.

B. Strengths of the Bolsheviks

1. **Lenin's undisputed leadership**.
   (a) He had created a **well-organised elite party**. This was crucial when everything collapsed in 1917. In 1903 there had been a split of the Social Democratic Party. Lenin strongly believed in organising an elite party while the Mensheviks wanted to organise a mass-based party.
   (b) Lenin **'timed' the revolution**. In September 1917 the Bolsheviks for the first time held a majority in the Soviets. Lenin realised that the party had a unique opportunity. Lenin now claimed: "*history will not forgive us if we don't seize power now*".
   (c) Lenin **communicated well with the masses: April Theses**:
      (i) Bread (to workers), Peace (soldiers), and Land (soldiers).
      (ii) 'All power to the Soviets' (appealed to left-wingers).
   (d) Lenin had strongly advocated a policy of non-co-operation with the PG. It resulted in 'clean hands', i.e. the Bolsheviks could not be blamed for the failure of the government.
2. **Bolshevik Red Guards** were important both during the Kornilov revolt and in the October Revolution. It was the only coherent and disciplined group in Russia when the army and political life disintegrated in 1917.

C. Other factors:

It is clear that the Provisional Government didn't come to power in a **favourable situation**. The impact of World War I cannot be underestimated. The new government also suffered from old thorny questions like the land question which was not easy to solve during a war.

Conclusion: It was a result of weaknesses of the Provisional Government/strengths of the Bolsheviks and other factors.

14. Evaluate the importance of Lenin in the Bolshevik seizure of power.

(Describe the importance of Lenin by weighing up his contributions and other factors. Points to consider are listed below.)

A. Yes, Lenin was important:

1. Lenin had organised a tight revolutionary party ever since the party split in 1903: the idea of an elite party. He was the undisputed leader of the party.
2. Lenin returned in April 1917. Explain his April Theses and how his policy of non co-operation with the Provisional Government would later pay off, i.e. to have 'clean hands'.
3. Lenin was able to communicate with the masses. He used effective slogans ('bread, peace, and land') and oratorical powers.
4. He timed the October coup.
5. It proved to be important to have a tightly organised political party in the chaos that existed in the autumn of 1917 – that had been one of the ideas behind his decision to organise a party according to this principle.

B. There were other factors as well which finally led to the Bolshevik seizure of power:

1. **Trotsky's** organisation of the October coup is often emphasised when discussing the reasons for the success.

Weaknesses of the Provisional Government:

2. The Government had no real authority i.e. the **Dual power**. The government was responsible for national questions while the Soviets controlled local power.
3. This Dual power can be clearly seen in the famous Order Number 1 from March 1917
4. They **continued the war**. Why? The Provisional Government had no money i.e. they needed Western capital. They also believed in a victorious war.
5. They **put off land reform**. Land was by far the most important question to poor peasants who made up the army. The PG feared that starting a land reform would make peasants desert the army
6. **Elections were also postponed.**
7. The economic crisis was intensified as the war went on. There was hyperinflation.
8. The PG was a **coalition** and had problems agreeing on a policy. When Russia needed a strong leadership it had a weak government.

Other factors:

9. It is clear that the Provisional Government didn't come to power in a **favourable situation**. The impact of WWI cannot be underestimated. The new government also suffered from old thorny questions like the land question which was not easy to solve during a war. This of course helped Lenin and the party.

Conclusion: It was a combination between strengths of the Bolsheviks and Lenin, weaknesses of the Provisional Government and some other factors, which led to the Bolshevik seizure of power, i.e. Lenin's success. It must, however, be concluded that Lenin was of major importance in this process. The Bolsheviks went from obscurity to power within a year.

Chapter 8: Lenin

Issues

Apart from the coup, which is mainly discussed in other topics, the most significant discussion is how we shall judge Lenin as a politician after the revolution.

When Lenin and the Bolshevik party came to power in October 1917 they had three major problems to solve:

1. **How should they end the war?** Lenin had promised in his April theses to bring the war to an end and after having continued to criticise the Provisional Government for their continuous involvement in the war, it was now necessary to bring it to an end.

2. **How should they establish political control in the country?** After the coup in October they had some control but it took them another week to establish control in Moscow. In rural areas peasants were opposing Bolshevik policies of a state controlled economy i.e. that the land the peasants had seized in 1917, should now be transferred to state ownership. Of course, the old ruling class was also against a communist regime.

Figure 8.1: **Vladimir Lenin**

3. **How should a planned economy be implemented?** In other words, how should the means of production, land, and factories, be transferred to state ownership? The Bolshevik regime had no resources to compensate the owners and was not willing to do so, since they considered that the wealth that landowners and factory owners were in control of, had been created by the toiling masses. So, the means of production must be brought under control without compensation to the previous owners.

8.1 How the war was ended

On 25 October, the day after the coup, the new regime issued the **Decree on Peace**. The decree called for a peace settlement without land transfers and financial indemnities. Lenin saw the war as an attempt by imperialistic rulers to extend their power, but realised that the war could open opportunities for the party. After the Bolshevik party had seized power, it was absolutely necessary to seize control of other parts of Russia and therefore consolidate their control. In doing so, WWI had to be brought to an end. Trotsky was Commissar for Foreign Affairs (foreign minister). He was responsible for the peace talks, which started at Brest-Litovsk in December 1917. He tried to spin the peace talks out since both he and Lenin expected a left-wing revolution in Germany. The Spartacist Uprising in 1918/19 indicates that the situation in Germany and Europe after the war was volatile. But his tactic of delay didn't pay off and when no agreement was reached, the Germans launched a new offensive in early 1918, which forced the Bolshevik to sign the Treaty of Brest-Litovsk in March 1918. The Bolshevik regime needed to end the war to consolidate its own power in Russia. Russia lost in the treaty:

- Poland, Estonia, Latvia, Lithuania, Finland, the Ukraine and Georgia;
- about 33% of the population;
- about 33% of its arable land; and
- about 75% of its coal and iron resources.

Lenin concluded: *"A disgraceful peace is proper, because it is in the interest of the proletarian revolution and the regeneration of Russia"*.

8.2 How should they establish political control?

(a) The Bolsheviks had criticised the Provisional Government for delaying elections to a Constituent Assembly. Elections to this assembly had been scheduled to November and due to this previous attitude, elections were allowed in November. In the elections it was clearly shown that the Bolshevik party was mainly an urban or workers party. The Social Revolutionaries, a peasant party, got 53% of the votes while the Bolsheviks only got 24%.

This is strong evidence that the Bolsheviks had no majority support when they seized power in October. When the Assembly met in January 1918 Lenin and the Bolsheviks sent in Red Guards to **close down the Assembly**. Lenin, of course, had no interest in a body in which the Bolsheviks had only a minority. From an ideological point of view, Lenin had no interest in supporting a Western style of parliamentary democracy. The party and Lenin were heading for Soviet rule controlled by the Bolsheviks and the 'dictatorship of the proletariat'.

Lenin concluded: "[the Assembly was] *an expression of the old relation of political forces"* and *"a republic of soviets is a higher form of democratic principle than a customary bourgeois republic with a Constituent Assembly"*.

(b) In December 1917 the *Cheka*, or the secret police, was set up. The Bolsheviks deliberately used **terror** as a means in the political struggle. The estimated number of victims varies between 150,000–300,000. Trotsky concluded: *"We shall not enter into the kingdom of socialism in white gloves on a polished floor"*.

(c) In 1918 the **Social revolutionaries and the Mensheviks were expelled from the Soviets**. When the NEP was introduced in 1921, the Soviet Union was formally made a single party state.

Questions about how and when a single party rule or dictatorship was established are common (especially in Paper II). If this is asked about Lenin's/Mussolini's/Hitler's regime you can't end your answer by writing up to the October coup/when Mussolini was appointed Prime Minister in 1922/when Hitler was appointed Prime Minister in 1933. In the Russian example you must end your story in 1921 when a single party rule was formally established. In Italy, all other parties were outlawed in 1926. In Germany you must include the Enabling Act, the Gleichschaltung policy, and the Night of the Long Knives. When Hitler was appointed Prime Minister in 1933 he was a leader of a weak coalition and no dictator. After the Night of the Long Knives in 1934, he made himself both Prime Minister and President – i.e. Führer – and hence a full dictatorship had been established.

(d) Lenin had organised an elite party where membership was restricted to a few. In 1917 the party had agreed on a policy called **'democratic centralism'**. It means that the party was allowed to discuss and debate matters of policy and direction, but once the decision of the party had been made by majority vote, all members were expected to uphold that decision. As Lenin described it, democratic centralism consisted of 'freedom of discussion, unity of action'. This policy was further strengthened in 1921 when the NEP was introduced. A **'ban on factionalism'** was introduced which meant that no groups with views opposing the party line were allowed within the party.

(e) **Victory in the Civil War 1918–20 is the main explanation as to why the Bolshevik could establish political control.** The Civil War started due to the following reasons:

- The **Treaty of Brest-Litovsk** had pulled Russia out of the war and was opposed by many, especially leading generals in the army. Many Russians disliked the Bolsheviks' acceptance of giving up territories in the west.
- The new Bolshevik regime had also started to **nationalise** parts of industry without offering compensation.
- Many **nationalities** within the empire saw an opportunity to gain freedom when central power collapsed.
- Conservative groups wanted to **restore Tsardom**.
- **Social revolutionaries and Mensheviks** had been expelled from the Soviets in 1918 and **opposed Bolshevik dictatorship**.
- Western powers wanted Russia to **rejoin the war** against Germany and supported the White forces (USA, Britain, France, Italy, Japan). Another reason for foreign intervention was that the Bolshevik regime refused to **pay back foreign loans**.

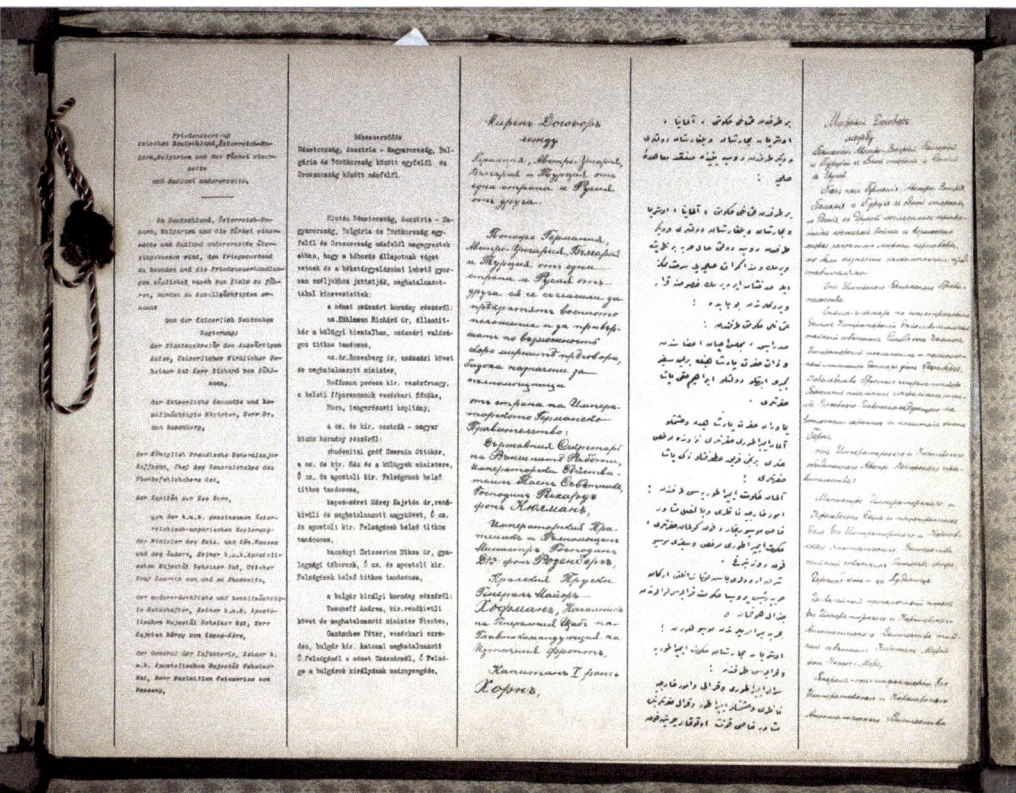

Figure 8.2: **Photocopy of the first two pages of Brest-Litovsk Peace Treaty between Soviet Russia and Germany, Austria-Hungary, Bulgaria and Turkey, March 1918**

Why did the Bolsheviks win the Civil War?

- The **White forces were divided** in their intentions and lacked a single command. There were foreign troops, tsarists, different nationalities, groups supporting the Duma etc. The White forces were spread out over thousands of miles and different commanders did not co-ordinate their attacks.
- The support from **foreign powers was half-hearted**.
- In contrast the **Red forces controlled central areas** of Russia and could effectively use the railway system. They also controlled the industrial areas of Russia.
- While the White forces were divided in most aspects, the Reds were united. They were effectively led by the War Commissar, **Leon Trotsky**, i.e. they had a single command. He built up the Red Army into a disciplined and effective force.
- While the White forces never managed to raise more than 650,000 soldiers, Trotsky was able to build up the **Red Army** into a mass army. In April 1919 it was made up by 500,000 soldiers and in June 1920, there were 5 million men in the Red Army.
- The Bolsheviks could claim that they **defended 'mother Russia' against foreign intruders**.
- Even if some peasants supported the Social revolutionaries in the Civil War, defending the peasants right to the land, many peasants feared the Whites because they expected that **land would be given back to the nobility**.

So the outcome of the Civil War can be described as a result of the **strengths of the Bolsheviks and weaknesses of the White forces**.

8.3 How was a planned economy introduced?

A planned economy means that the means of production must be transferred to state ownership. As has been previously stated the regime had no resources to compensate landowners and factory owners for the value of the factories/land. So it had to be confiscated, which to some extent explains both the setting up of the Cheka in 1917 and the start of the Civil War in 1918. Lenin's economic policy can be summarised in three different stages:

8.3.1 State Capitalism October 1917 to June 1918

Lenin's economic plans before the revolution had been more theoretical than practical. State Capitalism was a **mixed economy** where some parts were nationalised, such as banks and the railway system, while other parts remained in private hands.

8.3.2 War Communism 1918–21

In 1918 War Communism was introduced. Lenin claimed that it was a temporary policy to handle problems caused by the Civil War. Others argue that it was a first genuine attempt to introduce a Bolshevik economic programme i.e. a radical left-wing policy. When it failed it was explained as a temporary policy necessitated by the Civil War. What were the key features of War Communism?

- **Far-reaching nationalisation** of industries and banks.
- **Private trade was outlawed**.
- The **currency was made worthless** by the mass printing of money. Wages were paid in kind.
- Food and **grains were seized from the peasants without compensation**. This policy of food requisitioning was ordered to feed the urban population and the Red Army.

Results: Peasants saw no reason to produce food that was confiscated by the regime. The result was a terrible famine which killed around 7,500.000 million people. The grain harvest in 1921 was only 50% of the 1913 level. The industrial production had fallen to 20% of the 1913 level. The famine also led to a large scale migration from the cities and the urban population declined with 33% between 1917 and 1920. There were widespread strikes against the Bolshevik regime. But most of the food went to the growing Red Army, which of course was very important during the Civil War. About 60% of the food from the food requisitioning policy went to the army.

8.3.3 The New Economic Policy (NEP), 1921–28

In February–March 1921, sailors at the naval base Kronstadt revolted against the Bolshevik regime. The revolt was brutally suppressed but Kronstadt had traditionally been seen as a Bolshevik stronghold (see the July days in 1917), and the revolt alarmed Lenin: *"It illuminated reality like a flash of lightning"*. He also explained the new policy as a temporary policy. *"Life has exposed our errors [...] There was a need of a series of transitional stages to communism"*. The main features of the NEP were:

- A new **tax system** was introduced at a lower level than before.
- A new **currency** was introduced.
- The **food requisitioning** policy was brought to an end.
- The peasants were allowed to **sell any surplus**, hence to be encouraged to produce more.
- Smaller and medium size **factories could be privately owned** while larger factories and industrial concerns were still controlled by the state. According to Lenin *"the commanding heights of the economy"* were to remain under state control.

Results: In 1922, 88% of all enterprises were privately run but they employed only 12% of the workforce (because the major industries were still state owned). These figures exclude the agricultural sector. Notice that land in Bolshevik Russia was formally state property since the revolution, but the Bolshevik regime had realised that support was needed and allowed the peasants to **use it privately. The economy gradually recovered** and by 1928 the industrial output had reached the 1914 level and the recovery had been even faster within the agricultural sector. Many Bolshevik members were horrified by these concessions towards capitalism and considered the NEP as an **'economic Brest-Litovsk'** since Lenin's Russia was dominated by an agricultural sector, which was run by private owning peasants and within the industrial sector private enterprises were increasing in number.

8.4 Marxism-Leninism

Lenin was a devoted Marxist – he believed that the only way of bringing the class struggle to an end was worker's control of the means of production. By controlling the factories, the bourgeoisie had oppressed the masses who were not fully compensated for their work in the factories. A necessary change was to be accomplished through a revolution when the working class would topple the bourgeoisie. Marx wrote: *"The history of all human society, past and present, has been the history of class struggles"*. After the revolution, a period of 'dictatorship of the proletariat' would make the bourgeoisie realise the benefits of socialism and the society would finally develop into a classless society, communism. Lenin made significant contributions to this theory; hence we use the term Marxism-Leninism. It was Lenin who developed the practical tools as to how the working class should overthrow the ruling bourgeoisie. What were the main features in Lenin's ideology?

1. **The idea of an elite party.** In 1902 Lenin published his most important work *What Is To Be Done*. In this document he outlined the idea of a tightly organised party made up by professional revolutionaries. Membership should be restricted to a few and this group of dedicated revolutionaries should act as *"the proletariats advance guard [...] Just as a blacksmith cannot seize the red hot iron, so the proletariat cannot directly seize power"*. This idea had two major consequences. First, the fact that the party had no majority support when they seized power was not seen as a problem by Lenin. The proletariat, or the masses, were to be led by the 'advance guard' into realising the path

to revolution. The second consequence was that Lenin rejected Marx's idea of a period of capitalism and a middle-class dominated parliamentary democracy, before a true socialist revolution. This will be explained in the next point.

2. This idea of an elite party caused a split of the Russian Social Democratic party, at a party conference in London 1903. The Bolsheviks supported the idea of an elite party while the Mensheviks supported the idea of a mass-based party.

3. It is interesting to notice that Lenin's elite party was the only well-organised and coherent political group in Russia in the autumn of 1917, when everything else seemed to be disintegrating.

4. **The idea of capitalism developing into socialism could take place much sooner than expected.** The Mensheviks and many Bolsheviks thought that the February Revolution was an equivalent to the French Revolution, when the bourgeoisie had toppled the nobility. The reason for this was that one mode of production, agricultural production and feudalism, had been replaced by industrial production, hence a new ruling elite had emerged. This would lead to a period of capitalism where the bourgeoisie would be the oppressing class. This period would be ended by a working class revolution, which would finally bring the means of production into the hands of the masses, which would result in an end to class struggle. Lenin rejected the idea of the necessity of a period of capitalism. He argued that the elite party could lead the masses into a revolution, earlier than Marx and the Mensheviks had envisaged.

5. **The role of the peasantry.** In 1917, Lenin came to realise that the peasantry could act as a revolutionary class, in spite of his earlier ideas in *What Is To Be Done*. This was a departure from Marx's ideas. The peasantry made up 80% of the population in 1917 and had started to seize land illegally after the February revolution. Lenin consequently adapted his theory to circumstances in Russia and by accepting that the peasants could be a revolutionary class, Russia didn't need a long period of capitalism before a mass-based revolution could take place.

6. Lenin believed in a highly-centralised party. In 1917 the party had agreed on a policy called **'democratic centralism'.** It meant that the party was allowed to discuss and debate matters of policy and direction, but once the decision of the party had been made by majority vote, all members were expected to uphold that decision.

Now, when you have read the text:

1. Study the questions that follow (but not the answers!)
2. Copy a template and outline your answer.
3. Compare your answer with the one given and analyse any possible differences.

15. To what extent was Lenin a successful politician?

(Show his successes and failures.)

Yes, he was successful:

Before 1917 and in 1917/revolution:

1. Lenin had **organised a tight revolutionary party** ever since the party split in 1903: the idea of an elite party. He was the undisputed leader of the party.
2. Lenin returned in April 1917. Explain his **April Theses** and how his policy of non co-operation with the Provisional Government would later pay off, i.e. to have "clean hands".
3. Lenin was able to **communicate with the masses**. He used effective slogans ('bread, peace and land') and oratory powers.
4. He **timed the October coup**.
5. It proved to be important to have a tightly organised political party in the chaos that existed in the autumn of 1917 – that had been one of the ideas behind his decision to organise a party according to this principle.
6. The Bolshevik party was able to seize power in October even though they had **no majority support**.

After the October coup:

1. Russia was able to **withdraw from WWI**. Even if the terms of the Treaty of Brest-Litovsk were harsh, it was necessary for the survival of the revolution.
2. Lenin and the party were able to **establish political control** in Russia. This was of course due to many other factors than just Lenin's leadership but his role was of importance since he was the undisputed leader of the party. The decision to accept the peasant's seizure of land and to make a separate peace with Germany was very important in establishing political control.
3. Much of the economy was **transferred to state ownership** during Lenin's leadership. Even if the NEP was a departure to capitalism, the 'commanding heights' were still controlled by the state.

Lenin failed:

1. **War Communism** led to a famine, which probably killed 7.5 million people and it also resulted in strikes and revolts in the country. Some argue that this policy was not a temporary policy forced upon the party due to the Civil War. It was a genuine attempt to introduce a planned economy, **which failed**.
2. Ideologically, **the NEP must be seen as a failure**. In order to secure the survival of the regime and to create a recovery of the economy, Lenin had to revert to capitalism.
3. Lenin set up the Cheka in 1917 and used terror as a political means in the struggle. It can be argued that this **policy of terror laid the foundation** of a state that in the long term led to failure of the system. When Soviet archives were opened in the mid-1980s it was revealed that Lenin was far more ruthless than had been previously known.
4. Many historians argue that Lenin was responsible for Stalin becoming the new leader. It was Lenin who created a highly-centralised state, single-party rule, an oppressive system where media was controlled and who started to use terror. He laid the foundation for Stalin's rule.

Conclusion: From a Bolshevik point of view and from his own point of view he must be considered as very successful. He was able to organise and lead a small party into a position of controlling the country. He had no majority support but this was nothing he considered as a failure. The masses were to be led by the minority, his elite party. To some extent he was able to introduce a planned economy and Soviet control of the country.

Some argue that War Communism was a deliberate policy to introduce communism. If so, it was a failure. His most significant failure was probably that he had to revert to capitalism, via the NEP, in order to secure economic growth. The very fact that Stalin was able to succeed Lenin, can be seen as a failure even to Lenin.

Lenin brought communism to Russia, and many would argue that his contribution to Russia, in doing so, would cause a 70-year dictatorship which the country suffered enormously from.

16. Discuss to what extent Lenin followed his ideology.

(There are 'yes' and 'no' arguments. It is also very important to define his ideology in the beginning.)

A. Lenin's ideology:

1. Write about Marxism: **workers' control of the means of production,** the necessity of a **revolution** and the **dictatorship of the proletariat.**
2. Write about Lenin's idea of an **elite party**.
3. Write about Lenin's idea of the possibility of a **'premature' revolution**.
4. Write about his ideas of the role of the **peasantry**.
5. Write about his ideas of a highly-centralised state and the idea of **democratic centralism**.

B. Yes, he followed his ideology, i.e. Marxism-Leninism:

1. He believed in Marx's ideas about a **revolution, planned economy and the dictatorship of the proletariat.** This was to a major extent implemented.
2. He also implemented the idea of an **elite** party, which was his own ideological contribution to how power should be seized.
3. Lenin believed in **single party rule**, which he also implemented in 1918 when the Assembly was closed down and both the Social Revolutionaries and the Mensheviks were expelled from the Soviets.
4. Lenin believed that there was **no need for a capitalist period** in Russia before the toiling masses could seize power. This was implemented.
5. Lenin believed that the **peasantry could be a revolutionary class** in a mass-based revolution, which was implemented.
6. He believed in a highly-centralised state and **democratic centralism**, which was implemented.

C. No, he departed from his ideology:

The **NEP** was a clear departure from his ideology. By many Bolsheviks it was seen as an ideological "Brest-Litovsk".

Notice that even if Lenin devoted most of his life to implement a Marxist society, he could be very pragmatic (to act against his ideology). Examples of this are his willingness to give up land (the Treaty of Brest-Litovsk), his NEP and his unwillingness to collectivise without peasant support.

Conclusion: It must be concluded that Lenin to a major extent followed his ideology. His ideology must be referred to as "Marxism-Leninism", i.e. an extension of Marxism. But he could also be pragmatic and the NEP is a good example of this pragmatic approach

Chapter 9: The Causes of WW I

Issues

The origins of WW I are a complicated issue, which not only involve several countries but can also be traced back to events which occurred in the 19th century. Historians are divided. Opinions vary from those who claim that Germany deliberately planned for a war years before the conflict started (Fritz Fischer), to those who say that it was an accident or *"a tragedy of miscalculations"* (Turner). We need to outline the main causes, but first we will identify a few key issues:

- To what extent is it possible to blame Germany for WW I?
- Was WW I a result of miscalculations and misunderstandings?
- Was WW I caused by problems in the Balkans?

9.1 Long-term causes

1. **Industrialisation** (it can be discussed if this is a 'cause' or rather a factor which set the scene):

    (a) **Domestic consequences**: The industrialisation process resulted in people moving to cities and an increase of education. Awareness/class consciousness grew. Germany, Austria, the Ottomans and Russia, four great powers, were all autocracies. The economic and social development destabilised their political system. New groups, liberals, workers and national minorities, wanted rights/power. It created political tension in these countries and the rulers were questioned. It has been argued that some rulers saw a war as a way out of domestic problems.

    (b) It also changed **the balance of power between states**.

% of national production coming from industry in 1910	Britain	Germany	Austria	Russia
	75%	70%	47%	30%

    If some states, like Germany, are growing in power and other states, like the Ottomans, are weakening, this would affect the balance of power. Would a stronger state expand at the expense of a weaker one?

    (c) It is also clear that industrialisation made it possible to build up much stronger armies and fleets. The **arms race** destabilised the political situation.

2. **The decline of the Ottoman Empire.** The Turks had controlled the Balkans for centuries but now their power was in decline. Their empire was referred to as 'the sick man of Europe.' There was a **power vacuum** in the Balkans.

3. **Nationalism:** The 19th century was the era of nationalism. Nationalism in this context means that a group of people, a nation, with a common sense of belonging to the same

national identity, should also form a state. This sense of identity could be based on culture, religion, language, ethnic background and traditions. This belief could both unite (Italy and Germany) a country and split a country (Austria). In the Balkans, due to Russian support, Serbia, Bulgaria, and Montenegro had become independent in 1878. What was to come next?

4. **The growing strength of Germany**. In 1914 Germany was the most powerful industrial state in Europe. The Kaiser, Wilhelm II, wanted to expand its influence. He wanted a 'rightful place in the sun' by launching his 'Weltpolitik' in the 1890s.

5. **The Alliance system**: the Dual Alliance 1879 (Ger+Au-H), The Triple Entente (Fr+Ru 1894, Br+Fr 1904, Br+Ru 1907). It could set off a chain reaction. (Note! If you get a question about the importance of the alliance system, you need to study the terms of the most important treaties. Not all of them were binding.)

6. **The naval race/arms race** between Germany and Britain (and other Great Powers). At the end of the 19th century and beginning of the 20th century, Germany started to build a fleet. The British viewed this as a major threat to their colonial Empire.

9.2 Short-term causes

1. **The Bosnian crisis in 1908** (it can always be discussed if this is a short- or long-term cause). Austria made a secret agreement with Russia allowing the Austrians to annex Bosnia if the Russians were given access to the Dardanelles. When the Balkan powers found out about the annexation they reacted strongly. There were 3 million Serbs in Bosnia. Germany supported Austria. Russia, after the defeat against Japan in 1905, couldn't risk a war and didn't get support from the other great powers about getting access to the Dardanelles. The result was that Austria annexed Bosnia, but that Russia was still shut out from the Dardanelles. Hereafter both Russia and its junior ally Serbia would be determined to avoid further humiliation.

2. **The Balkan Wars in 1912 and 1913.** A Balkan league was formed by the Balkan states and in 1912 they attacked Turkey. Serbia more than doubled its size but it didn't get Albania which would have provided an outlet to the sea. Austria had mobilised twice with the support of Germany which meant that Russia didn't dare support its ally Serbia. The result of the two wars was still that Serbia had been strengthened. It was now determined to stir up trouble among Serbs and Croats in Bosnia. Austria was equally determined to put a stop to its ambitions.

3. **The crown prince of Austria-Hungary, Franz Ferdinand,** was assassinated by the Black Hand from Serbia. The Serbian government had some foreknowledge of the assassination.

Figure 9.1: **The first page of the edition of the** *Domenica del Corriere,* **an Italian paper, with a drawing of Achille Beltrame depicting Gavrilo Princip killing Archduke Francis Ferdinand of Austria in Sarajevo.**

4. **The Blank Cheque:** Austria was prepared to crush Serbia. Before doing so, it wanted support from its main ally, Germany. The Kaiser gave the Austrians unconditional support. Why? Did he do it because he had to support his only firm ally? Did he do it hoping that there would only

be a limited Balkan War? After all Russia had not supported the Serbs during the Bosnian Crisis nor during the Balkan Wars. Or is Fischer right in arguing that Germany wanted a general war 'sooner than later'?

5. **The Austrian ultimatum** was deliberately written so that Serbia would not be able to accept it and that there would be a war with Serbia.

6. **The mobilisation race**: Germany had a war plan called the Schlieffen Plan. The Germans planned to defeat France within a few weeks (as in 1870), while Russia was still mobilising. After that, Germany would defeat Russia. On 30 July the Tsar finally ordered full mobilisation (i.e. against both Austria and Germany), without declaring war. If Germany accepted a Russian mobilisation, Russia would be fully mobilised by September. Thereafter the Schlieffen Plan could no longer work. It was thus impossible to just stand by and watch a Russian mobilisation without a declaration of war. Russia did not realise that its mobilisation made war unavoidable from a German point of view. Germany now declared war on both France and Russia. A J P Taylor has emphasised how a diplomatic manoeuvre from Russia, to show its support for Serbia, resulted in an undesired war.

7. **The alliance system** was now set in motion and dragged Europe into a general war. Not every alliance was a clear commitment to support your ally, but many were. Britain had promised to support Belgian neutrality. When Germany went through Belgium, it dragged Britain into the war.

9.3 What can different countries be blamed for?

Russia: As the largest and longest established Slavic nation, Russia tried to bolster its declining reputation both domestically and amongst the new Slavic Balkan states by championing the idea of Pan-Slavism. Russia and the Tsar had been humiliated so many times. In 1878 the Western powers had forced Russia to give back land to Turkey after the Russo-Turkish War. Russia had been defeated by Japan in 1905. During the Bosnian crisis in 1908 and twice during the Balkan Wars it had been unable to support its ally. The crisis of 1914 was its last chance to gain some influence in the Balkans and perhaps to get control of the Dardanelles. The Tsar was prepared to risk a war.

Austria: Containing more than 13 different nationalities, Austria was a multicultural state in decline as there was no firm political control in the Balkans and Austria wanted to expand its influence in the area to stem the tide of nationalism. It was looking for a 'preventive' war against Serbia – no matter the consequences.

Germany: Germany and Kaiser Wilhelm wanted to expand German influence and prestige. In the 1890s it launched its 'Weltpolitik'. There is no doubt that Germany wanted to be influential beyond its boundaries: its colonial policy, its naval build up, and its aggressive foreign policy are just some examples. By giving Austria the **Blank Cheque**, it can be argued that Germany made it clear that it wanted to risk a war. One school of historians also argues that the growth of domestic opposition, from liberals and socialists, made the Kaiser declare war. Germany had been united in 1871 due to a war. This could happen again.

France: France had been defeated by Germany in the war of 1870–71. France knew that alone it wasn't strong enough to defeat Germany in a new war. It therefore settled its disputes with former enemies like Britain and Russia, just to create an alliance which was strong enough to win a war against Germany. France was the architect behind the alliance against Germany. In Germany, press and politicians complained of 'encirclement'. The other powers, led by France, had formed a ring of enemies around Germany.

Serbia: Extreme nationalism and governmental foreknowledge/secret police involvement in the assassination.

9.4 Historiography

As already mentioned, historians are divided over the reasons for WWI.

Fritz Fischer argues that Germany deliberately planned for the war. They wanted a war sooner rather than later because they feared a Russian rearmament which had stated in 1908. The Kaiser also believed that a successful war might ease domestic tension.

A J P Taylor argues that the mobilisation race went out of control. A process that was not initially intended to create a war, had this effect. He also argues that many states went to war out of a feeling of weakness. Austria-Hungary had to control Balkan nationalism if the empire was to survive. The Tsar had to show his reliability as an ally and had been humiliated in 1904 (the Russo-Japanese War), during the Bosnian crisis in 1908 and during the Balkan Wars. Both France and Germany felt that they had to support important allies. Taylor also argues that the alliance system played a minor role. Many of the terms were informal and loose (like the Entente between France and Britain) and the fact that Italy just left its alliance when the war started, shows that we can't consider the alliance system as the 'driving force' behind the war.

Gordon Martel emphasises the blame of nationalists in the Balkans, i.e. Austria-Hungary and Serbia, for causing the war.

L C F Turner argues that it was not a deliberately provoked war. It was caused by 'a tragedy of miscalculations'. Would Russia support Serbia? What did Germany expect when supporting Austria? Did Russia realise the implications of its mobilisation?

Of course there are many historians who advocate a 'mixed responsibility' as reason for the war.

> Now, when you have read the text:
> 1. Study the questions that follow (but not the answers!)
> 2. Copy a template and outline your answer.
> 3. Compare your answer with the one given and analyse any possible differences.

9. THE CAUSES OF WWI

17. To what extent was Germany responsible for the outbreak of WWI?

(It is a 'to what extent' question. It means that you have to write two parts in the essay. One showing German responsibility, and one showing 'other factors'.)

Germany's responsibility:

1. **The Schlieffen Plan** aimed to eliminate France first, taking advantage of the slow Russian mobilisation and then turn on Russia. Germany had signed a treaty where it promised to respect Belgium's neutrality. By invading Belgium, Germany made Britain enter the war = general war.

2. The '**Blank Cheque**' Germany promised to support Austria whatever policies it chose. Germany had backed up Austria firmly since the Bosnian crisis in 1908. This support was unconditional. Examples:

    (a) During the Bosnian crisis in 1908, the German Kaiser wrote a letter to the Russians where he demanded that Russia should accept the Austrian annexation of Bosnia and end its support for Serbia. Otherwise *'events would run their course'*, meaning Wilhelm threatened with war.

    (b) During the Balkan Wars the German Kaiser gave unconditional support to Austria in its attempts to block Serbia from the Adriatic Sea: *"Whatever comes from Vienna is for me a command"* the Kaiser said.

    Many argue that the **Blank Cheque**, given in the critical situation that existed in 1914, is evidence that the Kaiser wanted a general war.

3. '*Weltpolitik*' = an aggressive German foreign policy: Bismarck had limited Germany's role in Europe after the Franco-Prussian War in 1870. He was not interested in colonies, or navy, but in status quo. Kaiser Wilhelm's Weltpolitik starting in the 1890s, was something different: the Kruger Telegram, colonialism, the building of the Baghdad-Gulf railway, the building of a German fleet, the Moroccan Crisis 1905, the support of Austria, the Agadir Crisis 1911, The Zabern Affair 1913, The Schlieffen Plan, are all examples of Wilhelm's Weltpolitik.

    Germany's and Wilhelm's desire for an empire and a world role disrupted and threatened the international status quo. Britain sided with France as a result of the German naval build up.

4. **The rise of militarism** in Germany during the rule of Kaiser Wilhelm II contributed to the outbreak of WWI. The best evidence for this military power overriding the political decision makers is the Potsdam War Council. Fischer has shown how German generals and the Kaiser were prepared to declare war on Britain without consulting the government.

5. **Domestic consideration *and* the Fischer Thesis,** i.e. how to escape the threat from socialists and liberals. Germany deliberately planned for WWI and the best evidence is the Potsdam War Council. Why did Germany want a war?

    (a) Economic change had created a middle and working class wanting to change the constitution and giving the Reichstag political power. The economic and social development in this growing state, unbalanced its political system. The Junkers and the generals had considerable influence in Wilhelm's Germany. During Wilhelm's rule there was a 'rise of militarism', i.e. military leaders and the Kaiser became more powerful at the expense of the civilian government. But the growth of socialism challenged the conservative political power and German leaders feared revolution. Germany had been united through a war in 1870–71 and there was a tradition that the country could be united through nationalism. The Kaiser deliberately chose war to escape domestic problems. Germany was responsible, according to Fischer, for WWI.

(b) The second reason for Germany wanting a war 'sooner than later' was Russian rearmament. Russia had been rearming since the Russo-Japanese War in 1904–05 and the Bosnian crisis in 1908. Within a few years, Russia would be much stronger.

6. **Germany** went through Belgium when it attacked France. This dragged Britain into the war.
7. It was Germany who first declared war on both France and Russia.
8. **The September Programme** from 1914 showed the German war plans. It outlined aggressive growth both in the West and in the East.

No, the war was not a result of Germany's policies:

1. **Industrialisation** led to (a) tension in many countries i.e. new groups wanted power which led to domestic tension, and (b) it affected the international balance of power.
2. **The power vacuum in the Balkans** due to the decline of the Ottoman Empire.
3. **Nationalism** and imperialism in many countries led to the war. In Russia, pan-Slavism (the idea to unite all Slavs) had a lot of support. France wanted revenge for the 1870/71 defeat. Balkan nationalism was very strong.
4. **Austria-Hungary** wanted a war against Serbia no matter what the consequences would be.
5. **The mobilisation race** went out of control.
6. **The alliance system** led to a war that no one had prepared for.

Conclusion: summarise your main points and base your answer upon them. It is possible to answer that the war was to some extent caused by Germany but there were other factors as well, and there is no 'absolute' answer. What you have to do is to support your answer in the conclusion.

18. Discuss whether WWI was a result of miscalculations and misunderstandings.

(You can find yes- or no arguments for this. Write a balanced argument with the arguments below.)

Europe really did stumble into this conflict (support Turner's view):

1. It can be argued that few expected the **Russians to support Serbia**. Why? They did so neither in 1908 nor during the Balkan Wars, so perhaps the Russians would back off again. Both Austria and Germany had good reasons for believing that it would be a 'local Balkan war'.
2. Russia was not aware of how its **mobilisation** affected Germany. The Schlieffen Plan gave no alternatives for Germany: it could not just stand and watch Russian mobilisation, because it needed to defeat France *before* it defeated Russia. The result was that Germany declared war on Russia and France.
3. Germany didn't expect Britain to defend **Belgium**.
4. Was Germany aware of the crucial importance of its **naval build-up** and its aggressive foreign policies? It turned a potential ally, Britain, into an enemy.
5. It was a naïve thought that 'successful little wars' would ease **domestic tensions**. Berlin, Vienna and St Petersburg misjudged this policy and it finally led to the collapse of the three empires.

No, Europe did not stumble into this conflict:

1. Industrialisation changed the balance of power/domestic problems.
2. The decline of the Ottomans.
3. An era of colonialism/imperialism/nationalism/pan-Slavism.
4. The alliance system.
5. The arms race/naval race.
6. The growth of Germany/the aggressiveness of Germany and the Kaiser/the Fischer Thesis.
7. The problems in Austria with different nationalities.
8. The humiliation of Russia: in 1878 (Congress of Berlin after the Russo-Turkish War), 1904/05 Russia was defeated by Japan, 1908 the Bosnian Crisis when Russia did not get access to the Dardanelles and lastly in 1912/13, when Russia could not give any support to Serbia at the time of the Balkan Wars.

It was the long-term causes which turned the assassination into such a critical deed.

Conclusion: Summarise the main points of the essay. As you may know by now it is impossible to give you 'the answer' to this question, but my personal opinion is that it was not only an accident that the Balkan question erupted again in 1914 and that the Great Powers were involved in this conflict. The policies of several key states are a little too clear cut for us to consider the outbreak of war a misunderstanding.

Chapter 10: The Peace Settlements

Issue

How justified was the Treaty of Versailles in dealing with Germany?

The **settlements of the Paris Peace Conference**, (the Treaty of Versailles, Saint-Germain-en-Laye, Trianon, Neuilly and Sèvres), have been criticised many times. This is perhaps understandable especially if we take into account the difficulties facing the peacemakers:

1. **Four empires had fallen**, Russia, Germany, Austria-Hungary and the Ottoman Empire. In these territories there was a strong desire for national self-determination. It was impossible to satisfy all the demands. In Austria-Hungary there were at least 13 different nationalities. For a number of reasons it was impossible to give each nationality a territory and recognise it as a state.

2. **The victors** had very different experiences from the war and were consequently very **divided** in their intentions.

3. Europe had suffered enormously from this war, which killed 9 million people. At the end of the war the **Spanish flu** killed additional millions. Much of Europe was in ruins and peace would bring economic hardship: **there was no time for endless discussions**.

4. **After the Communist Revolution in Russia** in 1917 a Civil War followed in 1918. In early 1919 German communists revolted in the Spartacist Uprising. This new 'disease' from the East scared many in the West.

Figure 10.1: **The Paris Peace Conference: signing of the Treaty of Versailles in the Hall of Mirrors**

10. THE PEACE SETTLEMENTS

10.1 Background to the Peace Conference

When the war started **few of the states had declared any clear war aims**. Austria wanted to stem the tide of Serb nationalism. In September 1914, after the war had started, Germany presented its '**September programme**'. It was extensive, ambitious and aggressive, and outlined a German '*Mitteleuropa*', but also with conquests both in the West and in the East. France should more or less be transformed into a German vassal state.

Some historians have argued that many went to war out of a 'feeling of weakness'. Some rulers had domestic problems and saw war as a solution. Others just thought that they needed to support an ally. If so, the aims were often not publicly and clearly expressed.

The Entente powers wanted to defeat and control Germany. But the territorial demands were less ambitious. **France** was, however, clear over that it wanted back Alsace-Lorraine and both punishment and protection of Germany. To ask French taxpayers to pay for the damage caused by Germany in the North of France would be seen as madness, especially when France had been forced to pay an indemnity after the war 1870-71. In **Britain** there had just been elections with demands for 'hang the Kaiser'. On the other hand Lloyd George, the prime minister who had firm support from these elections, was concerned about the rise of Communism in Russia and the danger of punishing Germany at a time when communist uprisings were taking place in the country.

It was the US President Woodrow Wilson who most clearly had outlined his 'war aims'. This was partly paradoxical taking into account that the U.S. had been the least involved of the great powers and joined the war very late. **Wilson's 14-point programme** presented in early 1918:

Point 1 :	No secret diplomacy
Point 2 :	Freedom of navigation on all seas.
Point 3 :	Free trade among nations and an end to all economic barriers between countries
Point 4 :	Reduction of armaments and weapons to a level required for public safety.
Point 5 :	Fair and impartial decisions for the resolution of colonial claims
Point 6 :	Restoration of Russia's territories and freedom to establish and develop its own political system
Point 7 :	Preservation of the sovereignty of Belgium
Point 8 :	France should be fully liberated, its territory restored and be allowed to recover Alsace-Lorraine
Point 9 :	All Italians are to be allowed to live in Italy
Point 10 :	Self-determination should be allowed for all those living in Austria-Hungary.
Point 11 :	Self-determination and independence for the Balkan states and its borders re-drawn.
Point 12 :	Self-determination for the Turkish people and for Non-Turks under Turkish rule
Point 13 :	An independent Polish nation should be created which should have access to the sea.
Point 14 :	A League of Nations should be created.

Germany expected that a peace treaty should not punish the new democratic government. The Kaiser had fled the country and when the armistice was signed in November 1918, the new government had expressed a wish that it should be based on Wilson's 14 points.

The peace treaty was, however, never negotiated with Germany. The Germans referred to the treaty as a *'Diktat'*. The allied blockade was not lifted until July 1919, i.e. not until the peace treaty was signed. In 1918 alone 294,000 Germans died due to the effects of the blockade. Germany had no other choice than to sign the treaty.

10.2 Terms of the Treaty of Versailles

Most of the talks took place at the French foreign office in Paris. The various treaties are named after the places where they were signed, normally different palaces in Paris. That the Treaty of Versailles, the treaty dealing with Germany, was signed at Versailles, was very symbolic. It was here Germany had been proclaimed in 1871 and the Prussian king crowned Kaiser of Germany. The French prime minister Clemenceau was chairman of the conference, which was going to deal with the Germans.

1. **In Article 231** (The War Guilt Clause) it was stated that *"Germany accepts the responsibilities of Germany and her allies for causing all [...] the damage [...] and the war [...]"*. The final sum to be paid was unfixed and left to a commission. Germany should pay for direct damage but also less direct damage i.e. pensions and costs for orphans. The sum was fixed in 1921 to a total of £ 11,000 million, where half was supposed to be cash payment and half in goods. The size of the **indemnity** caused a major dispute not only in Germany, but also among the allies.

2. The **army** should be limited to 100,000 men and they should serve for 12 years, thus preventing a build-up of a trained reserve.

3. The size of the **fleet** was limited and Germany was not allowed to have **submarines or an air force**.

4. Germany lost all its **colonies**.

5. Germany was refused membership in the **League of Nations**.

6. The **Rhineland** should be a demilitarised zone and the Western allies should have troops there until 1930. The **Zaar** basin, rich of natural resources should be held by allied troops for 15 years and France should get the coal mined there during the first five years. Alsace-Lorraine was given back to France with two million people and three-quarters of Germany's iron resources. Germany also had to give up land in the East to the re-created Poland, hence dividing Germany in two pieces by creating the **Polish Corridor**. **Germany lost 13% of its territory, 12% of its population and 48% of its iron deposits** (part of this came from Alsace-Lorraine, taken from France in 1871).

If the **principle of national self-determination** were to be applied, that a lot of minorities in mainly Central Europe should be given the right to form a state, someone must provide this territory. So it was not only Germany who could complain that the peacemakers deprived them of land. Austria, Hungary, and the Ottomans suffered even more. It was a direct consequence of this idea.

10.3 The Treaty of Saint-Germain-en-Laye

In 1918 different national minorities in the Austrian-Hungarian Empire declared themselves independent – it was the end of the Habsburg Empire. The Austria which came out of the war was very different from Austria/Hungary which once entered the war.

1. The new republic was seen as the **successor to the empire** and had to pay reparations and was forced to limit its army to 30,000 men.

2. Considerable **territories were handed over** to many new states: Poland, Czechoslovakia, Romania, Yugoslavia and Italy. Hungary was also considered as a fully independent state. In total the country lost 15 million of its subjects and most of the industrial parts of the country. Austria was forced to recognise the independence of all these states in the Treaty. An economic union with Germany could be a possible solution to this new and difficult situation, but it was specifically forbidden in the Treaty.

10.4 The Treaty of Trianon

The treaty dealt with Hungary.

1. The country was seen as a **successor to the Austrian-Hungarian Empire**.
2. Consequently it had to pay an **indemnity and limit its army** to 35,000 men.
3. It had to give up **75% of its territory** and **lost 60% of its people**. Land was given to Austria, Yugoslavia, Czechoslovakia, and Romania. The country has been described as a 'pale shadow' of what it had been and was of course not satisfied with the terms.

10.5 The Treaty of Neuilly

In this Treaty, Bulgaria was forced to **give territories** to Yugoslavia and Romania. Land was also given to Greece, resulting in Bulgaria losing its **Aegean coastline**. As an ally of Germany, it was also forced to **limit its army and pay an indemnity** of half a million US dollars.

10.6 The Treaty of Sèvres and Lausanne

The Ottomans were comparable to Austria-Hungary: an old empire in decline, which had controlled vast territories. The situation was very complicated when the war ended because:

1. Russia had claims on territories but went through its revolution and Civil War.
2. The nationalist leader **Mustafa Kemal** emerged in Turkey.
3. Greece invaded **Smyrna,** which led to a nationalist revolt in Turkey.

In the Treaty of Sèvres the Ottoman Sultan agreed to give up all claims of non-Turkish territories. That meant the loss of the **Middle East**. Armenia was to be recognised as an independent state. Greece was given areas around **Smyrna for five years**. Most of the islands in the Aegean Sea were lost. **The Straits**, the outlet from the Black Sea, were to become international territory and demilitarised.

The outcome of the war and the Treaty was seen as a national humiliation and led to a national revolt led by Mustafa Kemal. The Greek invasion of Smyrna especially offended the Turks.

In March 1921, Kemal signed a treaty with Russia, which settled the border in Caucasus.

In August 1922, Greece had been defeated and there were new negotiations in Lausanne.

1. **Greece was forced to give back Eastern Thrace** and two islands, Imbros and Tenedos.
2. **The Straits** were still demilitarised but Turkey was given the right to close this outlet from the Black Sea in times of war.
3. **Foreign supervision of Turkish finance** was brought to an end.

The Turkey that we know today was to some extent born and the loss of territories in the Middle East and North Africa was of course of major importance.

The Democratic Republic of Armenia was formed and an independent Kurdish zone was proposed (these two soon collapsed). A mandate system under the control of the League of Nations was set up. Britain should administer Palestine/Transjordan, Mesopotamia (Iraq). Most of the Gulf was controlled by Britain. France controlled Lebanon and Syria. The only area controlled by the Arabs was what is today known as Saudi Arabia.

10.7 The Treaty of Brest-Litovsk, March 1918

This treaty was not a part of the Paris settlement, but it also played an important role in ending WWI.

The Bolshevik regime, coming to power in October 1917, wanted to end the war to secure the revolution in Russia. In December 1917 an armistice was signed. Trotsky was the Russian chief negotiator and wanted to delay an agreement because he hoped for a world revolution or that Germany would get more problems in the west, causing it to lose the war. This did not happen and in December 1917 the negotiations started with Germany and Austria-Hungary. Trotsky found the terms far too harsh and left the conference and declared 'peace without a Treaty'. The Germans didn't accept it and re-started the war. Revolutionary Russia could not fight a war and the Germans were soon only 100 miles from St Petersburg. Lenin used all his authority to convince a divided Bolshevik party to accept the terms. Trotsky signed the Treaty on 3 March 1918. It stated that:

1. Russia surrendered the Western part of the country i.e. **Estonia, Latvia, Lithuania and Poland. Areas in Southern Caucasus were to be given to Turkey. Finland, Georgia and the Ukraine** were going to be independent states.
2. 6,000 million marks should be paid in **reparations**.
3. Russia lost around **one third of its population, arable land and 80% of its coal mines**.

The price for peace was enormous. Why did the Bolsheviks sign such a Treaty?

1. They expected a **world revolution**, which would make the Treaty temporary.
2. It was necessary **to save the revolution**.

The Treaty of Brest-Litovsk was signed more than a year before the Paris Settlement. To the governments in the West it showed the greed of the Central Powers and made it clear that these powers, when they once would be defeated, should be held responsible and forced to pay their price for the war.

Taking into account the number of peace treaties, and that the map of Europe was totally redrawn, it is challenging to emphasise the key changes. If we make an attempt, be aware of that there are many views.

1. The creation of a number of **weak states** in central Europe, from Finland in the North to Yugoslavia in the South would play a major role in the future.
2. **That the Ottomans lost the Middle East** and that the territories were given to Britain and France as a part of the League of Nation's mandate system, had consequences which are difficult to oversee.
3. With hindsight it is difficult not to mention that the resentment in Germany over the Treaty and the financial burden it had to bear, in combination with all the weak states, were important building blocks in **bringing Hitler to power** and causing WW II.

> Now, when you have read the text:
> 1. Study the question that follows (but not the answer!)
> 2. Copy a template and outline your answer.
> 3. Compare your answer with the one given and analyse any possible differences.

19. To what extent is it possible to defend the way in which the Treaty of Versailles dealt with Germany?

(Structure: present the arguments for and against.)

Yes, we can defend this:

1. The indemnity and loss of population, territories and resources **did not prevent a German recovery**. In 1927 Germany's industrial production was back on the pre-war level, **supporting the claim that terms were not too harsh.** (This is a very complicated issue. One question is how much shall we link this recovery to the Dawes Plan, which resulted in US short-term loans being pumped in to Germany from 1924?)

2. Germany had forced France to pay an **indemnity after the Franco-Prussian War** in 1870–71. France did pay this indemnity of 200 million francs.
3. The North of France was in ruins after the war. The war had not been fought in Germany. The Germans should naturally also make a contribution to the rebuilding of France. **If Germany didn't pay – French tax payers would have to bear the full cost.** No French politician would have survived an election if it was accepted that Germany should not pay. It makes the indemnity highly justified.
4. Why should France not be allowed to take back **Alsace-Lorraine**, which had been taken from France in 1870–71?
5. In March 1918 Russia had signed the **Treaty of Brest-Litovsk** with Germany and Austria. The terms offered by these two states were much worse than those Germany had been offered by the allies. Russia lost 80% of its coal mines and one third of its population and farming land. Why show leniency to a Germany, which had offered Russia such terms?

No, we can't defend it:

1. **The indemnity was far too high**. The leading British economist at the time J M Keynes shared this view. It is a highly complicated issue to decide how accurate this view is, but it is worth noting that Keynes, who took part in the negotiations, later wrote a book about this where he criticised the Treaty. Keynes estimated that Germany could handle a sum of £ 2,000 million. British financiers estimated it to £ 24,000 million. The prime minister Lloyd George found it very difficult and complained: "*What is a poor politician to do?*" To this we must add that Germany lost 13% of its territory, 12% of the population and 48% of its iron deposits.
2. The idea of linking the indemnity to guilt for causing the war can be discussed. **How valid is the claim that it was only Germany and its allies who were responsible for the war** and had to take all the blame?
3. **The principle of 'national self-determination' was applied to many but not to Germany**. Eight million Germans lived as minorities in countries like Poland and Czechoslovakia. All those weak states with German minorities would later be one of the main reasons for WW II.
4. Why should the new democratic Germany not be a part of the **League of Nations**? It was a peacekeeping organisation and what was the logic behind keeping them out? This form of punishment is not 'justified'.
5. Yes it was correct that the terms of the Treaty of Brest-Litovsk were harsh. But it was the German general staff in **Kaiser Wilhelm's Germany who had formed these terms**. Why punish the new democratic Germany for what the Kaiser and his generals did?

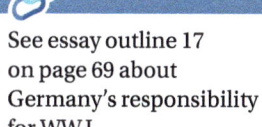
See essay outline 17 on page 69 about Germany's responsibility for WW I.

Conclusion: It is highly **complicated to decide if the indemnity was possible to pay** and how we should view the German recovery, which had been accomplished by 1927. The recovery has been used as evidence for that Germany could bear the indemnity. Even Lloyd George, the British Prime Minister, found it very difficult to estimate the sum Germany should pay. Another very **complicated issue is to decide how justified it was to blame Germany** and its allies for causing the war.

The fact that millions of Germans had to accept that they lived in other countries outside Germany, the War Guilt Clause, the refusal of not accepting Germany as a member of the League, cannot be described as 'wise'.

Summarise your key points and present your view.

HISTORY HL: EUROPE

Chapter 11: Spain 1918–39

Issues

Was the Civil War caused by domestic problems or shall we see it as a result of the struggle between democracy and totalitarianism in Europe before WW II? Why did the Nationalists win the Civil War?

11.1 Long-term causes of the Spanish Civil War

1. **Spain was a backward country**

   As late as in 1930, 46% of the workforce was still occupied with **agricultural production** and the country was one of the **poorest in Europe**. In the South, in Andalusia and Extremadura, vast private estates were often owned by absentee landowners and worked by armies of desperately poor landless labourers. There were more than two million landless labourers whom sought seasonal work and often earned less than £30 per year. It was a staggeringly unjust society. **The industrial sector was far too small**. As a result of this backwardness Spain was defeated in 1898 by the 'upstart' US in the Spanish-American War. It led to another disaster, Spain's loss of the remnants of their overseas empire: Cuba, Puerto Rico, and the Philippines. **'The Disaster of 1898'** was as much territorial as psychological and it had important long-term consequences i.e. Spain came to realise its own impotence and backwardness. The monarchy suffered from this development and a process started where some groups from both the right and the left would look at **alternative political solutions**.

2. **Spain was a divided country**

   (a) **Spain was divided politically:** Rich **landowners**, together with the **church** and the **army**, made up the **conservative right**, traditionally supporting the monarchy and the existing society. Historically they had been very reluctant to accept changes that would reduce their power/wealth and they made up a powerful ruling oligarchy.

   - The left was represented by agricultural workers, workers from the textile industries in Catalonia and workers in the iron, steel and shipbuilding industries in the Basque country. **Many workers supported radical left-wing solutions.**

   - **Liberals wanted constitutional reforms**, some even a **republic**.

   (b) **Separatism: In Catalonia and the Basque Country**, with distinctive languages and cultures, **separatists** demanded independence. In 1909 the army had been used to violently crush a revolt in Catalonia for an independent region.

   (c) **The political left was divided** which made it difficult to form a strong coalition against the political right. In Spain, the left was divided between socialists and communists. But there was a third very strong left-wing group, which had its stronghold in Catalonia: the Anarchists. It was unique in Europe. **Anarchists** reject the idea of political parties and a 'state' - the state was repressive - as the tool for ruling a country. Of course this made it very difficult to form a coalition. There was also a natural rivalry between these three parties due to their attempts to attract support from the workers, and this rivalry made co-operation difficult.

3. **King Alfonso XIII** (king of Spain 1902–31) was faced by a series of new challenges in the early 1920s:

- In **Morocco**, Spain was involved in its last colonial war. 12,000 soldiers were killed in one battle alone in 1921 which led to outrage in Spain.
- Spain was difficult to rule with a political left and right who were more than ever unwilling to co-operate. There were a number of **violent clashes** and the old party system began to crumble.
- After the end of WW I, where Spain had benefited from favourable trade conditions, there **were economic problems with unemployment**.
- **Separatists** in the Basque country and in Catalonia wanted **independence**.

Many considered the monarchy ill-equipped to deal with this difficult situation. Even the **king himself** was prepared to accept a strong leader i.e. he did not give full support to the parliamentary system.

11.2 Short-term causes of the Spanish Civil War

1. **The dictatorship of Primo de Rivera paved the way for Republicanism.**

    In September **1923 general Miguel Primo de Rivera** organised a *coup d'état*, with support from the king and the army. Rivera strongly believed that it was the politicians who had ruined Spain and that governing without them could restore the strength of the nation.

    - Primo de Rivera suspended the constitution and **dissolved the parliament** (Cortes).
    - He created a new 'apolitical' party, the Patriotic Union (UP).
    - Introduced martial law.
    - Censored the press.
    - Separatism in Catalonia was suppressed.
    - Workers also benefited from massive public works. The government financed such projects with huge public loans and it resulted in a decrease in unemployment.
    - The war in Morocco was brought to an end in 1927.
    - Primo de Rivera also imitated Mussolini's corporate system in Italy. Management and labour were organised in 27 corporations representing different industries and professions. Within each corporation, government arbitrators mediated disputes over wages, and other working conditions. This gave Spanish workers more influence than ever before, and this might be the reason why the Spanish Socialist Party and UGT (socialist union) agreed to co-operate with the government.

    His regime was conservative, authoritarian, and nationalistic and used the slogan 'Country, Religion, Monarchy'. He had some notable successes when even the socialists were prepared to co-operate with his regime. But by the late 1920s he was facing major problems:

    - Spain suffered from the effects of the world economic depression
    - Primo de Rivera lost the support from the army and the king
    - In January 1930, Primo de Rivera resigned and the king appointed men with a military background as the two next prime ministers. One major effect of the years with dictatorship was that both republicanism and socialism had gained in strength from opposing the dictatorship. It was a **dramatic transformation of the political system**.

HISTORY HL: EUROPE

Political life in the 1920s and early 1930s was increasingly polarised which finally led to the outbreak of the Civil War.

When municipal elections were held in April 1931 it was seen as a contest between monarchists and republicans/socialists. The result was a victory for the republicans, especially in the larger cities. **The king decided to leave the country in May 1931.**

2. **The Second republic 1931–33: Spain was turning to the left. The rule of the new government provoked the right.**

Apr 1931	Municipal elections won by republicans. King Alfonso in exile.
Jun 1931	Elections of a National Assembly confirmed a republican majority.
Dec 1931	Alcala Zamora new president and Manuel Azana new prime minister.

The new government presented their programme/constitution:

- Spain should be a **republic**
- The Cortes should be elected by **universal suffrage** every four years. The president should serve for six years.
- The government was given rights to **nationalise large estates and industries**.
- The principle of **regional autonomy** was recognised in the new constitution.
- Army officers and the clergy could not serve as president.
- **The church and the state should be separated** i.e. Spain had no longer an official religion. Freedom of worship and end of state support of salaries to the clergy. Compulsory religious education in schools was abolished and the Jesuits were banned.

Robert Wolfson concludes: *"Spain was to become a modern socialist state"*. This policy represented everything that the right hated.

The Socialist Party, the Radical Party and some supporters of Catholic Republicans supported this clear turn to the left. Supporters who were not socialists, came from the professional middle class and intelligentsia – people who had abandoned the right and the monarchy during the years of dictatorship.

The government and the Socialist Party had a difficult balance act when coming to power.

- **Many radicals**, like members of the socialist trade union UGT, **wanted a more radical policy**. But this could of course provoke other groups in the government.
- A radical left-wing policy would also **provoke the right**.
- **The anarchists**, represented by their labour organisation CNT were, according to their ideology hostile to all state power, making them **difficult to co-operate with**. The Socialists had also reasons to weaken their rival. Soon there were a number of clashes and the anarchists were alienated from the government. The anarchists were especially strong in Catalonia, where demands were made for regional autonomy. To some extent this was supported by the new government. Catalonia was given its own flag, president, and a parliament. This provoked the political right.

The opposition was now mobilising. Anticlericalism provoked many and dissatisfied Catholics merged with groups who felt that their wealth was threatened. The regime discharged 8,000 officers with full pay to assure that the army would be politically neutral. In 1933 a new mass Catholic-conservative party, **CEDA**, was formed. On the extreme right, **Carlism**, a very conservative party in the north which had been fighting liberalism for decades, gained new supporters. There were also the **Alfonists**, die-hard supporters of the king. The **Falange** was founded in 1933 by Primo de Rivera's son José

Antonio, following Italian fascism in their exaltation for totalitarian rule and use of violence.

A number of educational, religious, and agrarian reforms were carried out. The right was, however, partially able to successfully block a land reform in the Cortes. The regime also lacked the resources to implement such a reform. The slowness of the reforms affected the support for the government. In Catalonia, separatists thought that the reforms were far from enough. In January 1933 the army was responsible for a massacre of Andalusian villagers during an anarchist uprising.

3. **The right is coming to power again. Polarisation and political violence increased on both sides during 1933–35.**

   There were general elections in November 1933 and the **victory went to the right** i.e. the CEDA, the Radicals and parties from the extreme right. The tide had turned again in Spain. The main reasons were:

   (a) **frustration** over the slowness of the reforms promised by the government;

   (b) an almost unanimous refusal to vote from **anarchists**;

   (c) the **policies of the republican government** 1931–33 had alarmed the right;

   (d) **women participated for the first time** in general elections and they tended to support the centre/right.

The next two years were dominated by a number of coalitions from the right, increasingly dominated by the CEDA and their leader Gil Robert, but also giving a lot of influence to the extreme right. To the left, the years 1933–35 are known as 'the two black years'. Many reforms were reversed. Martin Blinkhorn concludes: *"…a course that could only have explosive consequences"*.

Dec 1933– Feb 1934 The most extensive anarchist uprising during the time of the republic, especially in Catalonia and Aragon, was suppressed with military force. During this period **socialism in Spain was radicalised**; some would use the term 'bolshevisation'.

Sept 1934 A new right-wing coalition came to power dominated by the CEDA. The socialists responded with a general strike.

Oct 1934 In Asturia there was an armed revolt, which has been described as *"the first round of the Civil War"* by Antony Beevor. Socialists and communists co-operated in a 'Workers' Alliance'. Catalonia declared itself independent. The actions of the left were crushed by the army with considerable bloodshed, and about 30,000 people were arrested.

Dec 1935 A third right-wing coalition fell from power. In the coming election a united left, a **'Popular Front'** emerged, wanting a return to the policies from 1931–33. The Popular Front was made up of Republicans, socialists, communists and anarchists.

CEDA was funded by considerable donations from landowners, industrialists and the Catholic Church. To each side, it was a question of either 'fascism' or 'Bolshevism' according to the propaganda.

- In the election in February 1936 the Popular Front won with a narrow margin. In the south poor peasants, expecting a land-reform, started to occupy large estates. Members of the CEDA Youth and the Falange stepped up anti-leftist terror.

On 17 July 1936 the army in Morocco and the Canary Islands revolted. This is the formal start of the Civil War.

11.3 The course of the Civil War

1936	July	Start of the revolt. Germany and Italy gave support to the Nationalists. **German airplanes transported Franco's army in Morocco to Spain.**
	Sept	Largo Caballero formed a government with Socialists, Communists, leftist Republicans and later Anarchists. **First meeting of the Non-Intervention Committee.**
	Oct	Franco head of the Nationalist state. **First Soviet aid reached Spain.**
	Nov	The Nationalists failed to conquer Madrid.
1937	Feb	Malaga conquered by the Nationalists.
	Apr	**Franco seized control of the Falange and united it with the Carlists.** The Nationalists started to attack the north.
	May	**Fighting started in Barcelona between communists/socialists and the POUM/CNT** (anti-Stalinists). This had a major impact in demoralising the left.
	Jun-Oct	**The North conquered.** Franco had abandoned the siege of Madrid to concentrate on the conquest of the North. It is generally considered as the **decisive turning point** because of the industries in the North.
1938	Apr	The Nationalists reached the Mediterranean, cutting in two areas controlled by the Republicans.
1939	Jan-Feb	**Catalonia conquered** by the Nationalists.
	March	**Madrid occupied** by the Nationalists.
	April	Civil War ended.

11.4 Analysis

When the revolt started the government was slow in taking action against the rebels. But by arming members of the UGT and CNT the Republican government was able to control key cities like Madrid and Barcelona. This resulted in a much prolonged conflict. It must be noted that it was **not the entire army who sided with the revolt**. In July 1936, the Nationalists had 62,000 officers and men, while the Republicans had 55,000. To this we must add Franco's forces in Morocco of 24,000 men.

The republican government expected help from the western democracies, especially France. But the French right and Britain refused to give help. The result was a **'non-intervention policy'**, resulting in the Spanish government being given little help while the Nationalists were given substantial aid from Italy, Germany, and Portugal. Between June and August 1936 Franco's African army was transported by German airplanes to mainland Spain – which was critically important in the beginning. The Soviet Union gave help and this help was important in the defence of Madrid in November 1936. But the **Soviets purged the POUM**, the anti-Stalinists or Trotskyists, which led to a Civil War within the left in Barcelona in May 1937. This split severely weakened the left. On the other hand Franco, with his control of the army, could unite the right. In April 1937, he issued the Decree of Unification, which gave him control of both the Falange and the Carlists.

In total, with Soviet help and foreign volunteers, 60,000 joined the international brigade supporting the Republicans. Italy supported the Nationalists with 75,000 men, Germany 15,000 men and Portugal 20,000 men. Apart from the number of men, material help was important. The Italian navy and the German air force were of major importance.

The casualties of the war were (from Hugh Thomas, *The Spanish Civil War*):

Republicans killed in action:	175,000
Nationalists killed in action:	110,000
Victims of the Nationalist terror:	40,000
Victims of the Republican terror:	86,000
Civilian deaths e.g. due to air raids:	25,000
Deaths due to disease or malnutrition	220,000
Total deaths:	**656,000**
Republican refugees:	440 000
Imprisoned Republican supporters:	200 000

There are few topics which have caused so many disagreements among historians as the Spanish Civil War. It should be noted that few historians actually question the need for reform in Spain. The issue has been *who was responsible for it going wrong*, i.e. what **led to a civil war**?

11.5 Historiography

1. When discussing the responsibility for the Civil War, many have blamed the right and mainly the CEDA.

    (a) It was the privileged groups in Spain who were **unwilling to accept the Republic** and the necessary redistribution of wealth, which the legal government advocated after 1931. These groups were also **responsible for the revolt in 1936**.

    (b) Some have argued that it was the leftist radicalisation from 1933, which led to the Civil War. Those defending the left argue that **the radicalisation was a result of a stubborn reluctance** from the right to accept changes after 1931. Blinkhorn writes: *"During 1934 the advantage in rural Spain was allowed to swing violently back to landowners, landlords and employers"* – this radicalised the left.

2. Those who defend the right argue on the other hand that it was the violent radicalisation of the left, for example anticlericalism and the armed revolt in Asturia in 1934, which was the key driving force in this process. Blinkhorn describes the policies of the Republican government of 1931–35 as *"an excessive emphasis on anticlericalism"*. CEDA, which could have developed into an ordinary Christian Democratic Party, **was forced rightwards by the conduct of the left**.

It should be noted that most historians today agree that the Civil War was caused mainly by domestic problems. Blinkhorn writes: *"On the right, while Italian and German agents were active in Spain and sympathetic to the Spanish Right, they cannot be said to have exerted pressure upon it or materially to have assisted it in subverting the republic."*

Another issue is the reasons for the Nationalist success:

- There is a consensus that the Nationalists did get a greater amount of **foreign aid**, and some argue this settled the war. This has, however, been questioned. Some argue that it was not the amount of aid, but more how and when it was delivered. Raymond Carr writes: *"it was less aid than the moral unity and logistic superiority of the Nationalists which was decisive in the long run."*
- Franco was much more successful in dealing with **internal factionalism** and the left was severely weakened from such factionalism. This view makes internal, and not external reasons, more important.
- Most agree that the Western democracies, with their **non-intervention policy**, betrayed the legally elected government in Spain.
- The main dispute has been over the impact of Soviet aid. How much had actions against the POUM **demoralised the left**? The USSR did not provide the Republican side with

enough resources and supported a conventional war against an enemy who always would be stronger. **This tactic was wrong and was decisive for the outcome.** Blinkhorn concludes *"Soviet aid to the Republic was principally calculated to prolong resistance, Axis help for Franco was aimed successfully to victory."*

20. Discuss the reasons for the Civil War in Spain in 1936.

(List the reasons for the Civil War.)

1. **Backwardness:** Spain was a backward country, which was less industrialised than many other European states. There were millions of desperately poor people. The loss of its colonies in 1898 can be seen in this light and it started a process where some groups started to look at alternative political solutions.

2. **The responsibility of the right:** The right in Spain, the army, rich landowners and the church, were not willing to give up their positions. Many argue that this reluctance is the main explanation to leftist radicalisation and violence after 1933. Spain was a staggeringly unjust society. But it was not only a question of wealth or religion. In the Basque Country and in Catalonia there were separatists who demanded independence. There was also, like in Germany and Italy after the war, a fear of Communism or Bolshevism. The right refused to accept this and organised a revolt in 1936 against a legally elected government.

3. **The role of the king:** When problems arose after WW I, King Alfonso XIII, was willing to support the coup by Primo de Rivera. The army and the king did not stand firm behind the parliamentary system. The church took also a firm stand behind the conservatives. It was a major strategic mistake by the king and it led to a dramatic transformation of the political situation – many became republicans.

4. **The responsibility of the left:** The new Republican government introduced a radical left-wing policy in 1931 which provoked the right. Some have argued that it was a misreading of the situation of anticlericalism. The church had considerable support through its church activities, education, hospitals, press and agricultural organisations, especially in rural Spain. The constitution of 1931 *"signalled an all-out legislative assault upon the Church's influential position within Spanish life"*, according to Blinkhorn. This together with other reforms led to a clear polarisation and that the right mobilising its forces. When the right won the elections in 1933 the left responded with strikes and even an armed revolt in Asturia in 1934. Some historians have argued, in contrast to point 2 above, that it was the conduct of the left, which forced CEDA to the right.

5. Some have argued that this conflict should be seen in a broader context, that it should be seen as a consequence of the **struggle between democracy and totalitarianism** that was raging in Europe at this time. Few historians support this view today. Most see the conflict as a result of domestic tension, which could be seen over a number of decades before 1936.

Conclusion: Emphasise domestic reasons when explaining this conflict. The responsibility between the right and the left has been widely debated. See points 2 and 4 above – two highly disputed points. Was it the reluctance of the right to give up their dominance, or was it the radicalisation and conduct of the left, which forced the right to move rightwards, which caused the Spanish Civil War? That is the key question.

21. Discuss the reasons for the Nationalist's victory in the Civil War.

(List the reasons and offer a balanced discussion about the reasons for the Nationalist victory.)

1. There seems to be a consensus amongst historians that the **Nationalists received more foreign aid**. Paul Preston writes: *"Franco could not have won the Civil War without the unstinting help of Hitler and Mussolini"*. But many have questioned whether it was the amount of aid, which was the key point, or if it was how the help was delivered and when. There are examples when the timing of the help seems to have been of major importance, like the air-transport of soldiers from Morocco in 1936. Hugh Thomas also emphasises **the timing of the aid** and gives examples when the Nationalists were given German aid when Aragon was conquered in 1938 and aid for the final campaign of the war. There are also examples where foreign help played a very strategic and logistically important role, like the Italian navy.

2. **Franco had a much more united force behind him**. When the Falange and the Carlists were brought under control with the Decree of Unification in April 1937, the Nationalists were more united than the Republicans. This fact has been more emphasised in recent research. Carr writes: *"It was less aid than the moral unity and logistic superiority of the Nationalists which was decisive in the long run."*

3. This unity did not exist to the same extent on the left. Soviet help was important but there were many anarchists and especially the **POUM** who were anti-Stalinists. It led to armed fighting between leftist groups in Barcelona in 1937. **This clash demoralised many Republicans**. There was also disagreement over how to administrate controlled areas. Some communists wanted collectivisation of land and state controlled industries, while others wanted a less radical policy so as not to alienate moderate groups.

4. **The extent and the nature of Soviet aid** have been discussed. Some have argued that the Soviets for strategic reasons just wanted to prolong the war and not win it. This would serve Soviet interests in Europe by maintaining good relations with Britain and France. It made the left fight a more conventional war against a stronger enemy: it made them fight a war impossible to win. Blinkhorn writes: *"Soviet aid to the Republic was principally calculated to prolong resistance, Axis help for Franco was aimed successfully to victory."*

5. **The non-intervention policy**, followed by most states (but not Italy, Germany and the USSR) resulted in the legally elected government in Spain receiving little help against a revolting junta. In combination with the fact that the Nationalists actually got help from mainly Italy and Germany, this affected the outcome.

Conclusion: describe the outcome as a result of a combination between **'strengths of the Nationalists'** and **'weaknesses of the Republicans'**. Recent research has more emphasised **internal reasons** (the split of the left and that the right was more unified). The importance of foreign aid can be discussed. The timing seems to be more important than the amount. The fact that most states in Europe followed a non-intervention policy also played a role.

Chapter 12: Mussolini and Italy 1918–39

Issues

How shall we describe the reasons for the Fascist seizure of power and how successful was the regime in transforming Italy?

It is nowadays common to label people with extreme right-wing views as 'fascists', however fascism has historically been used to describe a number of regimes. It is therefore necessary to define the term 'fascism' in an Italian context; there is some difficulty with this due to two reasons:

- There is no major theoretical work describing the ideas like Marx did for socialism/communism. Mussolini, however, made an attempt to define it in 1932 in his *Political and Social Doctrine of Fascism*.
- Mussolini constantly changed his policies in order to gain support.

But there are some basic features:

Figure 12.1: **Benito Mussolini dressed in the Fascist uniform.**

1. **Nationalism** was probably the strongest feature. They wanted to 'make Italy great again' after a period of weak governments. With the building of a strong superior state came the idea of **imperialism**, i.e. to acquire colonies.
2. Support for a strong and **authoritarian political leadership** embodied by **Il Duce**. Fascism was thereby non-democratic.
3. Support for a **totalitarian form of government**, i.e. a regime, which tried to control and mobilise the masses. In order to do so opposition, press etc. should be controlled.
4. To make Italy great again required **military strength**, territorial expansion and the use of **violence**. Mussolini stated that *"peace is absurd"* and as a result pursued an aggressive foreign policy.
5. In order to make Italy great again, the state must promote economic development and undertake a preparation for war. **Economic self-sufficiency** (**autarky**) was therefore necessary in making the state strong and ready for war.

6. **The idea of the corporate state**. Mussolini rejected the idea of ruling Italy through a parliamentary system in an attempt to avoid conflicts between labour and capital or the political left and the right. A number of branches were identified like industry, agriculture, and transport. A Chamber of Fasces and Corporations was set up with representatives from these branches made up by both employers and employed people. The corporate state was ideologically important but played a minor role politically.

Fascism can also be explained by emphasising what it stood against: democracy, parliamentarism, communism/socialism, egalitarianism. In many ways it was similar to Nazism, which evolved later in Germany but was not as obsessed with racism as the Nazis.

But in summary it must be concluded that Italian Fascism put less emphasis on ideology and was more a 'party of action' with the superior aim to seize power.

12.1 Why was Mussolini appointed Prime Minister in 1922?

Following the end of WWI, a number of events led to Mussolini's appointment as Prime Minister, with key developments shown in the following timeline.

1918		End of WWI.
1919		Resentment over the Treaty of Saint-Germain (Paris Settlement).
	March	Fascist left-wing movement founded in Milan (*Fasci di Combattimento*) but gained few votes in elections.
	Sept	D'Annunzio's seizure of Fiume.
		Land occupations, factory occupations.
1920		Wave of strikes.
	Dec	D'Annunzio expelled from Fiume.
1921		7% Fascist support in national elections. The Fascists now turned to the right, starting to support the monarchy/king and the church.
		Giolitti offered Mussolini to join the government. He refused to join as a junior partner.
1922	Aug	Socialists and communists called for a general strike against fascist violence – the strike was a failure.
	Oct 16	Fascists decided to plan an insurrection. The March on Rome 27–29 October.
	Oct 28	The King refused to sign a martial law. Prime Minister Facta resigned.
	Oct 30	Mussolini appointed PM.

12.2 The Fascist seizure of power

How shall we describe the Fascist seizure of power?

A. Strengths of the Fascists/Mussolini:

1. The fascist paper *Il Popolo d'Italia* was important in communicating the Fascist idea.
2. Mussolini sensed the mood of many Italians, charismatic, political flexible and pragmatic. He was a skilful journalist and orator who exploited middle and upper class fear of communism.

3. The Fascists offered 'law and order' and an alternative to communism.
4. Opportunism to attract support: in October 1921 a new programme was introduced which dropped earlier left-wing ideas, i.e. anti-clericalism and republicanism.
5. Strong local organisation – RAS.
6. Black-shirts: organised **'squads'** who attacked the socialists. In 1922 they numbered up to 250,000. This attracted support from conservative groups. Between 1920–22 Fascists killed more than 3,000 socialists.
7. Nationalistic appeal.

B. Weaknesses of the liberal government:

1. Historically there was a weak support for the political system. Until 1881 only half a million Italians had the right to vote out of a population of 32 millions. Liberal governments had a reputation for representing narrow class interests and the political elite represented mainly the upper classes and did little for the masses. Political leaders used bribery and vote-rigging to gain majorities.
2. There was also a rift between the church and the state due to the absorption of the Papal States by the new Italian kingdom during the unification of Italy in 1861-70. Until 1904 the church instructed Catholics not to vote in elections to the parliament.
3. The lack of political stability is reflected by the fact that between 1871 and 1900 there were no less than 22 governments.
4. The governments between 1918-22 were unstable. A proportional system of representation created a multi-party parliament with weak governments. There were five governments between 1918-22.
5. No strong coalition could be formed in the parliament due to the fact that the three largest parties were unable to co-operate. In the 1921 elections the Socialists (*Partito Socialista Italiano*, PSI) gained 123 seats, the Popolari (*Partito Popolare Italiano*, PPI) 108 seats and 'Giolittian Liberals' 60 seats – out of a total of 539 seats. The Popolari couldn't co-operate with the socialists due to the anti-clerical stand of the socialists. The Liberals couldn't co-operate with the Popolari due to their anti-clerical policies and the Popolari and the Liberals found it impossible to co-operate with the socialists due to their radical left-wing policies. The 1921 elections resulted in a parliament with 13 different groupings in the Chamber and it resulted in weak coalitions, which gave an impression of weakness at the top.
6. The government took no strong actions against occupations of factories and land, which made many middle- and upper-class Italians to turn to the Fascists.
7. The King didn't support the liberal government fully.

C. Other factors:

1. Resentment over the Paris Settlement. Italians felt that they had been betrayed by their allies in the Paris Settlement. 600,000 men had lost their lives and Italy was only granted South Tyrol, Trieste, and Trentino, but not Fiume and Dalmatia. Prime Minister Orlando was blamed by nationalists for not standing up for Italy's interests.
2. Fear of communism. WWI had brought Bolshevik victory to Russia. Communist uprisings in Germany and Hungary scared many middle and upper class Italians. The radical policy of the PSI resulting in both factory and land occupations in 1919 polarised the political life. Many saw the Fascists as the only alternative to the socialists (PSI) or the communists (*Partito Comunista Italiano*, PCI).
3. Inflation and unemployment after the war undermined the support for the government. Prices went up by 50% between 1918-20 and unemployment peaked in late 1921 with 2 million.

12. MUSSOLINI AND ITALY 1918-39

4. Law and order collapsed when there was a wave of strikes and occupations and when Fascist squads killed thousands of political opponents.
5. The King was weak and in 1922, when the Fascists had announced their march on Rome the King didn't give the liberal government support and invited Mussolini to form a coalition government in spite of the fact that the Fascists only had 7% support in the 1921 elections.

The approach used above to explain the seizure of power can be used on some other key topics in the IB course, e.g. the **fall of the Provisional government** in Russia, the **fall of the Weimar Republic** in Germany, the **Fascist seizure of power** in Italy and **Khomeini's revolution/fall of the Shah** in Iran:

1. **The Bolshevik seizure of power/fall of the Provisional government:**
   - Weaknesses of the Provisional government
   - Strengths of the Bolsheviks/Lenin
   - Other factors (impact of WWI)

2. **Fall of the Weimar Republic:**
   - Weaknesses of the Weimar Republic
   - Strengths of the Nazis/Hitler
   - Other factors (WWI and Wall Street)

3. **Fall of the liberal government in Italy:**
   - Weaknesses of the liberal government
   - Strengths of the Fascists/Mussolini
   - Other factors (impact of WWI)

12.3 How did the Fascists establish dictatorial power?

Partly as a consequence of the March on Rome in October 1922, some members of both the Liberals and Conservatives parties advised the King to appoint Mussolini to Prime Minister and the idea was to 'tame' him and use him to crush left-wing influence (a parallel to this can be studied in Germany in 1933).

Figure 12.2: **The March on Rome: Mussolini surrounded by Black-Shirts**

1922 On 30 October, the Italian king appointed Mussolini as Prime Minister of Italy. In the government there were 4 Fascists and 10 non-Fascists and in the parliament the Fascists only had 7% support. Mussolini could also be removed by the King who had the right to dismiss Prime Ministers. Mussolini had to be cautious and conciliatory.

The Italian king, in a decree of 25 November, gave Mussolini the right to rule Italy by dictatorial power for 13 months. It was an attempt to control violence and to restore order.

Leading members of the communist party arrested.

1923 The **Acerbo law** was passed with the support of the other parties in the coalition. The party that was given the largest number of votes in elections would be given a two-thirds majority in the parliament.

The Fascist party was merged with the Nationalist party which gave the Fascists more respectability.

1924 In the **elections of 1924**, the government (Fascists, national-liberals and some national-popolari) won 66% support after a very violent election campaign where also vote-rigging and bribery were used to gain necessary support.

A leading socialist Matteotti was murdered by Fascists and Mussolini's support was at risk. Mussolini survived the crisis and dismissed some radical Fascists at the expense of some respected nationalists. Lee concludes: *"The significance of the Matteotti crisis was enormous […] a turning point […] Once Mussolini had recovered […] he clearly had to do something more permanent to stabilise the political situation […] a second wave."*

1925 In January, Mussolini was given the **right to issue decrees**. By 1943 this had been used *more than 100,000 times*.

The King lost his right to appoint and dismiss ministers in the government and the **Prime Minister was made Head of State**.

Fascist violence described as a **reign of terror** started.

1926 The **OVRA** (secret police) set up.

All other parties outlawed.

The **Rocco Law** outlawed strikes and employers lockouts.

1928 A **new electoral law** introduced where the Fascist Grand Council was given the right to formulate a list of 400 nominees, which the electorate was invited to accept or reject *en masse*.

The other parties in the coalition and the political opposition to the left, underestimated Mussolini. The coalition parties supported the Acerbo Law in an attempt to establish a strong right-wing government, and the socialists made tactical mistakes during the Matteotti crisis.

12.4 The Fascist state – Mussolini: "I want to make Italy great again"

The **Corporate state**: In 1930 the National Council of Corporations was formed but it was not until 1934 that the first corporations were set up. By 1936, 22 corporations representing all major branches of the economic life had been formed and Mussolini claimed that it should replace the parliament. The idea was that different spheres of the economy should represent one corporation and representatives from both workers and employers should together resolve issues concerning their activities. In 1938–39 the parliament was replaced by the Chamber of Fasces and Corporations. In reality however, it did not play any major role in the decision making process in Italy and consequently had no real power.

Mussolini's economic power aimed at making Italy stronger and more self-sufficient (autarky) in order to support foreign wars and conquest. Autarky can be said to be the policy of a state when it seeks to be self-sufficient, e.g. replacing imported goods with products produced in the country.

In 1925 the **Battle for Grain** was introduced. Protective tariffs were introduced on imported grains, which led to that the import fell with 75%. As a result grain production in Italy doubled between 1923-38. But it was achieved at the expense of more traditional Italian agricultural production such as fruit, wine, olives and oil production. The policy also led to land in the South, less conductive to wheat-production being used. To the Italian consumer the policy resulted in higher food prices since the more expensive Italian production replaced cheaper grains from abroad. No structural reforms were undertaken within the agricultural sector, which resulted in that rich landowners continued to control most of Italy's arable land.

The **Battle for the Lira** was to Mussolini a question of national prestige. The regime decided to fix the value of the lira at an artificially high rate, which resulted in Italian products becoming more expensive abroad and the result was the exports fell from 44 million lire in 1925 to 22 million lire in 1938. An expensive lira would normally result in prices on imported goods going down, but the regime decided to introduce tariffs to stimulate domestic production and to promote the battle of grain programme.

The **Battle for Land** has for some aspects been described as quite successful. The malaria-infested Pontine Marches south of Rome were drained. However, it must be emphasised that, except for this success, little was achieved elsewhere.

In the **Battle for Births** the regime tried to achieve a rapid rise in the birth rate. Awards were given to prolific mothers and bachelors were penalised with high taxes. Abortions, sterilisation, and contraception were outlawed. A higher birth rate would give grounds for Italian claims for colonies but the campaign was a bitter disappointment to Mussolini. Even if the population did increase from 37 million in 1921 to 44 millions in 1941, this is explained by a fall in the death rate and a huge drop in emigration to the US. The birth rate in Italy fell from 147 births for every 1000 women in 1911 to 102 in 1937.

Figure 12.3: **A 20 lire coin from 1928**

Economic policy: In 1933 the **Istituto per la Ricostruzione Industriale (IRI)** was set up. The aim was to support and promote industrial growth during an era where the economies in the world were suffering from the Depression. There were both successes and failures in these policies. In many ways it led to the state rescuing both banks and industries from the effects of the Depression and by the late 1930s 20% of the capital of Italy's industrial companies was controlled by the government. The GNP grew by an average of 1.2% between 1922–40 in spite of the Depression and the drop of GNP during the worst years of the Depression. It was marginally better than most other Western European powers. There were notable industrial successes like the development of hydro-electric power, railways were electrified and the building of an autostrada network. But it must also be emphasised that the policy of autarky mainly failed and the aim to make Italy into a great industrial power was never achieved. In 1939 Italy produced 2.4 million tons of steel while Germany produced 13.4 millions tons of steel.

The overall conclusion about Mussolini's economic policy must be negative, even though we must take into account the world wide Depression. If we study the annual growth within the industrial sector we can conclude:

1901–25	1925–40	1940–52
3.8%	0.8%	3.5%

12.5 Mussolini and the Catholic Church

Probably the most important and lasting contribution of Mussolini to the Italian state was healing the rift between the state and the Church. For Mussolini it resulted in national popularity and support from the middle and upper classes in Italy – the groups from which he derived his support. The Church saw Mussolini as a guarantee against the godless doctrines of socialism. This support became even stronger during the Spanish Civil War where the clergy in Spain suffered from attacks from the Republicans, supported by the Soviet Union.

The Lateran Accords concluded in 1929 resulted in:

1. Catholicism was recognised as 'the only state religion'.
2. It recognised the Pope's sovereign rule of the Vatican City.
3. Religious education was made compulsory also in secondary schools.
4. Financial compensation was given to the Papacy for the losses of the Papal States in 1860 and Rome in 1870.

12.6 Control of media and education

To Mussolini with his background as a successful journalist, control of the media was important. But the state never owned more than 10% of the press but editors and owners were constantly subjected to pressure from the regime. From 1926 onwards it can be said that there was no real opposition press in Italy.

There was no major change in the structure of the Italian schools in the 1920s. In the 1930s however, there was a serious attempt to control education.

1. From 1929 all teachers were forced to take an oath of loyalty.
2. In 1931 all teachers associations merged into a Fascist Association and membership was compulsory from 1937.
3. The educational system was centralised.
4. Control of textbooks and the curriculum was important and textbooks became a state monopoly.
5. Glorification of the Duce was essential and Fascist virtues like patriotism and obedience were important. You should '*believe, obey, and fight*'.

Government control of education declined the higher up the structure you went. At universities there was an underground contempt for so-called fascist values.

According to Lee, "*education was not one of the more successful examples of indoctrination*".

The regime came also to place more emphasis on the organisation of youth groups outside the school, under the mantle of the Opera Nazionale Balilla:

- age 6-8: Children of the She Wolf (The Capitoline Wolf)
- age 8-14: Balilla (boys) and Little Italians (girls)
- age 14-18: Avanguardisti

Initially the process of youth organisations was very haphazard but the pace was gradually intensified and in 1935 membership became compulsory.

Impact: it is considered that a large proportion of the Italian youth responded enthusiastically to fascism but on the other hand it has been estimated that some 40% of the Italian youth aged between 8 and 18 managed to avoid membership.

12.7 Fascism and women

Employment: measures were taken to restrict female participation in working life. From their mid-20s women were excluded from 'unnatural occupations' and in the 1930s a number of edicts from Mussolini restricted the participation of women in most branches of employment.

In 1938, women were permitted to take up no more than 10% of the total jobs available.

Education: was seen as a training and preparation to stay at home. Women were excluded from prestigious posts in secondary schools. Surprisingly the number of women at universities increased in the 1930s. But this was due to a lack of other job opportunities.

Battle for births: Mussolini wanted to encourage the Italians to increase the birth rate: *'Go home and tell the women I need births, many births'* he said. Marriage loans were introduced, tax relief i.e. no income tax after 10 children, annual ceremony honouring the most prolific mothers (93 families in 1933 had 1,300 children!), increased taxation of bachelors, divorces were made illegal and abortions were banned.

Result: the birth rate actually declined probably due to economic problems in the 1930s and that many men were involved in the war.

Personal life: Fascists had strong views on what women should look like. It has been described by one historian as the 'Battle for fat'.

Politics: they Fascists were prepared to accept women being mobilised in political manifestations etc. but not in the decision making.

12.8 Fascism and the use of terror

Violence and terror were constantly used against political enemies, by the Black-shirts in the early 20s, and later by the secret police. Fascist squad violence was severely reduced after 1925.

The **Law of the Defence of the State** was passed in 1926 which made it possible to imprison people making attempts to form a political party.

In 1926, **OVRA** (Organisation for the Vigilance and Repression of Antifascism), the secret police, was formed.

In the 1930s, 20,000 actions were taken by the police every week. During the fascist period 5,000 people were imprisoned and 10,000 were in internal exile (on islands etc.).

But there was no Fascistisation of the legal system comparable to that in Germany and Russia. Of the 4,805 cases brought to court between 1927–40, 3,904 ended in acquittal. In the same period death sentences were carried out only 9 times. It has, however, been estimated that some 400 people were killed by the state for political reasons. Still this is not comparable to Hitler's Germany or Stalin's Russia. Of course, the scope for repression to many Italians was considerable. But the historian Cassel, concludes: *"The Fascist regime used terror, but was not in any real sense based on terror."*

12.9 Historiography and analysis

Marxist historians have seen Mussolini's seizure of power as a logical outcome and continuation of the Risorgimento (the unification). The Italian state had never been a true democracy or supported by the masses and this enabled conservative groups to bring Mussolini to power – a politician without mass support. Consequently they viewed Mussolini and the Fascist state as a tool of capitalist interests. Liberal historians have not acknowledged this link between the former Italian state and Fascist Italy. They identify a break between the two systems. They explain the emergence of the fascist state as a result of post-war economic problems and nationalist disillusionment after the war. Notice that we have a similar debate in Germany when discussing the Nazi seizure of power.

12.10 Mussolini's foreign policy

A. Both aggression and co-operation 1922–35

1922 The Corfu crisis: Italy occupied Corfu after the killing of an Italian general by Greek bandits. Italy left after actions from the League of Nations.

1925 Italy signed the Locarno Pact when Germany accepted its western borders.

1928 Italy together with some 60 other states signed the Briand-Kellog pact where they renounced the instrument of war for settling disputes.

1934 The Dolfuss affair: Austrian Nazis killed the Prime Minister of Austria, Dolfuss. Hitler mobilised his army and prepared to invade Austria. When Mussolini mobilised in the south, Hitler backed off.

1935 After the Dolfuss affair and when Hitler in 1935 declared that he would no longer observe the Treaty of Versailles, Italy, Britain and France signed the Stresa Front to safeguard the Treaty of Versailles.

B. The turning point 1935–36

In 1935, Britain signed a **naval agreement** with Germany allowing it to expand its navy. It was a violation of the Treaty of Versailles and Britain signed it without consulting its Stresa allies, Italy and France.

Italy invaded **Abyssinia** in 1935. Britain and France had given some secret understanding to Italy in the Hoare-Laval pact. When it leaked out to the press the governments came under pressure. Abyssinia was a member of the League of Nations and Italy was a founding member and a permanent member of the Council in the League. Britain and France now had to support sanctions against Italy. This was a major turning point to Mussolini and his route to a German alliance.

C. Turning to Germany from 1936

In 1936, the Spanish Civil War started. Italy intervened and supported the nationalists led by Franco. The same year we can see the first official sign that Italy was turning to Germany when the October protocols were signed. It was a commercial and friendship treaty. Why did Mussolini turn to Hitler?

- Mussolini felt betrayed by the Western powers in the Abyssinian affair.
- By being involved in both Abyssinia and Spain, Italy needed to resolve its problems with Germany in the north.
- Sanctions by the League affected Italian trade. The sanctions were, however, ignored by Germany who became a trading partner to Italy.
- Mussolini admired strength and from this aspect Hitler had much more to offer than the Western democracies.

1937 Italy signed the anti-Comintern pact with Germany and Japan.

Italy left the *League of Nations*.

1938 Mussolini and Italy had no objections to Germany's invasion of Austria and supported German claims on the Sudetenland at the *Munich conference*.

1939 April: Italy invaded Albania.

12. MUSSOLINI AND ITALY 1918–39

1940 Italy declared war on France two weeks before it surrendered.

Italy invaded Greece, which was a military disaster. Germany had to support Italy in Greece.

Italian troops invaded Egypt but were driven out by Britain.

1942 German-Italian troops defeated at El Alamein in North Africa.

1943 The allies invaded Sicily, which was the beginning of the end for Mussolini. He was deposed in 1943 and after returning to power with the support from Germany, was captured and executed in 1945.

There are **two major schools of interpretation** concerning Mussolini's foreign policy, which in many ways reminds us about the interpretations of Hitler's foreign policy.

The '**Intentionalist school**' (Knox) believes that Mussolini planned his aggression as a part of an intended plan to 'make Italy great again'. His cautious policy in the 1920s and his co-operation with the Western powers in the 1930s were a result of temporary measures. His ultimate aim was all the time to conquer land and to expand Italy.

The '**Structuralist school**' (De Felice) believes that Mussolini had no master plan for war nor an ideological view guiding him to expand, and that he just seized opportunities due to changing international circumstances. It is a parallel to WW II and Hitler where A J P Taylor argued that Hitler had no master plan for WW II, but only seized opportunities. Taylor also writes about Mussolini that he was *"without either ideas or plans."*

22. Examine the reasons for the Fascist seizure of power in 1922.

(Analyse the reasons from the model below.)

Some key events:

1918	end of WW I.
1919	resentment over the Treaty of Saint-Germain (Paris Settlement).
1919	Sept: D'Annunzio's seizure of Fiume.
1919	land occupations, factory occupations.
1919	March: Fascist movement founded in Milan but few votes were gained in the elections.
1920	wave of strikes.
1920	D'Annunzio expelled from Fiume.
1921	7% Fascist support in national elections. Turned to the right.
1921	Giolitti offered Mussolini to join the government. He refused to join as a junior partner.
1922	Aug: Socialists/communists called for a general strike against fascist violence – a failure.
1922	16 Oct: Fascists decided to plan an insurrection.
1922	27–29 Oct: the March on Rome.
1922	28 Oct: the King refused to sign a martial law. PM Facta resigned.
1922	30 Oct: Mussolini appointed PM.

Analysis:

A. Strengths of the Fascists:

1. The fascist paper *Il Popolo d'Italia* was important in the communication the fascist idea.

2. **Mussolini**: sensed the mood of many Italians and was charismatic. He was also politically flexible and pragmatic. He was a skilful journalist and orator who exploited middle and upper class fear of communism.
3. The Fascists claimed that they offered 'law and order' and an alternative to communism.
4. **Opportunism** in attracting support: In October 1921 a new programme was introduced which dropped earlier left-wing ideas i.e. **anti-clericalism and republicanism**.
5. The Fascists had a very strong **local organisation** – RAS.
6. Dedicated **black-shirts** were instrumental in the seizure of power: 250,000 men in 1922 organised 'squads' who attacked the socialists. This attracted support from conservative groups. Between 1920–22 Fascists killed more than 3,000 socialists.
7. **Nationalistic appeal** attracted support from right-wingers.

B. Weaknesses of the Liberal government:

1. Historically there was a weak support for the political system. Until 1881 only half a million Italians had the right to vote out of a population of 32 million. Liberal governments had a reputation for representing narrow class interests. Political leaders used bribery and vote-rigging and the political elite represented mainly the upper classes and did little for the masses.
2. There was also a rift between the church and the state due to the absorption of the Papal States by the new Italian kingdom during the unification of Italy in 1861–70. Until 1904 the church instructed Catholics not to vote in elections to the parliament.
3. The **lack of political stability** is reflected by the fact that between 1871 and 1900 there were no less than 22 governments.
4. The governments between 1918–22 were unstable. A **proportional system of representation** created a multi-party parliament which **resulted in weak governments**. There were five governments between 1918–22 and the 1921 elections resulted in a Chamber with 13 different parties/groups. It gave an impression of weakness at the top.
5. No strong coalition could be formed in the parliament due to the fact that the **three largest parties were unable to co-operate**. In the 1921 elections the Socialists (PSI) gained 123 seats, the Popolari (PPI) 108 seats and 'Giolittian Liberals' 60 seats – out of a total of 539 seats. The Popolari couldn't co-operate with the socialists due to the anti-clerical stand of the socialists. The Liberals couldn't co-operate with the Popolari due to the Liberals anti-clerical policies and the Popolari and the Liberals found it impossible to co-operate with the socialists due to their radical left-wing policies.
6. The government took **no strong actions** against occupations of factories and land, which made many middle- and upper-class Italians to turn the Fascists.
7. **The King didn't support** the liberal government fully.

C. Other factors:

1. **Resentment over the Paris Settlement**. Italians felt that they had been betrayed by their allies in the Paris Settlement. 600,000 men had lost their lives and Italy was only granted South Tyrol, Trieste and Trentino, but not Fiume and Dalmatia. Prime Minister Orlando was blamed by nationalist for not standing up for Italy's interests.
2. **Fear of communism**. WWI had brought Bolshevik victory to Russia. Communist uprisings in Germany and Hungary scared many middle and upper class Italians. The radical policy of the PSI resulting in both factory and land occupations in 1919 polarised political. Many saw the Fascists as the only alternative to the socialists (PSI) or the communists (PCI).
3. **Inflation and unemployment** after the war undermined support for the government. Prices went up by 50% between 1918–20 and unemployment peaked in late 1921 at 2 million.

4. **Law and order collapsed** when there was a wave of strikes and occupations and when Fascist squads killed thousands of political opponents.
5. **The King** was weak and in 1922, when the Fascists announced their 'March on Rome', he didn't give the liberal government support; he invited Mussolini to form a coalition government despite the Fascists only having 7% support in the 1921 elections.

Conclusion: It was a combination of weaknesses of the regime/strengths of the Fascists/other factors.

23. Evaluate the successes and failures of Mussolini's domestic policies.

(What were his aims – try to cover success both to Mussolini and Italy and write an account which discusses strengths and limitations.)

Aims:
- To establish political control.
- To crush the left.
- To 'make Italy great again'.

Successes:
1. Mussolini was able to abolish democracy and to create **a Fascist single party state**.
2. The political **left was crushed** (at least as a political force).
3. **Public work programmes** described as 'impressive' like draining marches and building motorways.
4. **Battle for Grain**: production doubled 1922–39 (at the expense of other crops).
5. **Pig iron and steel production doubled** 1930–40 (but Italy was still weak industrially).
6. Mussolini's aim for the economy was to create a **'third way'** a mix between capitalism and a state planned economy. The state office (IRI) controlled in 1939: 77% of the pig iron industry, 45% of the steel production and 80% of the naval production.
7. **The Lateran Treaty**: healed the rift between the state and the church and was politically a success for Mussolini.

Failures:
1. The growth of the economy was very low if you compare 1901–25 with 1935–40
2. Real wages fell.
3. **Battle for Births**: birth rate went down.
4. **Battle for Marches** reached only 1/20 of what was claimed.
5. **Battle for the Lira** made export too expensive and imported goods remained expensive due to tariffs.
6. The **Corporate** system didn't work in practice.
7. Agriculture: no major changes in the **pattern of ownership**.
8. Too dependent on imports i.e. **self-sufficiency failed**.
9. **Industrially, Italy was still weak**. He didn't 'make Italy great again.'

Conclusion: summarise your main points. His most notable success was the Lateran Treaty, that the left was crushed and a dictatorship was established. His main failure was probably that he was never able to make Italy 'great again'.

HISTORY HL: EUROPE

Chapter 13: The Weimar Republic 1919–33

Issues

There are two major views concerning the rise of Nazism/the fall of the republic. **One group of historians** is arguing that Hitler must be seen as a logical **continuation** of the militaristic and undemocratic tradition from Kaiser Wilhelm and Bismarck. A second view regards Hitler as an avoidable mistake, brought to power due to a combination of particular factors. Two such factors were the impact of WWI and the problems caused by the Wall Street Crash.

The German Second Reich collapsed in October 1918. When the Armistice was signed on 11 November, the Kaiser had abdicated and there was a new government that included Social Democrats. The end of Wilhelm's Second Reich was marked by both a revolution from above and below. General Ludendorff persuaded the Kaiser to hand over power to a civilian government and thereby preserve the reputation of the generals, who would thus not be implicated in the German request for an armistice. This transfer to a civilian government is referred to as the 'revolution' from above. In October, and later when the new government signed the armistice which made it clear that the war was lost, a revolution from below grew out of popular unrest. This was the birth of the Weimar Republic, which would last fourteen years and end in 1933 with the establishment of a single party rule – Adolf Hitler and the Nazi party.

13.1 The foundation of the Republic

In January 1919, elections were held to the new Reichstag. Germany at this time is normally described as a country with no democratic tradition where extremism can gain strong support. The support for the extremist parties was strong from the beginning and throughout the 14 years in which the republic existed, but it is also worth noting that 75% of the members of the parliament supported the new democratic constitution and the new government. The first government was a coalition between the Centre Party, the Democratic Party and the Social Democrats.

The new **constitution** is of major importance if you want to analyse the failure of the republic. Germany was a federation where each state had considerable power over education, police, etc. The Reichstag should be elected every four years with a **proportional system of representation**. 60,000 votes were enough to get one seat in the parliament. There was no threshold to win representation in the parliament and you could win a seat with only 0.4% support. In the 1924 elections, the Bavarian Peasants' League got 0.7% support, enough for 3 seats in the parliament. The result was a multi-party system and problems forming strong governments. Conservative Germans remembered the Second Reich as an economic success led by a 'strong' leader. It is understandable that when Germany was suffering from the impact of WWI and the parliament and the government was characterised by weak coalitions, it gave an impression of weakness at the top.

There are three remarkable things about the Weimar Republic:
- there were **21 governments in 14 years**;
- all were coalitions; and
- only 8 held a majority in the Reichstag.

The second part of the constitution which was of major political importance assessed the role of the head of state, the **President**. He would be elected every seven years and have considerable power. He would have the right to **appoint and dismiss the Chancellor**. Article 48 also gave the President special powers to rule the country by **decree** "*in the event that the public order and security are seriously disturbed or endangered*". There was no clear definition of how and when it could be used. This would have disastrous consequences for the republic after 1930.

13.2 The first crisis of the Republic 1919–23

Even if there was support for democracy in the first elections, there were many Germans who were resentful over how the war had ended. German troops were still on French soil when the **Armistice** was signed. This situation created a seedbed for the myth of the 'Stab in the back'. Many Germans had also hoped that the terms would be based on Wilson's 14-points, meaning that Germany would not be punished. But in the meantime the allied blockade of Germany, which as recently as 1918 had caused the death of an estimated 300,000 Germans, was not lifted. The **Treaty of Versailles**, which was finally signed in June 1919, was not a negotiated peace. The Germans called it a 'diktat' and Prime Minister Schiedemann, who was supposed to sign, was so horrified over the terms that he chose to resign. But due to the blockade the German representatives in Versailles had no alternative but to sign and take the blame for

Figure 13.1: **German states during the Weimar Republic period**

See "Chapter 10: The Peace Settlements" on page 72

signing the treaty. Subsequently, all through the Weimar period, German nationalists would attack the Weimar politicians for signing. According to the treaty, Germany and their allies had to take full blame for causing the war. They also had to pay an indemnity which would be fixed in 1921 at £6,600 million. The army was reduced to 100,000 men and they could have no offensive weapons such as air force, submarines etc. They lost their colonies and were refused membership of the League of Nations. The principle of national self-determination was not applied to Germany. About 8 million Germans would now be living in new states in Central Europe i.e. Poland, Czechoslovakia and Austria. The Rhineland was to be demilitarised. As a result of the Treaty, Germany lost 13% of its territory, 12% of its population, 48% of its iron ore deposits and had to pay the indemnity.

There are historians who argue that the republic was doomed as a consequence of the peace. Right-wing opposition would be constant and the reparation payments would cause major problems to the economy. **JM Keynes** wrote in *The Economic Consequences of the Peace* that the treaty would put too much strain on the German economy and that this would even threaten the prosperity of the victorious allies.

The first period of the Republic was marked by **putschism** (revolts). The first meeting of the parliament in January 1919 could not take place in Berlin due to a communist revolt. It had to meet in Weimar. The government was offered assistance from the army supported by ex-soldiers Freikorps. **The Spartacist coup** was bloodily suppressed and its leaders were executed while under arrest. In Munich, a Socialist Republic and later a 'Soviet', held power between November 1918 and May 1919, when it too was bloodily suppressed by Freikorps. In 1920 the government ordered the Freikorps to disband. This in turn led to a right-wing attempt to overthrow the Weimar Republic: **the Kapp Putsch**. When asked to support the government, the army answered that 'there can be no talk of letting the Reichswehr fight the Reichswehr'. It is significant that the German army was unwilling to defend the Weimar Republic against a right-wing coup. However, the Kapp Putsch failed due to a general strike by the Berlin workers. The period with attempted coups came to an end with the failed Nazi **Beer Hall Putsch** in November 1923. It is clear that the republic had many enemies both to the left and the right.

Figure 13.2: **Barricade in Berlin during the uprising, January 1919**

The period also witnessed many political assassinations. Both the leader of the Centre Party, Erzberger, and the Foreign Minister Rathenau, were assassinated.

As for the implementation of the Treaty of Versailles, the early years of the republic were marked by a **policy of obstruction**, i.e. to not co-operate in the implementation of the peace terms. In November 1922 the German government asked for a four year suspension of the reparations. The French responded by sending troops to the Ruhr area whereby the German government reacted by encouraging a passive resistance policy. Coal mining and industrial production fell to a minimum. As the government in this situation chose a policy of overprinting the mark, inflation would go out of control in the autumn of 1923. Small savers and Mittelstand (the middle class) lost life savings in a matter of days. Traditionally, these middle-class groups were supporters of parliamentary democracy, but their faith in the Weimar Republic was now seriously weakened.

13. THE WEIMAR REPUBLIC 1919–33

13.3 The Stresemann years 1923–29, years of recovery

The crisis brought Gustav Stresemann to power (Chancellor 1923 and Foreign Minister 1923–29) with his 'fulfilment' policy. Stresemann realised that Germany needed better co-operation with the Western powers.

A. How was the economy stabilised?

1. A new **currency**, the Rentenmark replaced the Reichsmark at the end of 1923.
2. The **Dawes Plan** was an agreement on reparations made in 1924. Short-term American credits were invested in German industry to enable Germany to recover and to pay their reparations.

B. How was the political situation stabilised?

1. **Stresemann was respected** by the conservative elite of Germany which still controlled influential posts.
2. In 1925 Field Marshal Paul von **Hindenburg became President** of the Republic. Hindenburg was the leading general from WWI and highly respected by patriotic German nationalists. Stresemann reflected that *"Germans want no president in a top hat. He must wear a uniform and plenty of decorations".*
3. In 1925 Stresemann signed **the Locarno Pact**. Germany guaranteed its western borders but said nothing about the eastern borders. The proposal was in line with Stresemann's **fulfilment policy**. He hoped that better co-operation with the Western powers would open up for a revision of the Treaty of Versailles in the East. By accepting the Treaty in the West, Stresemann risked a lot domestically. By German nationalists it was seen as a pathetic surrender. Internationally, it paid off, however, and in 1926 he was awarded the Nobel Peace Prize.

Did the 'fulfilment policy' pay off?

 ACHIEVEMENTS DURING THE STRESEMANN YEARS

1924 The Dawes Plan: better terms for the reparation payments plus US loans.

1926 Germany accepted as a member of the League of Nations.

   The withdrawal of British troops from Cologne.

1927 The withdrawal of the 'Inter Allied Control Commission' (the watchdog of the Versailles terms).

1929 French troops left Germany.

   The Young Plan further reduced reparation payments from 132,000 million marks to 37,000 million.

In 1927 Germany had recovered its pre-war industrial capacity. In the Reichstag elections in 1928, support for political extremism was reduced. The Nazis only obtained 2.6%. But there were still problems in Germany that could jeopardise the stability:

1. Even if support for extremism went down in the elections of 1928, the radical parties were still quite strong. The right-wing German Nationalists and the Communists together had 25% support.
2. With the Dawes Plan, the German economy had become over dependent on U.S. money. An economic crisis in the U.S. would affect the German economy severely. Stresemann concluded this in 1928 when he stated: *"Germany is dancing on a volcano. If the short-term credits are called in, a large section of our economy would collapse".*

This is exactly what happened after the Wall Street Crash in October 1929.

13.4 The second crisis of the Weimar Republic 1929–33

American short-term credits were now called in. It led to a massive **unemployment crisis** in Germany. It also led to a **political crisis**. The coalition parties lost to the extremes and especially the Nazis gained from the crisis. There is a clear correlation between **unemployment figures and the support for Nazism** as shown in the table.

Unemployment in Germany:		Support for Nazism:	
1929 July	1.2 million	1928	2.6%
1930	3.0 million	1930	18%
1931	4.1 million	1932 July	37%
1932 Jan	6.2 million	1932 Nov	33%
1932 July	5.5 million		

The polarisation, people turning to the extremes, eroded the support of the government. In March 1930 the Social Democrats left the coalition. This was a considerable turning point. Some historians argue that this was the end of the Weimar Republic. In a normal parliamentary situation, a government not possessing parliamentary support has to resign. However, the German constitution opened up for other ways of action. The country could be governed through **presidential decrees**. From 1930, the Prime Ministers would frequently ask the president for decrees to be able to govern the country. Consequently, the country would be led by an ageing president and parliament would lose significance.

	Number of presidential decrees	Number of sittings in Reichstag
1930	5	94
1931	44	41
1932	60	13

The period between 1930–33 witnessed three different Prime Ministers trying, with different means, to form a **strong government**. These governments can be referred to as 'presidential governments'.

13.4.1 Brüning, March 1930–May 1932

- Heinrich Brüning cut down government expenditures during the crisis and was referred to as the 'Hunger Chancellor'. When he failed to gain get support for his budget in 1930, instead of compromising in parliament, Brüning passed the budget through a presidential decree. He can therefore be blamed for initiating the use of **presidential decrees** and thereby undermining the authority of the Reichstag. The use of decree would now only increase.

- Thereafter Brüning announced **new elections in 1930**, in the hope of winning majority support in the parliament. This would prove to be major mistake, since these elections further increased the support for the extremes. Nazi support reached 18%. Brüning had to accept that the political extremism of the time would now be reflected in parliament. He had thus, by calling for elections, only worsened the situation.

- Brüning **banned the SA**, in order to reduce political violence.

- Brüning's anti-Nazi policy in combination with a proposal to break up bankrupt Prussian estates made advisors of President Hindenburg turn against him. In May 1932, Brüning was **dismissed** by Hindenburg.

13.4.2 Von Papen, May 1932–December 1932

- In May 1932 Franz von Papen was appointed Prime Minister with **very weak parliamentary support**. The government was made up by the elite, or 'barons' and was totally dependent on presidential decrees.
- He wanted to attract the support of the Nazis and therefore **lifted the ban on the SA.**
- **He deposed the Social Democratic government in Prussia** (two thirds of the Reich).
- He **offered Hitler** a position in the government. After new elections in July 1932, the Nazis had 37% support in parliament. Hitler demanded to be Prime Minister but this was turned down.
- Von Papen now hoped to use the army to restore order and set up some kind of **military dictatorship**. But Hindenburg feared civil war and replaced von Papen with von Schleicher, a top advisor to the President.

Figure 13.3: **Franz von Papen**

13.4.3 Von Schleicher, December 1932–January 1933

- Kurt von Schleicher tried to **split the Nazis** by inviting Gregor Strasser, a prominent Nazi politician, to join his government. He also wanted to **attract support from the political left** by using Brüning's ideas of a land reform. This strategy failed totally. Von Schleicher didn't receive any support in the parliament.

13.4.4 Hitler, Chancellor in January 1933

- It was von Papen who finally persuaded the president to appoint Hitler as Prime Minister. The idea was to **use the support of the Nazis** in the parliament to form a strong government and crush the political left. There were only 3 Nazis in the 11 man cabinet. The other ministers from the conservative elite were to **control Hitler**. Papen: *"Within two months we will have pushed Hitler so far into a corner that he'll squeak".*

13.5 The strengths of the Nazis

After the failure of the 1923 Munich Putsch, Hitler realised that he had to follow a policy of 'legality'. By the elections of 1932 he would be a strong leader in charge of the biggest party in parliament (37% support), while still standing outside the government. Hitler was a charismatic leader and an excellent orator. The party was well organised in different parts of Germany. The SA, the *Sturmabteilung* or Storm Department had been formed in 1920 and functioned as the original paramilitary wing of the Nazi Party. The SA was especially important during the political crisis after 1930. Goebbels was responsible for party propaganda and used new techniques skilfully. The Nazis sent mails to different groups using themes that would appeal to each group (farmers, businessmen, traditionalists). Hitler could use emotions or reason, when needed. One example is when he wanted to attract the support from the German industrialists after 1930, he temporarily played down antisemitism and used 'fear of communism' to attract support.

If you want to explain the fall of the Weimar Republic it is possible to write a chronological account describing:

1. The first crisis of the republic 1919–23
2. The recovery during the Stresemann years 1923–29
3. The second crisis of the republic 1929–33

The reasons for the final collapse can be described as a combination of '**weaknesses of the republic**', '**strengths of the Nazis**' and '**other factors**'.

Weaknesses of the Republic:

1. The constitution: the proportional system of representation resulted in weak governments. The possibility to rule by decrees weakened the parliament.
2. The new government had been forced to sign a peace treaty which affected the popularity of the government domestically and weakened the economy (the indemnity).
3. The conservative elite still held many influential posts within the civil service, the army and big business. There was no strong support for the republic or parliamentarism within this group.

Strengths of the Nazis:

1. Adolf Hitler was a skilful orator, charismatic, and had a strong political instinct.
2. Goebbels used propaganda skilfully especially during the election campaigns. The propaganda targeted particular groups emphasising different themes in order to appeal to different groups.
3. The Nazis were able to exploit all the important weaknesses of the Weimar Republic in their propaganda.
4. Hitler and the Nazis played down antisemitism and emphasised 'fear of Communism' when needed.
5. Millions of SA men were instrumental in the seizure of power.

Other factors:

1. There was no democratic tradition in Germany. That a man like Hitler could appeal to many Germans is more understandable if we take the 'tradition' of authoritarian leadership into account.
2. There was also a 'fear of Communism' in Germany which made many Germans turn to a right-wing party like the Nazi Party.
3. The Wall Street Crash cannot be underestimated if we want to explain the Nazi seizure of power. In the 1928 elections the Nazis only had 2.6% support. In 1930 this figure was 18%.

13.6 Historiography

> This kind of analytical approach is always very important to reach a higher grade.

There are two major views concerning the rise of Nazism/the fall of the republic. **One view** is arguing that Hitler must be seen as a logical **continuation** of the militaristic and undemocratic tradition from Kaiser Wilhelm and Bismarck. The democratic regime of Weimar went totally against this German tradition of authoritarianism and therefore finally collapsed in 1933.

A second view regards Hitler as an avoidable mistake, brought to power due to a combination of particular factors. Two such factors were the impact of WWI and the problems caused by the Wall Street Crash. Hitler was unique, especially his racism, and represents a '**break**' in German history and tradition. After all, there had been a parliament in Bismarck's Germany elected by universal suffrage. Democracy and the republic were not doomed due to old German tradition.

> Now, when you have read the text:
> 1. Study the questions that follow (but not the answers!)
> 2. Copy a template and outline your answer.
> 3. Compare your answer with the one given and analyse any possible differences.

24. To what extent did the Treaty of Versailles cause the fall of the Weimar Republic?

(Structure: show to what extent the Treaty of Versailles contributed to the fall of the republic and to what extent it did not.)

Yes, we can blame the Treaty:

1. The treaty created resentment in Germany. (Write one paragraph about the terms: the war guilt clause, the army, the indemnity, national self determination etc.)
2. The new democratic government was forced to sign this treaty. This weakened the republic.
3. German patriots blamed the new government for signing such a humiliating treaty and since many Germans resented the treaty, it affected the popularity of the government.
4. The indemnity which was a part of the treaty, led to financial problems. It led to the occupation of the Ruhr and the inflation crisis 1922–23. This crisis was solved through the Dawes Plan, which, however, created an over-dependence on American credits. As a direct consequence of this dependence, the 1929 Wall Street Crash would hit Germany harder than other comparable countries. The subsequent massive unemployment and political polarisation in Germany prepared the way to power for the Nazis.

No, it was not the Treaty:

1. Germany had no democratic tradition (a support of the continuity school).
2. The constitution: the proportional system of representation gave an impression of political weakness. Between 1929 and 1933 this impression was confirmed as parliament could not solve the political crisis. ***During its 14 years, the Weimar Republic had 21 coalition governments, of which only 8 held a majority***. The constitution made it possible to rule the country by presidential decree. This further weakened the democratically elected parliament.
3. The Wall Street Crash was crucial, but this event was totally independent of the Treaty of Versailles.
4. The strengths of the Nazis: Hitler, Goebbels, the use of propaganda, the SA.
5. The 'backstairs intrigue' (Alan Bullock writes: *"Hitler did not seize power; he was jobbed into office by a backstairs intrigue"*): neither Hindenburg, von Papen, von Schleicher, nor Hitler, supported the democratic system. It survived 1923 due to Stresemann and it collapsed in 1933 due to Hindenburg, von Papen, von Schleicher and Hitler and a backstairs intrigue between these men.

Conclusion: the fall of Weimar was a combination of '**weaknesses of the republic, strengths of the Nazis** and **other factors**' (mainly the Wall Street Crash and impact of the war).

25. "The constitution of the Weimar Republic played a major role in the fall of the Republic." To what extent do you agree with this statement?

(Write one part where you agree with the statement and a second part where you disagree.)

Yes, the constitution played a major role:

1. The proportional system of representation resulted in a multi party system. It would be enough to have 60,000 votes to get one seat in parliament. The result was a fragmentation of the parliament which resulted in weak governments. Many Germans who had no experience of democracy got an impression of weak political leadership. Especially if we take into account the major crises that the young republic had to face in 1923 and 1929.

2. The proportional system of representation led to the formation of weak coalitions. *In 14 years Germany had 21 coalition governments, of which only 8 held a majority.*

3. The constitution made it possible for the President to rule by presidential decree according to its Article 48. It was not clearly specified how this power should be used in times of crisis. From 1930 Hindenburg together with the Prime Ministers started to use presidential decrees extensively. In 1932 Hindenburg issued 60 decrees while there were only 13 sittings in parliament. It totally eroded the power of the parliament and can of course be clearly linked to the constitution.

No, there were other factors which had nothing to do with the constitution:

1. This was a country without any democratic tradition. It is an oversimplification to just blame the constitution. According to the 'continuity school' Germany had a long tradition of non-democratic rule, which is the reason for why democracy failed in Germany.

2. The Treaty of Versailles created so much resentment which weakened the government. The indemnity also affected the economy of the republic.

3. The Dawes plan, which can be linked to other factors than the constitution, made Germany over dependent of US money. *"Germany is dancing on a volcano"*, said Stresemann in 1928.

4. The Wall Street Crash is of vital importance if you want to understand the fall of the republic, i.e. the Nazi seizure of power. In 1928, the Nazis only had 2.6% support in the elections. The massive unemployment which was a result of the Wall Street Crash, led to a breakthrough for Nazism. In the 1930 election they got 18% and in 1932, when the unemployment crisis peaked, they got 37% support.

5. Adolf Hitler and the strengths of the Nazis is of course another major reason for the fall of the republic.

Conclusion: The constitution contributed to the fall of the Weimar Republic. It led to weak governments and presidential rule between 1930–33. It can also be argued that some of the points in the second part of this answer (no, it had nothing to do with the constitution) actually can be linked to the constitution. Weak coalition governments made the effects of the economic crises worse. The impression of weak governments made many Germans turn to a strong leader who criticised this system. So the constitution is one important point explaining the fall of the republic – but not the only one. It was a combination between weaknesses of the republic, strengths of the Nazis and other factors. We would conclude that the constitution was one important factor, but that it didn't play a *major* role.

13. THE WEIMAR REPUBLIC 1919–33

26. To what extent did the Wall Street Crash cause the fall of the Weimar Republic?

(Structure: show to what extent it caused the fall, and to what extent there were other reasons.)

Yes, the stock market crash led to the fall of the republic:

1. The crash led to an unemployment crisis.
2. The unemployment crisis led to a political crisis and an increase in support for Nazism (political polarisation). Explain how the inflation crisis in 1923 affected the middle class and how the unemployment crisis from 1929 affected the working class. The parliamentary system lost support. There is a clear link between unemployment figures and support for the Nazis after 1929.
3. The political crisis which started in 1929 led to an increasing use of presidential decrees.
4. After 3 years of presidential rule, the use of presidential decrees led to the acceptance of Hitler as Prime Minister. Leading politicians like President Hindenburg, von Papen etc. now accepted Hitler in order to get a strong government.

No, there were other factors apart from the Wall Street Crash, which led to the fall of the Republic:

1. This was a country without any democratic tradition. Use the arguments of the 'continuity school'.
2. The Treaty of Versailles created widespread resentment among the population. The war indemnity also had negative effects on the German economy. This weakened support for the republic.
3. The constitution lay the foundation for weak governments and rule through presidential decree.
4. The Dawes Plan made Germany over-dependent on US money. "*Germany is dancing on a volcano*", said Stresemann. The Plan is an isolated element which would aggravate the effects of the Wall Street Crash.
5. The strength of Adolf Hitler and the Nazis. Write about how Hitler's ideas appealed to the German population.
6. The fear of communism and lack of support for the Weimar Republic from conservative groups contributed to the fall of the republic.

Conclusion: Again there is a risk that you simplify the answer by not realising that one 'yes' explanation might affect a 'no' explanation (see also conclusion to question 25). It could be logical to argue, to give just one example, that the combination of a weak government (a 'no' argument) and the effects of the Wall Street Crash (a 'yes' argument), led to the fall of the republic. Therefore, again, we conclude that the fall was due to a combination of weaknesses of the republic, strengths of the Nazis, and other factors.

Chapter 14: The Third Reich

Issues

There are many possible issues to discuss concerning the Third Reich: how legal was the establishment of dictatorship in Germany? Another interesting topic is the recovery of the economy and what the driving force behind the attack on Poland in 1939 actually was.

14.1 How did Hitler succeed in establishing dictatorial power?

On 30 January 1933 Hitler was appointed Chancellor. It's very important to be aware the Nazi dictatorship was not immediately established after his appointment. At the time, there were only two other Nazis in the eleven-man cabinet (Göring and Frick).

Von Papen's idea was that the government should use and control Hitler: within two months *"we will have pushed Hitler so far into a corner that he'll squeak."*

- The government announced immediately that there would be **new elections in March**. The coalition wanted a two-thirds majority in the Reichstag in order to alter the constitution so that the government should be given the right to **rule by decree, i.e. to be able to pass laws without the support from the Reichstag.** The aim was to form a strong government, which could fight down the political left.
- The **SA**, the *Sturmabteilung* or Storm Department had been formed in 1920 and functioned as the original paramilitary wing of the Nazi Party. In the electoral campaign Hitler used the SA, which started a '**revolution from below**'. The SA was also used as auxiliary police in Prussia (two-thirds of the Reich) with the order that *'failure to act is more serious than errors committed in acting'*. In February and March, SA and

Figure 14.1: **Adolf Hitler and Ernst Röhm inspecting the SA in Nuremberg in 1933**

SS squads started to take over power in town halls, police headquarters and newspapers. It is described by Morris as a 'terrorist revolutionary movement'.

- On 27 February there was a **Fire in the Reichstag**. Hitler blamed the communists, and the day after the President issued a decree which suspended civil rights. It led to mass arrests of communists one week before the election. Noakes and Pridham describe the decree of 28 February as *"the most important single legislative act of the Third Reich."*

- The government didn't get a two-thirds majority in the elections in March. But after negotiations with the Catholic Centre Party a majority was secured to pass the **Enabling Act**. It gave the government the right to rule by decree for four years. If the Chancellor signed the decree the law went into effect the next day. Hitler now started to issue decrees without consulting the non-Nazi members of the government. The decrees (laws) were called Führer Edicts. With the Enabling Act, Hitler was able to Nazify Germany within months – something the non-Nazi members of the government had not foreseen.

- The Nazification or co-ordination of Germany is called the *Gleichschaltung*. The timeline of the most important laws is:

LAWS ENACTED

1933 **Civil Service Law**: Jews and officials suspected of disloyalty to the regime could be dismissed.

Law against the Formation of Parties outlawed other parties i.e. made Germany a single party state i.e. the Nazi party was the only legal party.

The Reich Press Law made editors responsible for what was printed in their newspapers.

1934 **Law for the Co-ordination of the Länder** abolished the individual states and centralised power to Berlin.

The Nazi Labour Front replaced the old trade unions.

All teachers had to join the **National Socialist Teachers League**.

1936 **The Basic Gestapo Law** put the Gestapo above the law.

- **The Night of the Long Knives**. In 1934, there was only one remaining power centre which Hitler didn't control and that was the presidency. The President had the right to appoint and dismiss the Chancellor and had also the right to rule by decree. In early 1934 it was known that President Hindenburg was seriously ill. Hitler didn't want to risk a conservative politician becoming a new President – someone who could challenge Hitler's power. Hitler also had an internal problem: the leader of the SA, Ernst Röhm, wanted to rebuild the army by using the SA. German generals and officers, among them President Hindenburg, detested the SA-men who had no genuine army background. Many in the SA were also supporters of socialist ideas. Hitler solved this dilemma in his own way when the SA leadership was executed during the Night of the Long Knives. Hitler claimed

Figure 14.2: **Adolf Hitler at the Nuremberg Rally, September 1935**

that Röhm had planned a coup and the old President congratulated him after the action was completed. When Hindenburg soon passed away, Hitler issued a decree which merged the offices of Prime Minister and President and called it Führer. The army gave Hitler support after he had crushed the SA and there was no remaining power structure left which Hitler did not control. Hitler was now the dictator of Germany.

If you ever get a question about how dictatorships were introduced in Bolshevik Russia, Fascist Italy or in Nazi Germany, you should not end your story with the October Revolution, the result of the march on Rome, or Hitler becoming Chancellor in January 1933.

- The Soviet Union became a single party state after the Civil War when the NEP was introduced in 1921.
- The fact that Mussolini was appointed PM in 1922 did not mean that he was a dictator. This happened instead step by step and in 1925 he gained the right to rule by decree.
- Hitler became dictator of Germany after having passed the Enabling Act in March 1933, the *Gleichschaltung* policy and the Night of the Long Knives – you must end that story in 1934. It is very important that you show an awareness of this in order to write a good answer.

How legal was the Nazi seizure of power?

Yes, it was legal:

1. The president who appointed Hitler had been elected in democratic elections.
2. The Nazi Party was by far the largest party in the Reichstag.
3. When the Germans were deprived their civil rights after the Fire of the Reichstag, a decree was issued according to Article 48 in the constitution. It was legally correct to issue such a decree.
4. The Enabling Act was passed with a 2/3 majority in the parliament, which was legally correct. It gave Hitler dictatorial power. The Nazification, which followed had a legal base.

No, it was not legal:

1. In March 1933 SA and SS squads simply took power in town halls, newspapers, etc. This violent revolution from below is described as a '*terrorist revolutionary movement*'.
2. After the Reichstag fire, it was mainly communists who were arrested. The decree to protect the state was used against 'selective groups.'
3. The idea behind Article 48 was to defend democracy against future enemies – not to abolish democracy.
4. Illegal methods were sanctioned by Göring when the SA formed an auxiliary police i.e. state violence was used against the opposition to the left.
5. Social democrats were intimidated during the Reichstag vote for the Enabling Act.
6. The Night of the Long Knives: around 200 SA men were killed to secure power.

Lee: "*It becomes perverse to call it a legal revolution*".

14. THE THIRD REICH

14.2 The pattern of dualism in the Nazi state

When examining the administration of the Third Reich, historians have debated why administration was so poorly organised. Some have even argued that Hitler was a weak dictator:

1. At **central level** government departments and ministries had to compete with rival Nazi institutions. Two examples:
   (a) the Foreign Office had to compete for power with the Nazi Bureau of Foreign Affairs;
   (b) the Minister of Transport had to compete with the Nazi General Inspector for German Roads.
2. After 1934 the **SS/Gestapo** infiltrated all state organs, which undermined the authority of other organs.
3. In **local administration**, local administrators had to compete for power with Nazi provincial chiefs (Gauleiters).

It led to confusion in the administration and Hitler never clarified who had supreme power. Irving concludes "*Hitler was probably the weakest leader Germany has known in this century*".

WHY DID HITLER ALLOW SUCH A SYSTEM?

View 1: **Ignorance** – Hitler was **lazy** and didn't care about administration.

View 2: **Social Darwinism** – by creating rival institutions, 'the fittest would survive.'

View 3: A **dual pattern** would give Hitler more power – it was a deliberate '**divide and rule**' policy (otherwise known as 'divide and conquer', from Latin *divide et impera*).

Views 2 and 3 make Hitler stronger and are possible to combine. It was a deliberate policy.

Hitler's authority was never questioned so one group of historians conclude that he was a strong dictator. But it was not made clear whether the party was superior or subordinate to the state, neither at national nor regional level.

Notice that laws in Germany were issued by the Führer and the parliament had no real power. In 1936 the government met only 4 times and not at all after 1938. The Führer-princip stated that someone at a lower level in the organisation must strictly follow a principle of obedience to superiors and at the top was the Führer. So the Nazi state from a political point of view was a highly personalised dictatorship but without an effective leadership.

14.3 The economy

When Hitler came to power he had no clear economic policy, but some basic ideas can be found in the book *Mein Kampf* that he started writing in 1924, like **autarky** and political and economic expansion in the East.

1. **Hitler's economic policy 1933–36 – 'partial fascism'**
   (a) job creation schemes were introduced;
   (b) attempts to control wages and to eliminate trade unions;
   (c) Schacht was President of the Reichsbank and Minister for the Economy: bilateral trade agreements with Balkan countries and South America were concluded. In the New Plan (1934) import and foreign exchange were regulated.

See further discussion of Hitler's policies and writing on page 136.

2. **1936 – The Four Year Plan**

    (a) self-sufficiency (production of substitutes);

    (b) preparation for war (It was stated that *"Germany must be operational for war within 4 years"*);

    (c) Göring was responsible for the economy and Schacht resigned in 1937, i.e. a Nazification of the economy.

3. **1939–41 Blitzkrieg**

    From an economic point of view the war was an attempt to win in a brief conflict without full economic mobilisation. A 'plunder economy' in invaded countries would maintain high consumption in Germany.

Hitler's economic policy must be seen as successful. Unemployment went down from more than 6 million in 1932 to 200,000 in 1938 when there was a shortage of skilled labour. The GNP was 72 billion Reichsmarks in 1928, 44 billion in 1933 and 80 billion in 1938. It must, however, be emphasised that the Nazis were helped by a growing world economy.

14.3.1 Nazism and 'big business'

The co-operation of 'big business' was vital in order to achieve economic recovery and rearmament. It is interesting to note how much of the economy was under monopoly control in the Third Reich, since the Nazis constantly attacked monopolies, during the power struggle. The percentage of the German economy under monopoly control rose from 40% in 1933 to 70% in 1937.

Conclusion: the power of 'big business' was left untouched in Nazi Germany (or even increased).

14.3.2 Nazism and small businesses

Artisans and small business owners were important to the Nazis in their seizure of power and the Nazis promised to close down department stores.

However, many small companies were absorbed by big companies growing in strength, and 20% of all small companies were closed down in the late 1930s.

14.3.3 Farmers

Farmers were described as 'heroes' by Hitler.

1. Tariffs were introduced to protect German peasants. From 1933 to 1937, prices increased by 20%.

2. The Hereditary Law (1933) guaranteed the control of the land to small scale farms – land could not be sold, mortgaged or closed due to debts.

3. All peasant debts were temporarily suspended between March and October 1933.

14.3.4 Workers

Political rights were destroyed by the Nazi regime:

1. SPD and KDP were dissolved.

2. Unions were replaced by the Nazi Labour Front.

But unemployment fell from 6 million to 200,000 between 1932–38 due to:

1. The world economy improved.

2. Rearmament (government spending in 1933 was 1.9 billion Reichsmarks, and 17.2 billion in 1938)

3. Job creation programmes (8.6 billion in 1932, 29.3 billion in 1938).

4. Conscription was reintroduced in 1935.
5. Women were partly excluded from the working life (marriage loans). However, by the later 1930s women had regained their position but now more women had lower level jobs.

Note that real wages fell in Germany in the 1930s (except for skilled workers), taxes were higher and hours worked per week increased by 15% between 1932-39 - but there was full employment.

14.4 Social life in Nazi Germany

The family was described in Nazi propaganda as '*the germ cell of the nation*'.

To strengthen families, loans were given to newly married couples. Abortion clinics were closed and women giving birth to many children were rewarded with the 'Mother's Cross.' The birth rate increased substantially in the 1930s (990,000 in 1932, 1.28 million in 1937). It is also worth noting that there was compulsory sterilisation of people with mental retardation, handicaps etc.

Youth: by 1939, 90% of the young Germans were members of the **Hitler Youth**, a Nazi youth organisation that had expanded membership through the late 1920s and 1930s and taken over many of the pre-existing youth groups. Camps were organised mainly for indoctrination, physical fitness etc. Girls joined the League of German Girls. Lee, however, concludes that: "*its success [...] appears to have been limited*".

Women: according to Goebbels the main task for women was to be "*beautiful, to bring children into the world*." Women were expected to be wives and mothers. They lost qualified jobs but the number of women in employment increased from 5 to 7.4 million due to an increase of the demand for labour in the late 1930s. Highly qualified women never regained their status.

14.5 Nazism and education

Important changes:

1. In 1934 the system of Länder was abolished (the federation) which led to a centralisation of power and more educational conformity. As a result the Reich Ministry for Education was established in 1934.
2. The curriculum was changed and History, Biology and PE became more important at the expense of the other sciences and humanities.
3. In 1933, 'The Ministry for People's Enlightenment and Propaganda' was established. One important aim was to control media and education. Hitler once stated: "*When an opponent declares 'I will not come over to your side,' I calmly say: 'Your children belong to me already'*".
4. Membership in the Nazi Teachers Association was compulsory.
5. Teachers were recruited for their ideological reliability. Their main obligation was to 'defend without reservation the Nazi state'.
6. Universities were deprived of their 'senate authority' and the state controlled appointments of rectors.
7. Dismissal of 'unreliable' teachers. 45% of all university posts changed between 1933-38.
8. Abolition of 'Jewish Physics' of Albert Einstein.

It is generally agreed that there was a serious decline in educational standards in primary and secondary education.

14.6 Indoctrination and propaganda

1. The Ministry for People's Enlightenment and Propaganda was set up in 1933 headed by Goebbels. A series of 'chambers' controlled press, radio, theatre, music, creative arts and film.
2. The Reich Press Law issued in October 1933 stated that all editors must be loyal to the Nazi state and made them personally responsible for what was written in their papers.
3. Increased access to radio sets: from 25% in 1932 to 70% in 1939, which was the largest proportion in the world.
4. The 'German News Agency' (DNP) provided 'correct' news to all journalists. In 1933 there were 4,700 daily newspapers from a variety of political views. In 1945 82% of all newspapers were state owned.

14.7 Relationship with the churches

Germany has traditionally been divided between Protestants and Catholics. Both welcomed the Nazi regime because of its anti-communist stand.

The Protestant church was centralised into a '**Reich Church**' in 1933 under the control of the Nazi Reich Bishop Müller. One sect, the **German Christians**, combined Christian beliefs with racism and Fuhrer worship. In opposition to this Nazification, pastor Niemoller founded the **Confessional Church**, which the majority of the priests joined – this organisation was never Nazified.

The Catholic Centre Party had supported the Enabling Act, in return for 'religious guarantees.' In the Concordat (1933) an agreement between the state and the Church was reached promising freedom of worship, protection for schools, etc. In return, the Church promised to withdraw from political life.

The Nazis violated the agreement, attacking especially the church youth organisations and soon public trials were held discrediting even nuns and monks. In 1937 the Pope abandoned his neutrality and issued an encyclical called *With Deep Anxiety*.

Conclusion: The Clergy managed to maintain a considerable influence and there was no significant Nazification of the Church. But the Church never challenged the regime politically.

14.8 The legal system/apparatus of coercion and terror

The legal system was profoundly altered and Nazified. The government controlled the judiciary and judges were appointed on basis of loyalty.

The decree after the Reichstag Fire in 1933 allowed indefinite detention without a trial. It led to the first concentration camps being opened the same year.

Police and terror

The SS/Gestapo was a 'separate organisational framework' and was put above the law in the Basic Gestapo Law in 1936. The SS (Schutzstaffel) was founded in 1925 and Gestapo was set up by Göring in Prussia in 1933. Himmler became the head of SS/Gestapo in 1933. The organisation penetrated the army, controlled concentration camps and infiltrated the civil service. While the Gestapo was the secret police that hunted down enemies of the Nazi state, the SS was a specially trained elite division of the military, which participated in everything from invasions to crimes against humanity. The Gestapo was a part of the SS. The Nazi state was based on terror. By July 1933 Germany had over 26,000 political prisoners and between 1933–45 800,000 Germans were detained for resistance. Edward Crankshaw concludes that the SS/Gestapo was a 'highly professional corps.' Recent studies (Robert Gellately) have, however, refuted this view. The Gestapo was insufficiently equipped, understaffed, inexperienced officials replaced those who were conscripted and the total membership of the Gestapo was only 32,000. The reason why the Gestapo worked was rather a compliant population with lots of 'informers.'

14.9 Antisemitism

1. In 1933 the SA organised a one-day boycott of Jewish businesses.
2. The Civil Service Law from 1933 excluded many Jews from the Civil Service.
3. In 1935 the Nuremberg Laws deprived the Jews their citizenship and civil rights.
4. After the Kristallnacht in 1938 'The Decree on Eliminating Jews from German Economic Life' was issued which excluded Jews from many professions.
5. In 1942, at the Wansee Conference, the 'Final Solution of the Jewish question' was decided.

The background to the Nazi seizure of power can be studied in the text about the Weimar Republic. Hitler's foreign policy can be studied in the text about the background to WWII.

27. Discuss how Hitler achieved dictatorial power?

(Structure: this is a list question where you need to go beyond January 1933, when Hitler was appointed Chancellor.)

1. **Hitler was appointed** Prime Minister in January 1933 due to a combination of weaknesses of the Weimar Republic, strengths of the Nazis and other factors (the Treaty of Versailles and the Wall Street Crash). Don't overstate this point because it asks for *dictatorial power*.
2. **Elections were announced** immediately to March 1933. The plan was to secure a two-thirds majority in order to change the constitution so that the government should be given power to rule by decree.
3. Göring authorised the **SA to be an auxiliary police** in Prussia. The SA started a revolution from below in the spring of 1933 and harassed political opponents.
4. After the **Reichstag Fire** on 27 February a **decree was issued the next day which suspended civil rights**. Indefinite detention without trials were allowed and thousands of communists were arrested and placed in newly opened concentration camps. Noakes and Pridham describe it as "*the most important single legislative act of the Third Reich.*"
5. The government did not secure a two-thirds majority in the elections in March. By making a deal with the Catholic Centre Party a majority was secured. (The communists had been arrested and only the Social Democrats voted against.) The **Enabling Act was passed** in March. It gave the government the right to rule by decrees for 4 years.

Hitler now started to issue decrees without consulting the other conservative members in the government and started a Nazification process through the *Gleichschaltung* policy:

What do you need to control?
  (a) Civil Service: The Civil Service Law 1933.
  (b) Media: the setting up of the Ministry for People's Enlightenment and Propaganda and the Reich Press Law 1933.
  (c) Political parties: the Law Against the Formation of Parties 1933.
  (d) Unions: The Labour Front replaced the old unions in 1933.
  (e) To centralise power to Berlin: the federation was abolished in 1934 with the Law for the Co-ordination of the Länder.

(f) The right to use terror: the decree issued after the Reichstag Fire gave the regime an opportunity of indefinite detention without a trial. In the Basic Gestapo Law from 1936, Gestapo was put above the law, meaning no external control allowed.

The final step was taken in June 1934 with **the Night of the Long Knives**. The SA was a powerful organisation with more than 2 million members headed by Ernst Röhm. There was an internal dispute about a continuing Nazi revolution and Röhm's wish that a new German army should be built by the SA. There was also strong support for socialism in the SA and talks about a second revolution. President Hindenburg was an ex-general and army officers detested the SA-people. The President had a considerable power and could appoint and dismiss the Chancellor and still rule by decrees. When it was known that the President was seriously ill in 1934 Hitler solved the dilemma in his way. He blamed Röhm for planning a coup and executed most of the leaders of the SA in the Night of the Long Knives. With this action he gained the support of the army and when Hindenburg passed away **in August 1934, he merged the office of Prime Minister and President and made himself Führer of the German Reich.** With this he had total control.

Conclusion: summarise the points above. I would conclude that the Enabling Act was the most important step towards a dictatorship.

28. Discuss why there was so little resistance against the Nazi regime?

(List the reasons why there was so little resistance.)

Note that initially there were some opposition groups like the SPD and the KPD, Jews and later the White Rose, the Swing Movement and attempted military coups. However, they were all effectively controlled and eliminated.

1. There was an extensive use of **terror**. The Basic Gestapo Law of 1936 put the Gestapo above the law. The Nazi state was based on terror. By July 1933 Germany had over 26,000 political prisoners and between 1933 and 1945, 800,000 Germans were detained for resistance.
2. Effective control of **media** by 'The Ministry for Peoples Enlightenment and Propaganda' headed by Goebbels.
3. Support was given from '**big business**' due to the rearmament programme and the destruction of left-wing parties and unions.
4. Support from the **army** due to a) successes in foreign policy b) the rearmament programme and c) the Night of the Long Knives.
5. Many **workers** were satisfied with the decline of unemployment. Six million had been unemployed in 1932. In 1939 it was 200,000.
6. Tariffs protected agriculture and the Hereditary Law (1933) gave smaller **farmers** security of tenure.
7. 90% of the **German Youth** belonged to Nazi youth organisations by the late 1930s and were indoctrinated.

Conclusion: The Nazi regime was based on terror. Many groups were also able to improve their situation after the depression and occupation after the war. Examples are workers (unemployment), the army, big business and farmers. Media was strictly controlled.

It is probably also correct to state that after 1933, when conditions started to improve in Germany, there was a support for the regime.

Chapter 15: Stalin

Issues

There are many issues to discuss involving Stalin:

- how could he outmanoeuvre Trotsky?
- why did he end the NEP and introduce collectivisation/industrialisation?
- did he strengthen the USSR?
- who was responsible for the purges?
- what were the aims of his foreign policy?

15.1 The power struggle

There are many factors explaining why Stalin, considered by many as a 'grey blur' could outmanoeuvre Trotsky. The most important factors were:

1. Stalin had been **Party Secretary since 1922**. He could appoint people who were loyal to him to key positions at both central, regional and local level. By this he could influence the selection of delegates who were sent to Party Congresses. He was considered as being able to 'deliver votes' at the congresses. He was also a member of the Politburo since 1917 (key decision making body within the party) and the Orgburo. He had a party base – this is by far the most important reason.

2. In 1921 a **'ban of factionalism'** had been introduced. It meant that once a decision had been made by the party, a party member could not openly disagree. To Stalin and the General Secretary who could control votes at party congresses etc. this limited the possibility of any opposition.

Figure 15.1: **Soviet dictator Joseph Stalin**

3. 1924: Stalin was able to make the most out of **Lenin's funeral** setting himself as Lenin's disciple. Trotsky was tricked by Stalin into not attending the funeral.

4. **Party membership increased** from about 300,000 in 1922 to 600,000 in 1925 and the new members knew who to thank.

There were many other differences between Stalin and Trotsky, however.

Stalin	Trotsky
1. Bolshevik background/had a power base.	1. **Menshevik background**/no power base.
2. Worker	2. Intellectual/brilliant theorist/**intellectual arrogance!**
3. **Ruthless and wanted power.**	3. It was beneath his dignity to fight for power.
4. '**Socialism in one country**' – it was what the party wanted to hear after the Civil War. (= Slavophile?). Stalin: "*One Soviet tractor is worth 8 or 10 foreign communists*".	4. Supported the idea of "**International or permanent revolution**" – revolution should be 'exported' to other countries to secure the revolution.
5. Unscrupulous/how important was ideology to Stalin? Stalin referred to as 'the Red tsar'!	5. Dedication to ideology/**loyal to the Communist party**. Trotsky: "*one cannot be right against the party.*"
6. Stalin **General Secretary from 1922** could appoint his men – build a power base. Also a member of the **Politburo and the Orgburo** (as the only one).	6. With his Menshevik background and arrogance Trotsky had lots of enemies and no party base.
7. Could be very cautious when needed.	7. Outspoken/didn't watch his words.
8. Stalin exploited **Lenin's funeral** in the best possible way to promote himself.	8. Trotsky was **absent** (probably due to Stalin) – considered as very important.
9. Stalin was absolutely **determined** to achieve a dominant position.	9. Trotsky turned down Lenin's offer of becoming Chairman of the Soviet parliament. He also refused to attack Stalin when he had the opportunity (the Testament and the Georgian affair). **Did he want power?**
10. Stalin – "a grey spot" according to Trotsky i.e. he was underestimated. But he was a brilliant organiser.	10. Controlled the Red army – **fear of Bonapartism** i.e. many Bolsheviks feared that he would seize power by using the Red Army.
	11. Trotsky was ill from 1922.
	12. A Jew – according to Trotsky this was important because there was antisemitism even within the party.

In 1924, Lenin's political testament was revealed to the Central Committee. Lenin warned the party against Stalin. Kamenev and Zinoviev urged that it should not be general knowledge: they feared Trotsky more.

There were three different stages in the power struggle:

1. At the Party Congress in 1924 the **Triumvirate** (Stalin, Kamenev and Zinoviev) could easily outmanoeuvre Trotsky by controlling the party.

2. In 1925 Stalin's 'socialism in one country' attracted the support of the political 'right', e.g. Bukharin, and those who supported the NEP. Zinoviev, Kamenev, now together with Trotsky, formed a '**united opposition**' – the left wing advocating an ending of the NEP. Stalin could easily defeat them. He controlled the party and could accuse them of 'factionalism'. In 1927 they were expelled from the party.

3. When the political left was outmanoeuvred, **Stalin turned on the right** by making a clear 'left-turn'. He called for an ending of the NEP and rapid collectivisation in 1928. The 'right' and Bukharin who believed in the NEP couldn't oppose Stalin due to:

    (a) Ideology: the NEP was seen by many Bolsheviks as an economic 'Brest-Litovsk' (surrender).

    (b) The ban of factionalism, which made it difficult to organise an opposition.

    (c) Stalin controlling the party.

15.2 Stalin's economic policy

Lenin had introduced the NEP in 1921 in order to increase production. Small scale capitalism was allowed within both agriculture and industry and the economy which had suffered during the civil war, soon recovered. In the late 1920s the economy ran into troubles. Only 17% of the grain harvest reached the workers in the cities mainly due to the fact that state prices were too low.

Possible solutions:

1. capitalist way, offering better prices to peasants doing private farming.
2. to make agriculture state owned i.e. to collectivise agriculture. In a communist state this was ideologically more correct.

The Party Congress in 1926 had decided to undertake *"the transformation of our country from an agrarian into an industrial one, capable by its own efforts of producing the necessary means"*. Stalin preferred *"to squeeze out all capitalist elements from the land"*.

When collectivisation had been implemented there were:

- state farms (*sovkoz*) which were entirely state property and which handed over the production to the state, and
- collective farms (*kolkhoz*) where land and equipment were collectively owned by the peasants.

A kolkhoz was committed to deliver parts of its production to the state. 'Machine tractor stations' served the collective farms with heavy machinery.

Reasons for collectivisation

1. **The procurement crisis** (see above) resulted in that not enough grain was delivered to feed the population.
2. **Ideological reasons**: The NEP was seen by many Bolsheviks as an ideological embarrassment (an ideological Brest-Litovsk!). Agriculture must finally be nationalised and state controlled. In a Marxist state the future belonged to the urban workers.
3. **Political reasons**:
   (a) To **eliminate the Kulaks** as a class! The Kulaks and other peasants were no supporters of communism. To collectivise agriculture was a way to increase and tighten party control (notice that the concept of a Kulak class was a Stalin myth. A class of exploiting landowners didn't exist in the USSR).
   (b) Protests from workers in the towns due to the procurement crisis, was **dangerous politically**.
4. **Economic reasons**: Stalin argued that more would be produced and with a state controlled agricultural sector, it would be much easier to procure grain for the cities and for export. It is a fact that while the overall grain harvest declined in the early 1930s, state grain procurement did not!

   If collectivisation worked it would result in a more efficient agricultural sector which would provide:
   (a) the industries with **workers**;
   (b) **food for workers** and the peasant population;
   (c) the possibility to **export** grain which in turn would make it possible to buy foreign machinery;

To simplify it: there were **ideological, political and economic reasons**.

15.3 Impact of agricultural policies

Collectivisation was implemented with remarkable speed:

	Oct 1929	Sept 1930	1931	1933	1935	1936	1941
% of households collectivised	4	21	52	65	83	90	98

It led to an economic disaster – why?

1. It occurred **too quickly** which resulted in disorder. The peasants were not prepared to co-operate in the deliberate destruction of their wealth and traditional way of life.
2. Procurement **quotas set at far too high levels.**
3. **Rebellious peasants** slaughtered their cattle and burnt down their farms. Millions were either killed or sent to the Gulag. The loss of people and expertise resulted in a sharp decline of the production.
4. **Communist** party members, who were sent from the towns, **ignored farming techniques**.

Grain harvest	1929: 71 million tons	1935: 67 million tons
Cattle	1928: 70 millions	1932: 34 millions
Sheep and goats	1928: 146 millions	1932: 32 millions

This resulted in:

1. A disastrous **famine** (especially in Ukraine). The estimate of the number of victims varies but 10–20 million people is a common estimate. It can be described as a 'national famine.'

   Isaac Deutscher: "*the first purely man-made famine in history*".

   Conquest argues that the famine was a deliberate policy in the Ukraine to crush opposition and Ukrainian nationalism, i.e. a 'terror-famine' created by Stalin.

   Officially collectivisation was described as a success and problems were never publicly admitted. So the government could not appeal for assistance from the outside world (did so during the Civil War in 1921). Instead the USSR exported grain during the famine. Michael Lynch: a large proportion of the population "*was sacrificed on the altar of Stalin's reputation*". Stalin was the 'great planner'!

2. An enormous **migration** from rural to urban areas started (there was more food in the towns). Internal passports were introduced to control the population, since it destabilised society.

View 1:	Collectivisation was planned and productivity was even sacrificed to hunt down kulaks/peasants and class enemies.
View 2:	The implementation got out of hand due to local initiatives. Poorer peasants were encouraged to attack the kulaks and Medvedev concludes: "*collectivisation was a civil war between peasants*". Stalin called for a halt in the process in 1930 and accused NKVD of being 'dizzy with success' (it explains the figures from Sept 1930).
Historians:	Stalin has been credited for using agriculture to promote industrialisation. However, recent studies have shown that **hardly any capital flowed from agriculture to industry**. The transfer of peasants to industry was too rapid which resulted in administrative problems and worsening social conditions.

15. STALIN

Lynch: *"..a policy of state taxation of an uncollectivised peasantry would have produced a much higher level of investment capital"* and avoiding social dislocation and misery. This was the policy of the 'right' and Bukharin.

Lee: *"It is difficult to say anything favorable about Stalin's agricultural policies".*

15.4 Industrialisation

15.4.1 Reasons for industrialisation

1. **Military reasons**: In 1931 Stalin delivered his famous speech: *"We are fifty or a hundred years behind the advanced countries. We must make good this distance in ten years. Either we do this or they will crush us"*, referring to hostile western capitalist countries. Industrialisation was the same as security and survival.
2. **Economic reasons**: an industrialised economy produces more than an agricultural one.
3. **Ideological and political control**. Industrialisation would strengthen the working class at the expense of the peasantry. This would strengthen the communist party. According to Marx, communism should emerge in an industrialised society.

15.4.2 Impact of industrialisation

Five Year Plans 1928-32 and 1933-37 (a third 1937-42 was disrupted by the war) emphasised heavy industry (coal, oil, iron, electricity, etc).

It was a planned and centralised economy averaging an annual growth of 20%. There were failures, especially compared to the goals, but the **result is normally described as 'successful'** or **'substantial'**.

	First Five Year Plan
Steel	4 to 6 million tons
Coal	35 to 64 million tons
Pig iron	3 to 6 million tons

From IB examiners' report: *Candidates must find a way of remembering these figures.*

Second Five Year Plan: Heavy industry still important but new metallurgical resources such as lead, zinc, nickel, were now emphasised. Communications were now improved. Railways were largely double tracked.

Armament was now very important: it had consumed 3.4% or the total expenditure in 1933. In 1936 it was 16% and in 1940 it was 32% of government investments!

15.4.3 Living standards

Industrial workers suffered for the following reasons:

1. Workers were mobilised to remote areas.
2. Many times they worked with inadequate equipment without facilities and comfort.
3. In new industrial centres there was enormous overcrowding.
4. No priority was given to the production of consumer goods.
5. Workers were supervised by the NKVD and risked prosecution if targets were not met. After 1940 new labour legislation lengthened the working week from 5 to 6 days and made lateness for work by more than 20 minutes, a criminal offence.
6. The unions were used by the state to enforce its policy and not to represent the workers. Strikes were not permitted.
7. Real wages in 1937 were not more than 85% of the 1928 level.

Alexander Nove describes the years 1928–33 as *"the most precipitous decline in living standards known in recorded history"*!

Conclusion: The resources for industrialisation were **generated from within Russian society**. The achievements of industry were considerable but it had its price in living conditions.

WAS STALINISM NECESSARY?

Martin McCauley – YES:

The price in human suffering was high but it **saved mother Russia** in WW II.

Adam Ulam – NO:

An alternative policy with more private enterprise and taxation of an uncollectivised peasantry, would have strengthened the USSR even more. Stalin's policies were not only **wrong** from a **human point of view**, but also **economically**.

15.5 The purges

There was a long-standing tradition of using terror in Russia. The Tsar's secret police, the Okhrana, had used terror and Lenin set up the Cheka in December 1917. During the Civil War terror was used as a deliberate means. After an attempt to kill Lenin the Red Terror was intensified in the summer of 1918. The purpose was to terrify all hostile social groups. Estimates today put the number of victims at 300,000.

- **1928** The Shakhty affair: Stalin claimed that he had discovered an anti-Soviet conspiracy among the mining engineers of Shakhty. It led to a trial.

- **1932** Ryutin, a right-wing Bolshevik had publicly attacked Stalin. The same year there was a trial against the 'Ryutin group'. Between 1933–34 one million party members were expelled, i.e. one third of the total membership, on the grounds that they were 'Ryutinites'.

    In November Stalin's wife, Nadezhda, committed suicide. She was depressed by the excesses of the collectivisation and supported Bukharin who thought that the ravages of the countryside had gone too far.

- **1934** The Congress of Victors (17th Party Congress). Many believed that it was now possible to slow down the pace of the collectivisation and industrialisation. Kirov, the Leningrad party boss, said *"the fundamental difficulties are behind us"*. Stalin opposed this and wanted to push ahead. There was a split in the Politburo. Provincial delegates asked Kirov to take over as General Secretary. Kirov got a long standing ovation and both Stalin and Kirov were given the title of Secretary of Equal Rank.

After the Congress **Kirov was assassinated**. Many historians suspect that Stalin ordered the killing. Khrushchev stated in his Secret Speech in 1956, that Stalin was almost certainly behind the killing. Out of the 1,996 delegates who attended the Congress of Victors, 1,108 were later executed. Out of the 139 members to the Central Committee, elected at that gathering, 98 were executed!

The Kirov affair is seen as a major turning point: Before the Kirov assassination industry and plant managers had been the victims. Now Stalin started to purge the Bolshevik Party. This was the beginning of the Great Purges. It started with thousands of the Leningrad Party being purged. The murder was seen as a widespread conspiracy against the Soviet state.

15. STALIN

The Party purged: in 1935, Stalin turned on the left-wing opposition of the party. Zinoviev and Kamenev were arrested and the first 'show trials' took place. The last show trial, or period of terror took place in 1937–38. The Rightists, those who had supported the NEP, were accused. Bukharin and the former head of the NKVD, Yagoda, were sentenced.

In 1937 the **Red Army was purged**: 75 of the 80-man Supreme Military Council were executed. It has been estimated that 90% of all Russian generals were executed. 35,000 officers in total were either imprisoned or executed.

The people were purged: historians tend to concentrate on the show trials, the attack on the army etc. But the Russian population suffered from the purges and what happened at central level was copied at local level. It has been estimated that one in eighteen of the population were arrested and almost every family suffered from the purges. In 1988 KGB (NKVD) archives were opened; the result according to Michael Lynch:

- 1934: one million people arrested and executed in the first major purge;
- by 1937, 17 to 18 million had been transported to labour camps. 10 million of these died;
- by 1939 another 5–7 million people had been 'repressed' (3 million of these died in camps or were executed).

The purges continued after this. If we add victims of the famine to this list (Deutscher: *"the first purely man-made famine in history"*), probably **more than 20 million people died**, due to Stalin's policies.

Deutscher argues that the purges, in a longer perspective created *"a grotesque fear of initiative and responsibility in all grades of the administration"*.

Causes of the purges:

1. **Stalin's paranoia**.
2. **Stalin's desire for power**: by wiping out all old Bolsheviks and supporters of Kirov, he secured absolute personal power. He turned on his own party. Neither Lenin nor Hitler did anything comparable.
3. **Economic reasons**: to get a disciplined workforce and slave labour in the Gulag.

 MAJOR INTERPRETATIONS

The orthodox view:

Stalin was responsible. Also referred to as the '**intentionalist school**', i.e. Stalin intended or planned the purges. It is a 'top-down' approach. Richard Pipes is one among many representing this school.

The revisionist view:

The system is mainly responsible. Also referred to as the '**functionalist school**' and a '**bottom-up**' approach. Terror was not new in Russia. The Tsars had used it and Lenin had used it. The Soviet state was not as totalitarian and controlled as expected. At local level there were thousands of 'little Stalins'. Party officials, NKVD, poor peasants (remember Medvedev's writing about a war between peasants) were all involved, and the purges were a result of a system and a tradition. Stalin is definitely not without responsibility but his personality alone is not a sufficient explanation to the scale of the purges – blame the system. It was not possible for Stalin to control the implementation of orders and 'little Stalins' exceeded his orders. J. Arch Getty is one important historian who argues for the revisionist school.

It might be noted that the purges all ended with Stalin's passing away in 1953, hence giving support to the intentionalist school. If the system was the driving force it should have continued after Stalin's death. The opening of Soviet archives during the 1980s has also supported this view.

15.6 Society and culture

15.6.1 Social changes

Early Bolshevik policy: virtue of equality in wages, military ranks etc. Stalin revived differences as a part of his economic policy. The concept of family was restored and it was much more difficult and expensive to get a divorce, and abortions were made illegal after 1936. There were also rewards for mothers who bore many children.

15.6.2 Education

Education is a typical example of Stalin's conservatism. Early Bolshevik education had been based on group-based activities and had favoured relaxed discipline. From 1934 Stalin changed this:

- examination and grades more important;
- more formal 'one-way' teaching;
- full authority to teachers;
- school uniforms;
- compulsory pigtails for girls;
- Tsarist past more important in history;
- academic qualification when selecting pupils for higher education (and not class background).

Note: it must be concluded that Stalin's regime improved education: compulsory primary education was introduced in 1930 which increased the number of pupils from 9 to 18 million (1920 to 1933). Secondary pupils rose from 0.5 to 3.5 million (1922 to 1933). About 75% of the population was illiterate in 1917, but illiteracy was rare when WWII started. In 1940, USSR had 70,000 public libraries.

15.7 Bolshevik/Stalin's foreign policy

It is possible to describe the evolution of Stalin's foreign policy in three stages.

15.7.1 Stage I: Early development

In 1922, two nations outcast after the war – Germany and communist Russia – ended their isolation by signing the **Treaty of Rapallo**. It led to economic and military co-operation.

Stalin was committed to '**socialism in one country**' and showed no interest in Comintern activities. (The **Communist International**, abbreviated as **Comintern** was an organisation which should promote the expansion of communism globally.)

When Nazis and Fascists grew stronger, Stalin turned down ideas from communists in the west calling for joint action between social democrats and communists, against Nazis. Stalin referred to social democrats as 'social fascists'.

15.7.2 Stage II: 1933 Hitler becomes Chancellor: a turning point

Litvinov, Russia's foreign minister, advocated collective security against fascist expansion.

15. STALIN

- **1934** Russia joined the **League of Nations** the policy of attacking western social democrats as being social fascists was overturned. Now left-wing parties should form 'popular fronts' to fight the spread of fascism.
- **1935** The Soviet Union and France signed a mutual assistance pact with Czechoslovakia.
- **1936** The Spanish Civil War was a dilemma to Stalin. Many left-wing Europeans saw it as a chance to fight back Fascism. Stalin, on the other hand, feared that a successful soviet intervention would alarm Britain and France so that they would form an anti-Communist alliance with Germany and Italy. Stalin intervened but acted cautiously in Spain.

  Hitler marched into the Rhineland.
- **1938** March: Anschluss.

  The **Munich agreement**. USSR was not invited to the conference.
- **1939** March: Germany took most of the rest of Czechoslovakia. France and Britain now gave a guarantee to Poland. The USSR now became an important potential ally to both Britain and France *or* Germany in the case of a war over Poland.

Stalin's/USSR's position in March 1939

- No real strong ally.
- Knew that 'Lebensraum' was Russian territories.
- Japan in the East had joined the anti-Comintern pact in 1936 (there were major battles with the Japanese in 1938 and 1939. In July and August 1939 the Japanese suffered 61,000 casualties!)
- The USSR had not been invited to Munich.
- After purging the Red Army, the USSR needed time.
- Germany, and not Britain and France, could be prepared to make a deal over territories in Eastern Europe.
- If Britain and France fulfilled their obligations to Poland, the USSR could stand aside while the capitalists fought each other.
- Germany was USSR's major trading partner.

In April, Litvinov proposed an alliance with Britain and France but talks led nowhere. Several proposals 'went unanswered' according to Lynch.

15.7.3 Stage III

Molotov, who had criticised Litvinov's policy of collective security, was appointed foreign minister in May 1939.

In August, Anglo-Soviet negotiations broke down. One reason was that Britain would not put pressure on its ally Poland to give Soviet troops right of passage across Polish territories. Britain didn't believe in a Nazi-Soviet pact.

On 23 August, the Molotov-Ribbentrop Pact was signed: Hitler didn't risk a two-front war and with the treaty he probably expected that there would be a second Munich, i.e. that Britain and France would not support its ally. With Russian support he could now overcome a WWI-type Anglo-French blockade. But his ultimate aim of defeating the USSR had not changed!

The Nazi-Soviet pact (a non-aggression pact and not a military alliance): the treaty committed both countries to refrain from aggression and observe neutrality in conflicts involving a third part.

HISTORY HL: EUROPE

A secret protocol defined future 'spheres of influence' which gave USSR eastern Poland, Estonia, Latvia, and Bessarabia (part of Romania). There were also economic agreements.

 STALIN'S FOREIGN POLICY

Two major interpretations

View 1: The policy for collective security arose from a genuine fear that the **Nazis** were dangerous. Hitler had clearly stated in *Mein Kampf* that 'Lebensraum' was to be found in the USSR. In this view Stalin is more defensive wanting protection.

View 2: Stalin always preferred co-operation with Germany and his ultimate aim was to **manoeuvre the capitalist states into a mutually destructive war,** which would enable USSR to expand. A Br/Fr/Ger understanding was the nightmare of Russian diplomacy and this was also the idea behind the Rapallo agreement of 1922. The attempt with collective security was followed only when an agreement with Germany looked impossible (Robert Tucker). This view makes Stalin look more aggressive.

29. Discuss why it was Stalin, and not Trotsky, who succeeded Lenin.

(This is formally a 'list' question where you must show Stalin's strengths and Trotsky's weaknesses, but let's start by emphasising some major events in their careers and then compare the two.)

Events:

1905   Trotsky the leader of the St Petersburg Soviet during the revolution (being a Menshevik at the time).

1903   After the split of the Social democratic party in 1903, Lenin became the leader of the Bolsheviks. Trotsky now became an independent socialist – he did not join the Menshevik party as expected.

1912   Stalin a member of the Central Committee.

1917   May: Trotsky returned from exile. From now on a Bolshevik.

1917   Stalin Commissar (= Minister) for Nationalities.

1917   Trotsky organised the October Revolution (Where was Stalin during the revolution?).

1918   Trotsky created the Red Army.

1921   Victory in the Civil War – Trotsky seen as the victor! When NEP was introduced in 1921 the party also decided to impose *a 'Ban on factionalism'.*

1922   Lenin *and* Trotsky both ill. Stalin appointed *General Secretary.*

1923–25   The Triumvirate = Zinoviev, Kamenev, and Stalin against Trotsky.

1924   Lenin died. Stalin made the most out of the *funeral.*

1925   Trotsky resigned as Commissar for war. 'The United Opposition' formed by Zinoviev/Kamenev/Trotsky.

1927   Both Zinoviev and Trotsky expelled from the party.

1928   Trotsky banished to Central Asia.

1929   Stalin attacked the Right i.e. Bukharin. Trotsky: exiled abroad and later killed.

Analysis:

Strengths of Stalin (there are more points in the text):

1. In 1922 Stalin was appointed **General Secretary**. He was now able to control nominations to Party Congresses etc., i.e. he could control them. This, in combination with the ban on factionalism from 1921, was a very powerful weapon. Once the party had made a decision, you could not openly oppose such a decision. Stalin had a **power base**.
2. Stalin was underestimated but he was a very skilful administrator.
3. His policy of 'socialism in one country' attracted much more support after the Civil War, than Trotsky's international or permanent revolution.
4. He was able to make the most out of Lenin's **funeral**, like giving the most important speech, while Trotsky was absent.
5. **Party membership increased** from about 300,000 in 1922 to 600,000 in 1925 and the new members knew who to thank.

Weaknesses of Trotsky (there are more points in the text):

1. He had joined the party in 1917 after years of disputes with Lenin i.e. he **had no party base**.
2. Trotsky was a brilliant orator but also sometimes **arrogant** and did not always watch his words.
3. Trotsky controlled the Red Army and there was a fear that he would use the army against his rivals (**fear of Bonapartism**).
4. Politically, his ideas of an **international revolution attracted less support** after the Civil War than Stalin's 'socialism in one country'.

Conclusion: It was a combination of Stalin's strengths and Trotsky's weaknesses.

30. Evaluate whether Stalin's domestic policies strengthened the USSR.

(Show arguments where you examine how the USSR was strengthened and also arguments where you show how the policies weakened the USSR.)

Yes, it strengthened the USSR:

1. The **industrial sector** grew substantially in the 1930s. Five-year plans were introduced from 1928 (1928-32, 1933-37). Figures showing the growth of heavy industry in the first Five-year plan: steel 4 to 6 million tons, coal 35 to 64 million tons and pig iron 3 to 6 million tons. Even though targets were never met both the first and the second five-year plans were very successful in terms of economic growth.
2. **Armament was very important in the 1930s**: it had consumed 3.4% or the total expenditure in 1933. In 1936 it was 16% and in 1940 it was 32% of government investments. So from a military point of view the USSR got stronger.
3. Stalin's regime improved **education**: compulsory primary education was introduced in 1930 which increased the number of pupils from 9 to 18 million (1920 to 1933). Secondary pupils rose from 0.5 to 3.5 million (1922 to 1933). 75% of the population had been illiterate in 1917 but illiteracy was rare when WWII started. In 1940, USSR had 70,000 public libraries.
4. **Historiography**: McCauley argues that *"one may dismiss Stalin as a tyrant [...] on the other hand it is possible to argue that he rendered the Soviet people a service* [if it hadn't been for Stalin it would have] *succumbed to the German onslaught of 1941."*

HISTORY HL: EUROPE

Stalin weakened the USSR:

1. **Historiography**: Ulam argues that an alternative regime would have strengthened the USSR and that **Collectivisation** weakened the USSR. Production went down and millions were sent to the Gulag prison camp system or died in the famine. The idea was that collectivisation should promote industrialisation but no resources went to the industries. Lee writes: *"It is difficult to say anything favorable about Stalin's agricultural policies"*.

2. Millions were killed in the **purges**. 98 out of 113 members from the Central Committee elected in 1934 were executed. 75 of the 80-man Supreme Military Council were executed. It has been estimated that 90% of all Russian generals were executed. Millions of ordinary citizens were purged as well. It has been estimated that one in eighteen of the population were arrested and almost every family suffered from the purges. The number of victims, if we include the number of those who fell under the collectivisation, is probably not less than 20 millions. Crankshaw even argues that the famine in the Ukraine was planned to crush peasant and Ukrainian resistance i.e. a terror famine. Deutscher argues that the purges, in the long term, created *"a grotesque fear of initiative and responsibility in all grades of the administration"* which took generations to cure.

3. Resources for industrialisation were generated from within the USSR. It was the Russian population who had to pay the price in terms of terror, famine and severe **living conditions**. Nove describes the years 1928–33 as *"the most precipitous decline in living standards known in recorded history"*.

Conclusion: Morally his regime can never be defended. In terms of economic development there are totally opposing views. Make your own judgment and back up your argument.

Chapter 16: The League of Nations

Issue

What were the reasons for the failure of the League?

16.1 Foundation of the League of Nations

In January 1918 the US president, **Woodrow Wilson**, outlined the idea of an international peace keeping organisation in his 14-point programme. There had been similar suggestions by other statesmen earlier, but the peace conference in Paris gave Wilson a golden opportunity. He was seen as an idealist by the other peacemakers at the Paris Peace Conference, and had to give up many of his points. The idea of this peacekeeping organisation was, however, accepted and became a part in all the different peace treaties that were signed in Paris. Wilson was highly optimistic and described WWI as '*a war to end wars*'.

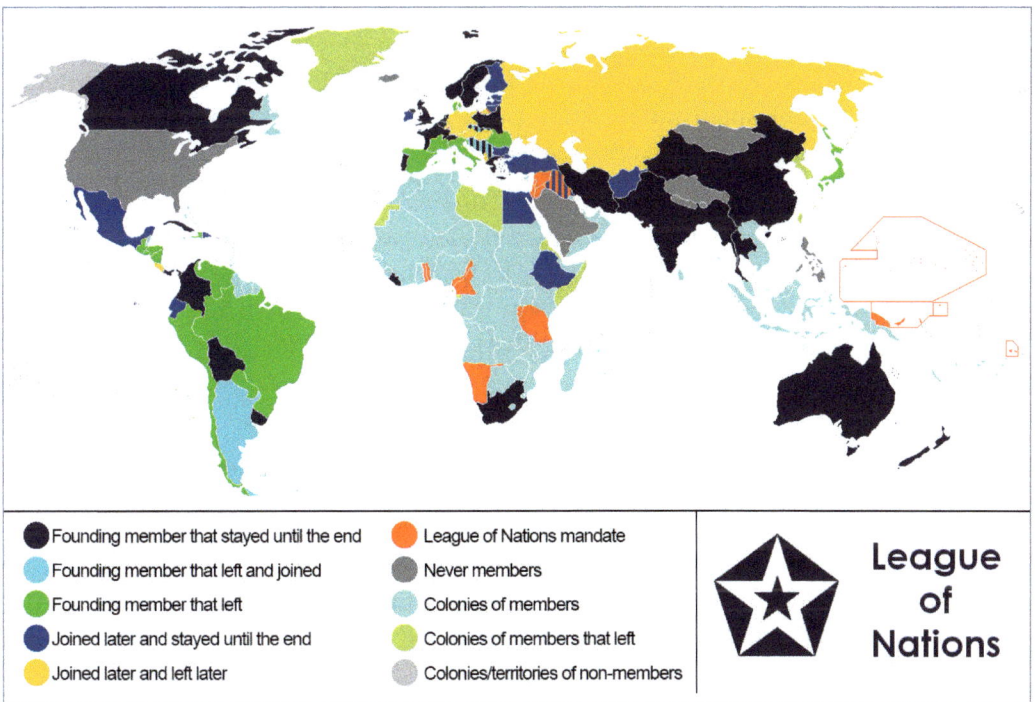

Figure 16.1: **Anachronistic world map showing member states of the League of Nations from 1920 to 1945**

HISTORY HL: EUROPE

16.1.1 The aims of the League

1. To prevent **wars**. Article 10 of the Covenant stated: *"The members of the League undertake to respect and preserve against external aggression the territorial integrity and existing political independence of all members of the League".*
2. To promote international **co-operation** through its various organisations.
3. To promote **arms reduction** and control of arms manufacturing.

Every member state promised to register their international agreements at the League to prevent secret diplomacy. They also promised to bring any dispute with another state to the League for decision. The League could also impose economic sanctions and if it didn't work members had to supply armed forces against the aggressor. The League had no military troops of its own but they should contribute with armed forces in collective actions against an aggressor.

16.1.2 The organisation of the League

1. The **Assembly**: every member was represented in the Assembly, which decided the general policy and the budget. A **unanimous vote** was required **on important decisions**, i.e. a **veto** right to each member. It planned to meet at least once a year.
2. The **Council**: it was made up by permanent members/great powers and chosen non-permanent members. Decisions **on important questions** had to be **unanimous** i.e. a **veto** power. The first permanent members were **Britain, France, Italy and Japan**. All these four powers played a major role when the League collapsed in the 1930s (the Manchurian occupation and the invasion of Abyssinia). This smaller body was to deal with specific political disputes and crises.
3. The **Secretariat**: responsible for the **implementation** of decisions made by the League.
4. The **Court of International Justice**: according to the covenant, members should bring their disputes to the court.

There were also a number of different committees, normally referred to as 'special departments', to deal with specific problems. The **International Labour Organization** should work for better working and living conditions. The **Health Organization** and the **Mandate Commission** were other important organisations within the League.

The League came into existence formally on 10 January 1920. Forty-two nations were members from the beginning in 1920. There were, however, several nations that didn't join, or were not allowed to join, the organisation. The US Senate refused to ratify Wilson's Treaty and consequently the US didn't join. This was of course a major blow to both Wilson and the League. Germany and Russia were not allowed to join the organisation.

16.2 Early successes – the 1920s

The early years of the League in the 1920s are normally described as a success.

1. Danzig was established as a free city controlled by the League.
2. Upper Silesia was divided between Poland and Germany after a plebiscite in 1921.
3. Aaland was handed over to Finland in 1921 after a dispute with Sweden.
4. Austria was given financial help when it was close to collapse in 1922.
5. The League could prevent hostilities between Greece and Bulgaria.
6. The most important achievements of the League were probably accomplished by the different organisations and committees. The **International Labour Organization** prodded governments into improving working conditions. It put pressure on member states to agree on 8-hour working days, annual paid holidays, the right to form trade unions, that no one should be employed full-time before the age of 15. The **Health**

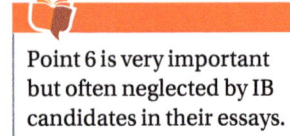

Point 6 is very important but often neglected by IB candidates in their essays.

Organization was very successful in combating different diseases. The **Refugee Organization** was very important helping refugees and prisoners of war, after WWI. The **Mandates Commission** supervised and administrated areas taken from Germany and Turkey after the war.

There were some early failures as well: Vilnius was taken from Lithuania by Poland. Corfu, a Greek island, was bombed by Italy after an incident. Italy ignored decisions made by the League.

16.3 Failing major tests – the 1930s

Mussolini concluded correctly "*The League is all right when sparrows quarrel. It fails when eagles fall out*". Among the 'eagles' to fall out in the 1930s were the four first permanent members of the Council: Britain, France, Japan and Italy.

1. **Japan invaded Manchuria**, a part of the Chinese Empire, in 1931. It was the first time the League was faced with aggression by one of its major powers. This was exactly what the League should prevent. It was a moment of truth. The League condemned Japan and ordered the troops to leave, which it refused to do. When the League suggested that Manchuria should be governed by autonomous Chinese administration in October 1932, it was rejected by Japan. Instead, it simply left the organisation in 1933.

2. One of the most important aims of the League was to promote **disarmament**. A Disarmament conference had started in 1932. Germany had joined the League in 1926. When Hitler came to power in 1933 it became even more important to reach an agreement. Germany demanded parity with France and Britain at the conference. In practice this meant rearmament of Germany, living under the restriction of the Treaty of Versailles, and disarmament of France. When this was refused Germany left both the League and the Disarmament conference in October 1933.

3. **Italy invaded Abyssinia in 1935**. There are many parallels to the Manchurian crisis: one important member of the league was violating the independence of another member state. Italy was a Stresa Front ally of Britain and France. They were anxious to maintain good relations with Italy, who at the time was no ally of Germany. Italy was, on 7 October, declared the aggressor and the League now decided to impose sanctions. Unofficially however, the two powers later sanctioned the aggression in the Hoare-Laval Pact. Abyssinia was a member of the League and when the acceptance leaked out to the press in France and Britain, it led to a major outcry. Hoare was forced to resign and King George V remarked: "*No more Hoare to Paris*". Britain and France now actively supported the sanctions on Italy, by sending a naval squadron to Alexandria. The damage was, however, irreparable. Three of the four first permanent members of the Council had been prepared to violate the independence of another, weak, member state in Africa. Another fatal consequence was that Italy drew closer to Hitler.

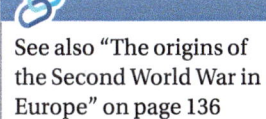
See also "The origins of the Second World War in Europe" on page 136

4. Few members brought their disputes to the Court of International Justice.

Why did the League fail?

1. There were serious **weaknesses in the covenant**. **The veto power** in the Council and the Assembly limited its power.
2. **Important countries were absent**. It was of course a major blow when the most powerful state in the world, and the initiator of the League, the US, didn't join. It affected the organisation both economically and psychologically. It was also a weakness that two of the most powerful states in Europe, Germany and Russia, were not members from the beginning. Germany joined the League in 1926 but left again in 1933. The same year Japan left the League due to the Manchurian occupation.

Figure 16.2: **The Gap in the Bridge: cartoon about the absence of the USA from the League of Nations**

3. The League was a **part of the Paris Settlement**, which was deeply resented, especially in Germany but also in Italy. It weakened the authority of the League.

4. It had **no military troops** of its own. It can always be discussed whether a peacekeeping organisation should be armed. Wilson refused it; but it can be argued that a strong military capacity could have deterred an aggressor.

5. With the Manchurian occupation, and the Abyssinian attack it was clear that **Japan, Italy, Britain and France**, had all contributed to weakening the authority of the League. These four states had been the first permanent members of the Council.

Now, when you have read the text:

1. Study the questions that follow (but not the answers!)
2. Copy a template and outline your answer.
3. Compare your answer with the one given and analyse any possible differences.

31. Discuss why the League of Nations was set up in 1920 and what the results were.

(Discuss the reasons for setting up the organisation and in the second part you are supposed to analyse the effects of its work.)

Why was it set up?

1. Clearly the **effects of WWI** led politicians like Woodrow Wilson to propose a new order. Similar suggestions had been made by politicians like Robert Cecil from Britain, Jan Smuts from South Africa and Leon Bourgeois from France

16. THE LEAGUE OF NATIONS

2. More specifically the aims were:
   - To prevent **wars**. Article 10 of the Covenant stated: *"The members of the League undertake to respect and preserve against external aggression the territorial integrity and existing political independence of all members of the League"*.
   - To promote international **co-operation** by its various organisations.
   - To promote **arms reduction** and control of arms manufacturing.
   - It should also supervise territories controlled by the League after the Paris Settlement.

Effects:

It had some *early successes*:

1. Danzig was established as a free city controlled by the League.
2. Upper Silesia was divided between Poland and Germany after a plebiscite in 1921.
3. Aaland was handed over to Finland in 1921 after a dispute with Sweden.
4. Austria was given financial help when it was close to collapse in 1922.
5. The League could prevent hostilities between Greece and Bulgaria.

   The most important result of the work of the League, especially taking into account the collapse of the organisation in the 1930s, was the work of the 'special departments':

   - the **International Labour Organization** prodded governments into improving working conditions. It put pressure on member states to agree on 8 hour working days, annual paid holidays, the right to form trade unions, that no one should be full-time employed before the age of 15;
   - the **Health Organization** was very successful in combating different diseases;
   - the **Refugee Organization** was very important helping refugees and prisoners of war, after WW I;
   - the **Mandates Commission** supervised and administered areas taken from Germany and Turkey after the war.

   However, there were some *notable failures*:

   - **Japan invaded Manchuria**, a part of the Chinese Empire, in 1931. It was the first time the League was faced with aggression by one of its major powers. When the League proposed that Japan should leave Manchuria, Japan left the League. The League had failed in a major test
   - One of the most important aims of the League was to promote **disarmament**. A Disarmament conference had started in 1932 but failed to reach an agreement. Hitler could now continue his rearmament programme.
   - **Italy invaded Abyssinia in 1935**. Again an important member of the League invaded a weaker member and the League was unable to prevent it. It led to a split between Italy and Britain and France. It made Italy turn to Hitler.
   - In the Western democracies, pacifist opinion strongly believed in the League. It was **one reason for the appeasement policy** in the 1930s. Expectations had been raised for a new order and the 1920s had proved that the organisation worked. It affected the political situation in countries like Britain.

6. Is it possible to argue that the failure of the League then led to WW II? It is perhaps possible to argue that the failure was **one reason for WW II, but it was far from being the most important one**.

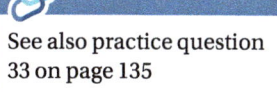
See also practice question 33 on page 135

Conclusion: Emphasise the success of the special departments. This is normally described as a success. The League clearly failed in its main task: to prevent future wars. We would not, however, conclude that the failure of the League was one of the major reasons for WW II.

32. "The League of Nations failed due to its own weaknesses." To what extent do you agree with this statement?

(Show in the first part the effects of the weaknesses of the organisation. In the second part you are supposed to show some other factors which might explain its failure.)

Yes, it failed due to its own weaknesses:

1. There were **weaknesses in the covenant**. **The veto right** in both the Assembly and the Council made it very difficult to take actions against aggressors.
2. Members didn't bring their disputes to the **Court of International Justice**. That was not intended from the beginning.
3. **The League had no military troops**. A strong and powerful military organisation would have been useful in times of crisis. A resolution in 1923 had also made it clear that it was up to each nation to decide if they wanted to take part in military actions by the League. It was very difficult to organise military actions due to these rights.
4. It was clear that the League was weak due to the fact that major world powers did not join the organisation. How could it be possible to exercise real influence if major world powers were not behind the organisation or if they left the organisation, which they could easily do? It was for obvious reasons a **voluntary organisation** and this made it weak, lacking the support from important states.

No, there were other reasons for the failure:

1. In 1921, 26 out of 28 European states were democracies. In 1940 only three remained. In other words, the League had to operate in a very difficult time dealing with men like:
   - Adolf Hitler who had clearly outlined, in both Mein Kampf and the Second Book, that he was going to war. It is possible to write a lot showing how Hitler's actions made war inevitable.
   - Mussolini wanted to 'make Italy great again'. He was, like Hitler, not prepared to accept any limitations from a peace-keeping organisation.
   - Stalin and the USSR joined the League in 1934 and were expelled after the attack on Finland in 1939. Again we have to be aware that this was a very ruthless dictator who didn't respect an organisation like the League.
2. **With hindsight it is easy to see that all the problems that could be solved by the settlement would lead to grievances somewhere.** It was not easy for an organisation like the League to be able to handle problems like this. One example is that 8 million Germans lived in weak states that had borders with Germany.
3. Even states like Britain and France were prepared to sacrifice the interests of the League for their own selfish needs. It was most clearly seen during the Abyssinian crisis. It was more important to maintain their relations with their Stresa ally, than to defend the principles of the League. Britain and France were by far the two most important members of the League and they were prepared to accept a violation of the independence of one member state.

Conclusion: There were weaknesses in the League which partly explains the failure i.e. the veto power. The main reason for the failure is, however, to be found outside the league. The situation in Europe in the 1930s was more important, by far, in explaining the failure, than the League itself.

16. THE LEAGUE OF NATIONS

33. To what extent was the failure of the League of Nations responsible for the outbreak of WW II?

(Show to what extent the League contributed to the war and in the second part of the essay, all other factors leading to the war.)

Yes, it is possible to blame the League for the war:

1. By the formation of the League, **hope was raised** that it would be able to prevent future wars. This had a profound effect on the pacifist opinion in many Western countries and contributed to the support of the **appeasement policy**.
2. The League failed in its attempt to achieve disarmament. When Germany left the Disarmament Conference in 1933 and continued its rearmament programme, it destabilised Europe.
3. The League was unable to prevent **stronger powers** from violating weaker states, or as Mussolini expressed it: *"The League is all right when sparrows quarrel. It fails when eagles fall out."* **Japan** was one of the permanent members of the Council when the League was formed. When it invaded Manchuria in 1931 and the League imposed sanctions, it just left the League. When **Italy** invaded Abyssinia in 1935, the League imposed economic sanctions but was unable to make Italy leave Abyssinia. When **Germany** invaded Austria and took over Czechoslovakia, the League was without any authority to prevent it. The League **had no means in its Covenant** to prevent actions like this. **No armed forces** and lack of tradition and authority, made it easy to bypass it.
4. It was also a very ineffective organisation where **unanimity** was needed both in the Assembly and in the Council, to reach a decision.

No, we can't blame the League:

1. We can't blame the League for the fact that important Great Powers chose to not join the organisation. The lack of authority is due to that countries refused to support the organisation. The US never joined, Germany left in 1933, Japan left in 1933 and Italy in 1937. **Blame the powers who did not support the League**.
2. It was impossible for any organisation to prevent and **control** a determined dictator like **Hitler**, from starting a war.
3. There were also other dictators who were more or less aggressive. **Mussolini** attacked Abyssinia, Albania and intervened in the Spanish Civil War. **Stalin** was prepared to sign a pact with his arch enemy. Ruthless politicians like this were not prepared to respect an organisation like the League.
4. **France and Britain**, the two most important members of the League and permanent members of the Council, made a **blunder** when they secretly accepted Italy's violation of another member state, **Abyssinia.** If anything, this weakened the authority of the League.
5. The **Paris Settlement** resulted in the creation of many new **weak states** in Eastern Europe, containing millions of Germans. It was not easy for any organisation or state, to prevent a future revision of this settlement.
6. **Britain, France, and the USSR** were not able to **co-operate** against such an obvious aggressor like Hitler. How could we expect the League to be able to do it?

Conclusion: The failure of the League is perhaps one minor reason for WW II. It is, however, clear that there were other far, more important reasons for this conflict; in particular Hitler.

HISTORY HL: EUROPE

Chapter 17: The origins of WW II

Issues

Most historians tend to agree that Hitler played a major role in the outbreak of World War II. The main issue discussed by historians concerning Hitler's involvement is a debate once brought up by A J P Taylor: Did Hitler have a **master plan** for WW II or did he just seize the opportunity offered by other great powers? The 'opportunity offered by other great powers' brings us to the second issue that will be discussed in this outline: The reasons and the effects of **appeasement**. A third factor, which is *common in IB questions* is the importance of the failure of the **League of Nations**. After having studied both WW I and WW II it might also be useful to compare and contrast the reasons for these two wars.

17.1 The origins of the Second World War in Europe

1. The **Paris Peace Conference** in 1919 resulted in five different treaties: The Treaty of Versailles (dealing with Germany), Saint-Germain (Austria), Neuilly (Bulgaria), Trianon (Hungary) and Sèvres (Turkey). The treaties have often been criticised. It has even been claimed that they led to World War II. It has been said that Ferdinand Foch, the Marshal of France stated, when he heard about the terms: *"This is not peace; it is a truce for 20 years"*. In what way can we argue that it contributed to WW II?

    - The **new democratic government** in Germany was **forced to sign** the treaty. It deprived Germany of most of its army and Germany had, together with its allies, to take the blame for causing the war and as a consequence pay an indemnity. Signing the treaty was seen as a betrayal by patriotic Germans and this weakened **support** for the new government. The indemnity that was fixed to £6,600 million put a lot of **strain on the economy**. It was partly due to economic problems that **Hitler** came to power in 1933.

    - **The principle of national self-determination** was not applied to Germany. A series of **weak states** were created in Central Europe containing German minorities. These groups of discontented Germans played a major role when Hitler expanded into Austria, Czechoslovakia and Poland in the mid-1930s.

    - The foundation of the **League of Nations** was included in each of the five peace treaties. The aim was *"to promote international co-operation and to achieve international peace and security"*. Should this organisation be able to promote international co-operation and peace?

2. **Hitler** was a long way from power in the 1920s. In 1924 he wrote **Mein Kampf** and, in 1928, **Zweites Buch** in which he outlined his foreign policy aims. It is worth asking how much attention we should pay to books written years before he had real power. In *Mein Kampf* we can read: *"First we have to crush France in the West and then conquer*

Hitler started writing *Mein Kampf* (in English: 'My Struggle') while in prison in 1924. By early 1925 it was still incomplete, so to avoid delay it was published as a first volume. A second volume followed, completing the book, in 1926. This second volume should not be confused with *Zweites Buch* (in English: 'Second Book'), which was written shortly after but never published in Hitler's lifetime.

17. THE ORIGINS OF WW II

Lebensraum in the East". *Lebensraum* was defined as 'Russia and its subjugated states'. In *Zweites Buch*, he provides us with a detailed plan of expansion.

(a) First a removal of the restrictions of Versailles, i.e. to reconstruct the army and to remilitarise the Rhineland.

(b) End of the French system of alliances in Eastern Europe and the establishment of German control in Austria, Czechoslovakia and Poland.

(c) Defeat of France.

(d) Defeat of the USSR.

(e) Contest for world supremacy possibly against Britain and the US.

As we can see all these points were implemented later, except for point (e).

1933 **Adolf Hitler** came to power in Germany and this dramatically increased the pace towards war. Already in February he informed his cabinet and his generals that rearmament was now the main priority i.e. a clear violation of the Treaty of Versailles. In October Germany left **the Disarmament Conference** officially because France rejected a proposal of parity between the French and the German armies. Hitler was, however, not prepared to accept any future limitations of his rearmament programme, which was the real reason for his departure. The same month Germany left the **League of Nations**. By these measures and the secret rearmament programme, it was clear that Germany was in a vulnerable situation.

1934 Hitler, anxious to cover his real intentions, signed a non-aggression pact with Poland which would weaken the French alliance system in Europe. Privately he declared: *"All our agreements with Poland have a purely temporary significance"*. The same year Austrian Nazis killed the Prime Minister of Austria and Hitler was prepared to invade. When Italy announced their support for Austria, Hitler backed down. He was still too weak.

1935 Hitler officially announced the existence of a **German Air Force** and **conscription** was reintroduced i.e. the military provisions of the treaty of Versailles would no longer be observed. Britain, France and Italy now formed the **Stresa Front** to safeguard the Treaty of Versailles (April 1935). However, already in June, Britain signed the Anglo-German Naval Agreement, which allowed a German navy to be 35% of Britain's, at the most. It was a clear violation of the Treaty of Versailles and it had been done without Britain consulting its Stresa front allies. Britain wanted to avoid a naval race as before WW I.

October: Italian troops invaded **Abyssinia**. Britain and France were anxious to maintain good relations with their Stresa-ally and were prepared to accept that parts of Abyssinia should belong to the invader (Hoare-Laval Pact, December 1935). When this leaked out to the press, Britain and France had to abandon its Stresa-ally and support sanctions from the League.

The Abyssinian affair was a major turning point in international affairs:

- It destroyed the Stresa co-operation
- It destroyed definitely the image of the League of Nations as an effective peace-maker.
- Italy was isolated and turned to Hitler. The **Rome-Berlin Axis** was signed in **October 1936**.
- Italian-German friendship totally changed the balance of power in Europe. It would lead to the **Anschluss** in 1938.

1936 **March**: while France and Britain were still distracted by the Abyssinian crisis and when the French government had just resigned, **Germany remilitarised the Rhineland**.

- Strategically this would block France from helping Czechoslovakia and Poland in the East.
- It clearly demonstrated the unwillingness of Britain and France to safeguard the Treaty of Versailles. Churchill claimed: *"There has never been a war more easy to stop"* referring to WW II and the lack of Anglo-French actions during the Rhineland crisis.
- To Hitler it was a success, which strengthened his position.

In the autumn, **the Spanish Civil War** started. Franco got firm support from both Italy and Germany.

The 'Rome-Berlin Axis' was formed and also the 'Anti-Comintern pact' between Germany and Japan.

'The Four-Year plan' was introduced in Germany where it was stated that *"Germany must be operational for war within four years"*. Rearmament and self-sufficiency were the aims.

1937 Hitler summoned a conference with his leading generals in which he outlined his plans for expansion in Eastern Europe. Colonel Hossbach's records from the meeting are known as the Hossbach memorandum. Hitler declared that he planned to invade Austria, Czechoslovakia and Poland. Russia is not mentioned as a target. How much attention ought we pay to these records that never were signed by Hitler? Lee argues that it *"clearly indicated a change in tempo"* and that Hitler was now more willing to take risks.

1938 **The Anschluss**: the incorporation of Austria had been stated on the first page of *Mein Kampf*. The importance of German minorities living in the weak adjacent states of Austria, Czechoslovakia and Poland would soon be visible and within two years and would lead to WWII.

The Anschluss clearly showed:

- the weaknesses of Britain and France, now without Italy;
- Germany and Italy now shared a border, with direct access to the Balkans, outflanking France.

In September Britain, France, Italy and Germany, agreed to hand over the Sudentenland to Germany in **the Munich agreement** i.e. the climax of appeasement.

Neither Czechoslovakia, nor its ally the USSR, were invited.

Figure 17.1: **Benito Mussolini and Adolf Hitler in 1938**

17.2 Effects of Munich

France, with treaty obligation to Czechoslovakia, had betrayed them. This resulted in the **destruction of the French alliance system** in the East

Czechoslovakia as a state was **doomed** after Munich. It lost 70% of its steel and iron resources and a defensible frontier against Germany; this agreement would encourage other nationalities within Czechoslovakia.

Suspicion on the Soviet side that the West believed that *"Hitlerism was better than Stalinism"*, was confirmed. A Russian diplomat said: *"We nearly put our foot on a rotten plank. Now we are going elsewhere"* referring to co-operation with the Western powers. It would **lead to the Molotov-Ribbentrop agreement.**

To Hitler it was another success. It might be argued that this made Hitler believe that the Western powers would never act to defend Poland.

In **March 1939** Germany took most of **the rest of Czechoslovakia**. Hitler had claimed that the Sudetenland was his last territorial claim in Europe. In April, Britain and France issued a guarantee to Poland and Romania i.e. the end of appeasement.

Stalin's position in April 1939:

- The USSR had **no real strong ally.**
- They knew that **'lebensraum' was Russian territories**.
- **Japan** in the East had joined the anti-Comintern pact in 1936. There were major battles with the Japanese in 1938 and 1939. In July and August 1939 the Japanese suffered 61,000 casualties.
- The USSR had not been invited **to Munich.**
- After purging the **Red Army**, the USSR needed time.
- Germany, and not Britain and France, might be prepared to make a **deal over territories** in Eastern Europe.
- If Britain and France fulfilled their obligations to Poland, the USSR could **stand aside** while the capitalists fought each other.
- Germany was the USSR's major **trading** partner.

Hitler's position:

- He was planning to **attack Poland**.
- With the Anglo-French guarantee there could be a **two-front war**, which must be avoided.
- Would there be a **new Munich** if he attacked i.e. no support from the Western democracies? If that was the case he could continue to attack the USSR later.

In April Litvinov, the Russian foreign minister, proposed an **alliance with Britain and France** but talks led nowhere. Several proposals "went unanswered" according to Michael Lynch.

In August: Anglo-Soviet negotiations broke down. One reason was that Britain would not put pressure on its ally Poland to give Soviet troops right of passage across Poland. Britain did not believe in a Nazi-Soviet pact.

In **August: signing of the Molotov Ribbentrop Pact**. Hitler did not want to risk a two-front war and by signing the treaty he probably expected that there would be a second Munich i.e. that Britain and France would not support its ally. With Russian support he could now overcome an Anglo-French blockade as in WW I. His ultimate aim of defeating the USSR had not changed. On 1 September, Germany attacked Poland and two days later Britain and France declared war on Germany.

HISTORY HL: EUROPE

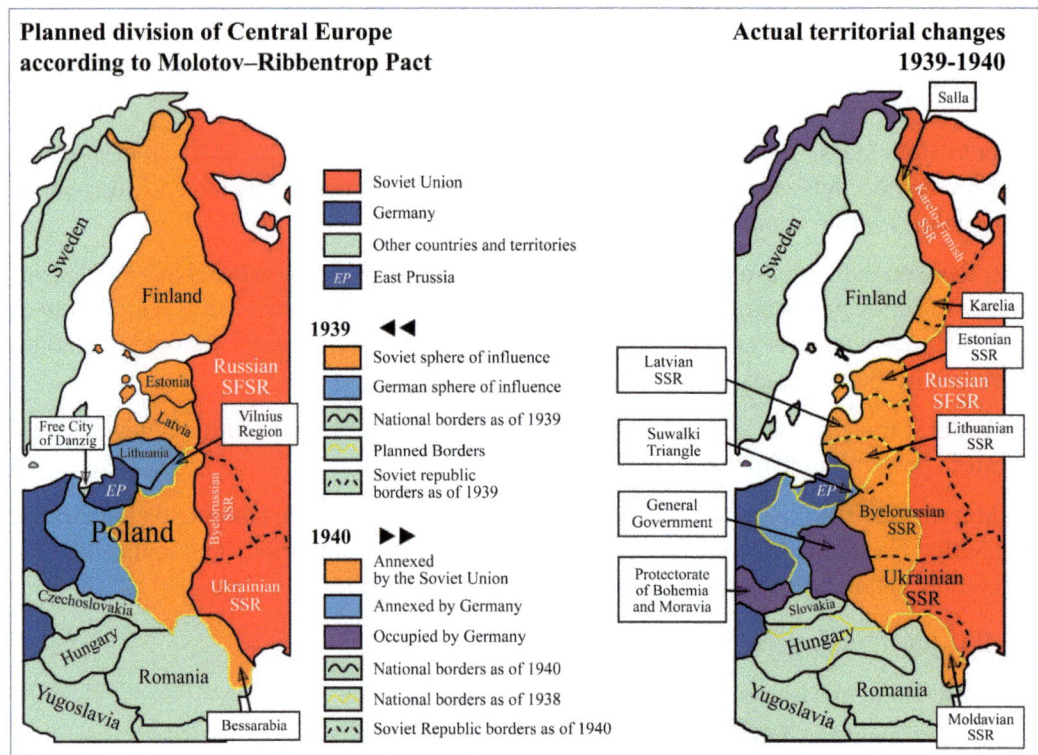

Figure 17.2: Molotov-Ribbentrop Pact—political map of Central Europe in 1939-40

With the outbreak of the war it was clear that **appeasement had failed**. The aim was to settle disputes by compromises and concessions to avoid war. The naval pact with Germany, the in-action over the remilitarisation of the Rhineland, Anschluss, and Munich, can be seen in this light.

17.3 Why appeasement?

1. Legacy of the Treaty of Versailles. Some argued that both Italy and Germany had genuine **grievances**. National self-determination was denied to Germany.

2. Memories from WW I:
   - Many leading politicians had been young men fighting in the **trenches** of WW I.
   - Wasn't the **Sudetenland the equivalent of Bosnia**? Chamberlain asked in 1938 if Britain should go to war "[...] *because of a quarrel in a far off country between people of whom we know nothing*". Why was it Britain's responsibility to defend territories in 'far off countries'?

3. The Civil War in Spain had clearly shown **the horrors of modern warfare**. War had to be avoided.

4. After the depression many thought that money could be needed for other things. There was a very **strong pacifist public opinion**. Every newspaper in Britain except for one supported the Munich agreement.

5. '**Better Hitlerism than Stalinism**'. Stalin was more feared than Hitler, and therefore some people were willing to give him give a free hand in crushing communism in the east.

6. Chamberlain was a **man of peace**: *"I myself am a man of peace to the depths of my soul"*. He gave the impression that Hitler could be trusted if disagreements could be solved.

7. Britain was **not militarily prepared** for a war in Europe. As a colonial power it had troops in Asia, India, and in the Middle East. A general war in Europe had to be avoided.

8. France was weak and divided and not ready for a war.

17. THE ORIGINS OF WWII

 APPEASEMENT

There are two major historiographical interpretations concerning appeasement:

The Orthodox view: Chamberlain was naive and fooled by Hitler. He made a major blunder in believing in agreements with a dictator like Hitler. Churchill said: *"There has never been a war more easy to stop"*. If Britain and France had reacted in 1936, war could have been avoided, i.e. blame the appeasers. They were 'guilty men'.

Revisionist view: As Prime Minister, Chamberlain was of course aware of Britain's military weakness and commitments to other parts of its colonial empire. By appeasement Britain gained time. These two years, 1938–39, were used for military preparations, which saved Britain.

With the outbreak of the war it was also clear that the **League had failed**. The League had suffered from the fact that important states did not join/were not allowed to join, the organisation from the beginning. The US, Germany and the USSR did not join in the beginning. Japan left the League in the early 1930s. It was also clear that important powers like Germany, Italy, and Japan had no intention to let the League challenge their national interests. The League also suffered from that all decisions in both the Assembly and the Council had to be unanimous.

17.4 Summary of possible reasons for WWII

1. Nazism meant war: once **Hitler** had come to power in Germany, a European war was inevitable as his plans were bound to conflict with those of other countries. Hitler had planned for this war and we can find the evidence in *Mein Kampf*, in *Zweites Buch*, and in his policies after seizing power. Hugh Trevor-Roper writes: *"Mein Kampf was a complete blueprint of his intended achievements"*.

2. The policy of **appeasement** encouraged Hitler to continue his plans for expansion of the Reich. In particular, the attitude of the western powers at Munich confirmed his opinion that they would not go to war with Germany in defence of an East European power.

3. The **Paris Settlement**: The erection of a series of **weak states** in Eastern Europe, (especially states that could not even agree with each other) brought about the war. There was no state, or block of states, to oppose Hitler in the very area that he had stated he planned to conquer. The Paris Settlement also **weakened the new regime in Germany** after WWI. The punishment of Germany in the Treaty of Versailles inevitably meant a hostile Germany that would, given the opportunity, attempt to redress its grievances.

4. The unavoidable **failure of the League of Nations** in Manchuria and Ethiopia/Abyssinia meant the end of collective security and, consequently, a return to the principle 'might is right'.

5. An **Agreement between Britain and France and the Soviet Union** would have prevented the outbreak of war. This agreement proved impossible only because of fear and suspicion of communism in government circles in Britain and France who, therefore, must take responsibility.

6. **Failed diplomacy**: Britain, France and Italy had signed the **Stresa front** to safeguard the Treaty of Versailles. Only months later Britain signed the **Anglo-German naval pact**, which allowed Germany to have a fleet that was 35% of Britain's fleet i.e. a violation of the Treaty of Versailles. Britain did this without informing Italy and France. The same year Britain and France first gave a secret understanding to Italy when it planned to invade **Abyssinia** and finally supported sanctions from the League against Italy. Did these policies to some extent explain why Mussolini turned to Hitler? The very fact that the

USSR was not invited to **Munich** was a major turning point of Soviet foreign policy. Stalin now abandoned the pro-Western collective security policy and turned to Germany in August 1939. Was it failed diplomacy which made Italy turn to Germany and the Soviet Union turn to Germany? This can of course be discussed but, if so, it must be seen as one point explaining the outbreak of WW II.

7. **Japan** occupied China in 1937 and attacked the US at Pearl Harbor in 1941. These are of course very important factors behind WW II.

8. **Stalin** made it possible for Hitler to start the war. By signing the Pact with his arch-enemy, Stalin made it possible for Hitler to attack Poland. Stalin's real intention, according to one school of historians, was to trick the Western powers into a mutually destructive war, hence claiming that Stalin's policy of collective security was a mask.

9. There was **no strong group of states guaranteeing the peace treaties** from Paris. The US never ratified the treaty and the USSR and Germany were pariahs. This was the difference between the Vienna Settlement (the Quadruple alliance) and the Paris Settlement and it partly explains why a new war took place so soon.

As you may be aware many of these points can be discussed. To be able to assess the importance of these points, it might be useful to outline some questions.

34. "Hitler planned and was responsible for WW II." To what extent do you agree with this statement?

(Write one part where you support the claim and one part where you disagree.)

Yes, Hitler planned the war

1. In *Mein Kampf*, Hitler talked a lot about a revision of the Treaty of Versailles, to unify all Germans and to acquire Lebensraum. Lebensraum was clearly defined as Russia and its subjugated states. It was also necessary to crush France. He had a Social Darwinist approach and regarded war as a natural means to expand.

2. *Zweites Buch (*Hitler's *Second Book)* from 1928 provides us with a clear programme of expansion. It is difficult to ignore the fact that what he wrote in 1928 was also implemented later when he came to power. With the Rhineland remilitarisation in 1936, Anschluss 1938, the Munich agreement 1938, the attack on Poland in 1939, France in 1940 and the USSR in 1941 he implemented the plans from *Zweites Buch*.

3. The **Four Year plan** in 1936 stated that Germany should be operational for war within four years. Economic self-sufficiency, which was emphasised in the Plan, was a preparation for war.

4. The **Hossbach memorandum**: Hitler outlined his war plans in central Europe to the High Command and after this declaration; his foreign policy became more aggressive.

Points 1–4 are points where Hitler *outlined his aims*.

5. His **rearmament programme** started immediately when he came to power.

6. He **left the League and the Disarmament Conference** in December 1933, clearly showing that these peace keeping organisations were not in line with his programme.

7. Conscription was re-introduced in 1935.

8. In 1936 German troops were ordered to remilitarise the **Rhineland.** In 1938 **Austria** was invaded. The same year Germany was given the **Sudetenland** in Czechoslovakia, after a crisis provoked by Hitler. It was his 'last territorial claim'. In March 1939, Germany took most of the rest of Czechoslovakia and attacked **Poland** in August.

17. THE ORIGINS OF WWII

9. Historiography: According to Hugh Trevor-Roper, *"Mein Kampf was a complete blueprint of his intended achievements"*. Alan Bullock's perspective is *"Yes, it was Hitler's war. He had a master plan and he also seized the opportunity"*.

No, it was not a planned war/the war was not only caused by Hitler:

1. The importance of the **Paris Settlement** cannot be ignored. All **weak states**, which were created at Versailles, destabilised Europe and the treaty also **weakened the new government** in Germany.
2. A stronger **League of Nations** could have prevented war – another weakness of the Treaty.
3. Blame the **appeasers**. Their policy opened up opportunities to Hitler. Churchill argues that "*There has never been a war more easy to stop*", indicating that an alternative policy in 1936 would have prevented the war.
4. **Britain** could have acted differently. First they made Italy turn to Germany with the Naval Pact and the Abyssinian affair. Then they made Stalin turn to Germany with the Munich agreement and by not responding to signals from the USSR, about forming a co-operation against Germany.
5. **Stalin** and the USSR must take part of the responsibility by concluding a pact like the Molotov-Ribbentrop Pact, with an aggressor like Hitler. Some historians believe that Stalin's main aim was to manoeuvre the capitalist states into a mutually destructive war.
6. Historiography: A J P Taylor claimed in his *Origins of the Second World War* that Hitler surely was partly responsible but that he did not have a master plan. There was no difference between Hitler and other German nationalists, like Wilhelm II. So when he saw an opportunity to expand, he just seized the opportunity like any other nationalist would do. Taylor argues that Hitler, when outlining his plans, was *"in large parts daydreaming, unrelated to what followed in real life"*. The opportunity to expand was offered by the appeasers. But note that Taylor didn't have access to *Zweites Buch* in the early 1960s.

Conclusion: There are two 'command words' that must be addressed in the answer. It must be concluded that Hitler was 'responsible'. Even if he did not plan the war and only seized the opportunity that was offered by the appeasers, he is still responsible for his aggressions. Did he have a 'plan'? Well, obviously A J P Taylor was able to present a convincing argument saying 'no', but be aware that he is quite alone in his opinion. One weakness with Taylor's argument is that he had no access to *Zweites Buch*. Most historians agree that Hitler had a plan for the war. Support your answer with some of the points above.

35. Discuss why Britain and France followed a policy of appeasement in the 1930s

(This is a list-question i.e. list all the reasons you can find explaining why appeasement was used by Britain and France and include different interpretations. Define the word 'appeasement' in your introduction.)

Introduction: Explain the term appeasement: a policy aiming at avoiding war, by giving way to demands from aggressive powers, provided that these demands were not unreasonable.

Examples of appeasement: no reaction against the German rearmament programme from 1933, the Anglo-German Naval Pact in 1935, Abyssinia, 1935, the Rhineland remilitarisation in 1936, Anschluss in 1938 and the Munich Agreement 1938.

HISTORY HL: EUROPE

Why?

1. **Legacy of the Treaty of Versailles.** Both Italy and Germany had genuine **grievances** over the Treaty of Versailles. National self-determination was denied to Germany and the indemnity had been criticised even in Britain by Keynes. To revise parts of the Treaty would lead to less aggression from Germany.

   There were memories from WW I:
   (a) many leading politicians had been young men fighting in the **trenches** of WW I – they knew the horrors of war;
   (b) wasn't the **Sudetenland the equivalent of Bosnia?** In 1938 Chamberlain asked if Britain should go to war "[…] *because of a quarrel in a far off country between people of whom we know nothing*". Why was it Britain's responsibility to defend areas in 'far off countries'? Britain's primary interest was still its colonies.

2. **The Civil War in Spain** had clearly shown **the horrors of modern warfare**. War had to be avoided.

3. After the Depression many thought that money could be needed for other things. There was a very **strong pacifist public opinion** in Britain. In 1935 the British Prime Minister, Baldwin declared after winning elections: "*I give you my word of honor that there will be no great armaments.*" The support for appeasement is also shown by the fact that every newspaper in Britain except for one supported the Munich agreement.

4. **'Better Hitlerism than Stalinism'.** Stalin was, by many, more feared than Hitler after the purges in the USSR, and to give Hitler a free hand in crushing communism, had support from many people in the West.

5. Chamberlain was a **man of peace**: "*I myself am a man of peace to the depths of my soul*". He gave the impression that Hitler could be trusted if disagreements could be solved.

6. Britain was **not militarily prepared** for a war in Europe. As a colonial power it had troops in Asia, India and in the Middle East. It is easy to find support for British military weakness if you study arms production. To give just one example: Britain produced 6,867 aircraft between 1936–38. Germany produced 15,953 aircraft. In 1938 Germany was the most powerful state in Europe. A general war in Europe had to be avoided.

7. There are two major historiographical interpretations concerning appeasement:
   - **The Orthodox view:** Chamberlain was naive and fooled by Hitler. He made a major blunder in believing in agreements with a dictator like Hitler. Churchill said: *"There has never been a war more easy to stop"*.
   - **Revisionist view:** Chamberlain was of course, as Prime Minister, aware of Britain's military weakness and commitments to other parts of its colonial empire. By appeasement Britain gained time. These two years, 1938–39, were used for military preparations, which saved Britain.

Conclusion: It is possible to find support for each side and perhaps even to reach a compromise: Chamberlain hoped for the best, but prepared for the worst.

36. Compare and contrast the reasons for WW I and WW II.

(In a question like this you are supposed to show similarities and differences. Don't write the story of WW I, then the story of WW II, and then emphasise the similarities and the differences. You will not have time for this. Write one part showing similarities between the two wars and a second part, showing the differences.)

Similarities:

1. **Power vacuums and weak states**: in the Balkans there was a power vacuum and weak states due to the decline of the Ottoman Empire. Who would fill this vacuum and control the area? Austria, Russia or the Balkan states? It led to a conflict.

    The Paris Settlement had created a series of weak states in Central Europe with millions of Germans. This was easy for Hitler to take advantage of.

2. **German aggression**: Kaiser Wilhelm wanted Germany's 'rightful place in the sun'. He had introduced his Weltpolitik in the mid-1890s and provoked other states and encouraged Austria to fight down Serb aggression. According to Fritz Fischer he deliberately planned for WW I.

    Hitler was clearly the aggressor behind WW II. We can find support for this in *Mein Kampf*, the *Zweites Buch* and his actions. Trevor-Roper: *"Mein Kampf was a complete blueprint of his intended achievements".*

    The 'continuity-school' argues that both Kaiser Wilhelm and Hitler had a desire to expand German territories.

3. **Nationalism**: it affected the actions of most states before WW I: Austria, Serbia, France, Germany and Russia (pan-Slavism). To Hitler a unification of all Germans and the expansion of Lebensraum was of primary importance. *"We demand the union of all Germans"* was written in the Nazi Party Programme from 1920.

4. **Racism**: It is possible to see traces of racism in Kaiser Wilhelm's policies. He saw a battle between Germans and Tutons (Slavs) as the major battle to Germany. To Hitler it was Arians against Slavs and Jews. (However, see point 5 in 'Differences'.)

5. **National minorities** played an important role in both conflicts: Serbs in Bosnia and Germans in Austria, The Sudetenland and Poland were of major importance.

6. Both wars can to some extent be blamed on **dictators.** The Tsar, Kaiser Wilhelm, the Austrian Emperor, Hitler, Mussolini and Stalin were all to some extent dictators and played a role in these wars. There has never been a war between two democracies.

Differences:

1. It is easier to identify one **clear aggressor** in WW II: Hitler. It is possible to argue that it was more of a mixed responsibility behind WW I.

2. There **was nothing comparable to the Paris Settlement/Versailles** behind WW I. The 19th century had been a quite stable period.

3. There was nothing like **appeasement** or failure of the **League of Nations** before WW I.

4. The **alliance system** played a **more important role in WW I** than in WW II. It was, however, not without importance in WW II, i.e. Britain's and France's support for Poland

5. We can't compare the **racism** of Kaiser Wilhelm with that of **Hitler**. WW II was clearly a Social Darwinist and racial war, where Germans were going to expand at the expense of the Slavs. There was a difference in degree. This supports the **'break school'** comparing Kaiser Wilhelm's Germany and the Third Reich (see also questions about the Weimar Republic discussing the issue of continuity or break in German history).

6. **Domestic considerations** were more important in WW I. In Germany, Russia and Austria there was a feeling of going to war to preserve their empires related to problems within the empires. We don't see this pattern before WW II.

Conclusion: clearly there were both similarities and differences – and that is what you are supposed to outline in your answer. But it is interesting to notice and emphasise that in both cases there were **power vacuums/weak states** in which an aggressor wanted to expand into, very much due to **nationalism**.

Chapter 18: The origins of the Cold War 1945–49

Note that Paper 3 is related to an IB region – in this case, Europe. So, an answer in the exam must have a clear focus on Europe, even if the text in this guide occasionally tries to show a broader context.

Questions about the *reasons for the Cold War are frequent in IB exams*, in both paper 2 and paper 3.

If you analyse the questions it might be concluded that the main themes are:

- the Cold War was a result of WWII;
- it was a result of two different ideologies; or
- as a result of the development between 1945–49.

Historiography: this is a question where knowledge about different historiographical interpretations is very important. It invites you to be very analytical. Let's start by showing the main interpretations from a historiographical point of view.

ORIGINS OF THE COLD WAR

Orthodox view:	Stalin and communism was responsible for the Cold War. To Americans it was in the nature of communist ideology to make attempts to spread the ideal of communism. Marxist-Leninism was an expansionist, aggressive force and its aim was to 'liberate the masses' from capitalism. Stalin had also, throughout his career, clearly shown that he tolerated no rivals. His policy in Eastern Europe after the war is a very good example.
Revisionist view:	emerged from mainly American historians in the late 1960s. The US didn't realise how weak the Soviet Union was after WWII and how much stronger the Americans were. Russia had suffered enormously during WWII while the Americans not only experienced an economic boom, they also had a nuclear monopoly. Stalin realised Russia's weaknesses and his desire to control Eastern Europe was a defensive move to protect the USSR. How did the Americans use their superiority? They issued the Truman doctrine giving themselves a right to intervene everywhere. With the Marshall Aid programme and their economic 'open-door policy' they tried to control countries by economic dependence.

Post-revisionist view: with access to newly-released archives, a new school of Post-revisionist historians emerged in the late 1970s. The Cold War was a result of mutual misunderstanding and overreaction due to **fear**. The Americans didn't really understand the USSR's need for security against the West and its need for buffer-states and how their strength and 'open-door policy' affected the USSR.

The Russians were not aware of how their policy in Eastern Europe affected opinions in the West. It is clear that the development of nuclear weapons and their different ideologies resulted in a lot of mutual fear.

Defensive measures by one power were often seen as offensive by the other power. It was met by further measures and a dangerous cycle of actions and reaction came into being. The net outcome, especially if we take into account the development of nuclear weapons, was less security for both. This is called the **security dilemma**. So the Post-revisionist view argues that it was more miscalculations by both than aggression from one, i.e. a shared responsibility.

'Realpolitik' School: When discussing the Cold War it is clear that 'ideology' is a key word. It is therefore useful to be aware of the Realpolitik School, which dismisses the idea of the importance of ideology. It claims that many politicians act out of other reasons than ideology. Ideology is only an additional weapon deliberately used by the superpowers to rally the support of the nation. It is a propaganda tool and a mask used to get support while trying to fulfil their selfish interests. Economic pressure, military power and ideology were means used to achieve an aim. There are many examples where it is debatable whether ideology really was important. Examples of this might be the pact between the arch-enemies Germany and the Soviet Union in 1939 which led to WWII. Another example is Stalin's reluctance to support the communist side in the civil war in Greece in 1947 or, and this is a very good example, the US and Nixon's co-operation with both Red China and the USSR in the 1970s. Ideology did not matter as long as co-operation served a purpose. But it must also be noticed that to some politicians ideology might be very important.

18.1 Possible explanations for the Cold War

18.1.1 The Cold War as a result of two different ideologies

To be able to assess the importance of these ideologies, you need to be able to describe them. It is clear that the USSR's Marxism-Leninism and the USA's western liberalism, opposed each other in every vital aspect.

Political life: There was a multi-party system in the US, i.e. alternatives in elections, and in the USSR there was a single-party system. The communist party was considered to represent the masses so there was no need for other parties.

Economic life: In the US there was a market economy with private capitalism. The US also wanted an 'open-door' policy, where every state should be open to free trade. In the USSR it was a state-owned economy and a planned economy. The USSR thought that workers in capitalist countries were economically oppressed and should be 'liberated'.

Religion: In the US religion has a strong position even if religion is separated from the state. In the USSR the regime opposed the influence of the church and officially Marxism and the Soviet state were atheists.

Civil rights: Freedom of speech, the press, of worship i.e. individual rights, are considered as cornerstones in the constitution. In the USSR the state controlled the press. Officially this was 'the dictatorship of the proletariat' – the state ensured that media were controlled by the majority. Russians criticised the US for allowing a minority, i.e. rich capitalists, to control media. Consequently both accused the other side for having no individual freedom.

Consequently these two systems opposed each other in every vital aspect. **Both systems also wanted to expand.** The US thought that open societies with free trade were the best alternative. The USSR and the communist side thought that the masses were oppressed by capitalists in the west and should be liberated from this. **With two fundamentally different systems where each wanted to expand, a clash was inevitable.** This supports the view that the Cold War was a result of two different ideologies.

18.1.2 The Cold War as a result of WWII

Communism came to power already in 1917 in Russia. Even if there was tension between these two systems well before WWII, it must be concluded that the post-1945 development was very different. This has resulted in some historians wanting to emphasise the **effects of the war** as a driving force behind this conflict.

Remember that officially the two superpowers were allies during the war:

1. The war resulted in two victorious superpowers with totally opposing ideologies.
2. One of them had a nuclear monopoly.
3. **The USSR had suffered** enormously from WWII: 25 million people were killed, 1,700 cities and 70,000 villages were in ruins, 70% of its industries and 60% of its transportation facilities destroyed.
4. The US had experienced a wartime **economic boom** and industrial output increased by 90%.
5. Germany was crushed politically and economically when the war ended. There was an enormous power vacuum in the centre of Europe.
6. The Red Army had liberated and controlled most of Eastern Europe.
7. In Asia Japan had occupied **Korea, China, and Indochina**. Both Korea and Vietnam should be temporarily divided and later unified. Would it work? Would the civil war in China continue?
8. Events from the war had soured relations:

    (a) Even though the US and the USSR had been allies during WWII there were reasons for distrust not only from a political and ideological point of view. The USSR had signed the **Nazi-Soviet Pact** in 1939. The question of a **second front** in Europe had divided the allies. Stalin wanted help to ease the burden of the Red Army. It was not until 1944 that the Western powers finally invaded France. Was it a deliberate move to let the USSR bleed to death? For every American who was killed, 90 Russians died (300,000 compared to 25–30 million).

    (b) The War ended with the Americans dropping atomic bombs at **Hiroshima and Nagasaki**. The USSR had promised to join the Americans in defeating Japan, now the Americans dropped the bomb without informing their major ally. *"It was the last battle of WWII and the first battle of the Cold War"*.

Finally, there were two wartime conferences, which had a major importance, in Yalta and Potsdam.

18. THE ORIGINS OF THE COLD WAR 1945–49

Figure 18.1: **Atomic bomb mushroom clouds over Hiroshima (left) and Nagasaki (right)**

Yalta February 1945

Poland: the border was moved 300 kilometres to the West (Oder-Neisse line). A compromise was reached over the future government when Stalin promised that some members of the London government (pro-western) should join the Lublin government (pro-Soviet). **The Declaration on Liberated Europe** was signed by Stalin and the US, promising free elections in countries liberated from the Nazis.

Japan: Stalin promised to help the Americans in defeating Japan and to declare war two to three months after the war had ended in Europe.

United Nations: a renewed attempt at collective security was agreed upon and Molotov would attend the first meeting at San Francisco in April 1945.

Germany: should be de-Nazified and was divided into four zones of occupation: American, Russian, British, and French. Berlin was also divided into zones of occupation, which would later lead to the Berlin problem of a separate western zone within the eastern zone. Germany was to be governed by an Allied Control Commission with veto right to each power. The reparation issue was not solved but handed over to a Reparation Commission.

Yalta is *normally considered as a success*.

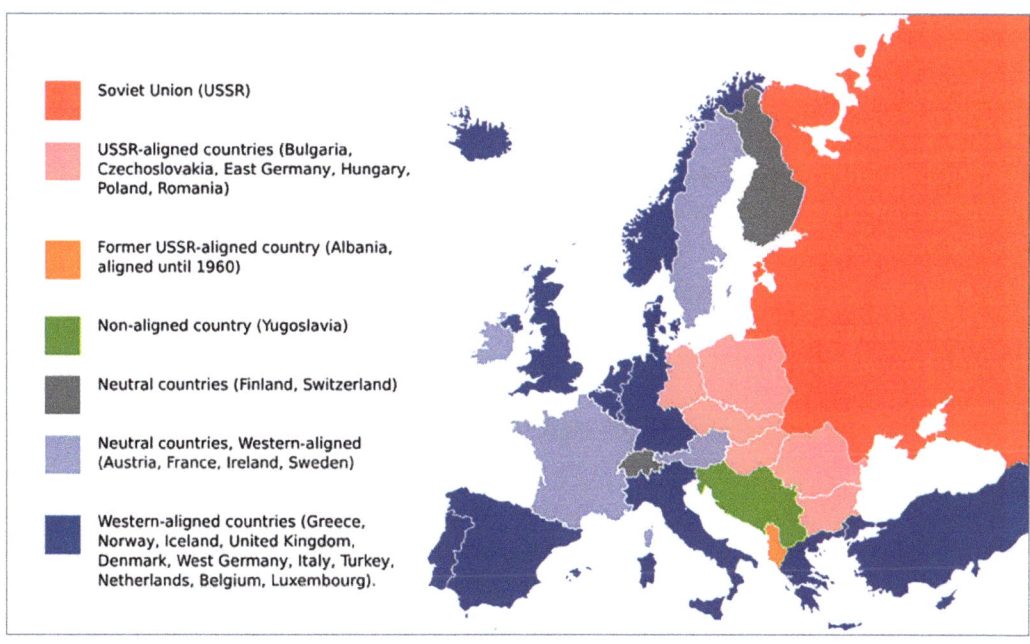

Figure 18.2: **Cold War map of Eastern and Western Blocs in Europe**

Potsdam July 1945

The war in Europe had now ended but Japan did not surrender until August 1945.

Reparations: No agreement was reached over reparations. Russia demanded some $20 billion from Germany, which was rejected by the Western powers. Russia was left to take what they could from their zone of occupation. Agreements made over Berlin which was a Western island in the Eastern Bloc.

Eastern Europe: Western leaders voiced objections to client governments set up by Stalin in Eastern Europe. There were 'sharp exchanges' and the West claimed that Stalin didn't follow the spirit of the **Declaration on Liberated Europe**.

Japan: The Potsdam Proclamation called for the unconditional surrender of Japan. Truman knew at Potsdam that the Bomb would work and wanted to end the conflict on his own terms. Stalin was prepared to take part in the defeat of Japan and did not desire a quick Japanese surrender.

Vietnam and Korea: Agreements were made to divide the countries temporarily and then unify them later. These two solutions did not work and it led to the two worst armed conflicts of the Cold War.

The Potsdam conference in *normally described as a failure,* with many disputes. Some historians even see the Potsdam meeting as the start of the Cold War.

18.2 Key developments following WWII

1946

Leaders in the West were deeply worried about the development in **Eastern Europe**: harassment, terror, and rigged elections produced a communist single party rule in countries like Bulgaria, Romania, Poland, and Hungary in 1946–47. It was a clear violation of the Declaration on Liberated Europe. In **China the Civil War** had restarted and in the south of China, in **Vietnam** a full-scale war between the French and Vietnamese communists and nationalists Việt Minh started. In 1946 we can see signs of a changing attitude in the West.

February: George Kennan's Long Telegram, a report written by a US diplomat which was widely circulated within US bureaucracy. It provided the intellectual basis for the 'doctrine' of containment', i.e. no long-term co-operation possible with the Soviet regime. Communism must be contained within its present borders. Marxist USSR was described as *"more dangerous and insidious than ever before."*

March: Churchill's Iron Curtain Speech appealed for a renewal of the Anglo-American alliance as a means of deterring Soviet expansionism. Revisionist historians argue that it was now that Stalin definitely decided to 'satellite' Eastern Europe.

In his **Stuttgart Speech the US Secretary of State Byrnes** announced that from September 1946 US would support for a revival of Germany, politically, and economically. *"The German people [...] should now be given the primary responsibility for the running of their own affairs."*

1947

In 1947 President Truman announced his **Truman Doctrine**. It was a **major turning point in US foreign policy** where isolationism and hesitancy towards the Soviet Union was replaced by containment of communism and a more active role in world affairs. It was intended originally for Greece and Turkey but was soon extended globally. It was the official start of the Cold War. *"One way of life is based upon the will of the majority....The second way of life is based upon the will of a minority. It relies upon terror and oppression...it must be the policy of the United States to support peoples who are resisting attempted subjugation by armed minorities or by outside pressures."*

18. THE ORIGINS OF THE COLD WAR 1945–49

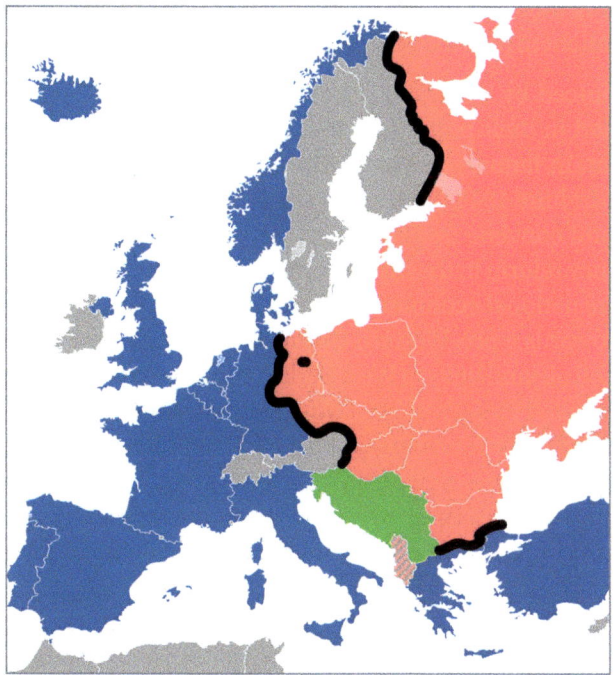

Figure 18.3: **The Iron Curtain depicted as a black line.**
Warsaw Pact countries on one side of the Iron Curtain appear shaded red; NATO members on the other are shaded blue. The black dot represents Berlin.
Militarily-neutral countries are shaded grey.
Yugoslavia, although communist-ruled, remained largely independent of the two major blocs and is shaded green. Communist Albania broke off contacts with the Soviet Union in the early 1960s, aligning itself with the People's Republic of China after the Sino-Soviet split; it appears red with grey-striped hatching.

The new American Secretary of state General George Marshall visited Europe in 1947 and was appalled at the economic situation in the Western democracies. **Communist parties** in these states had attracted substantial **support** in elections after the war. A major economic crisis might lead to a slump that **would affect America also** and it could make the Western democracies **succumb to communism**. The US now announced **the Marshall Aid programme** with economic aid to Europe. Marshall stated: *"Our policy is directed not against any country or doctrine, but against hunger, poverty, desperation and chaos."*

Initially it was offered to the USSR and its satellites, but it was soon rejected by Stalin. The USSR saw American aid as an attempt to create **economic dependence** that later would lead to political control, i.e. a new form of economic imperialism.

1948

Yugoslavia had been liberated from Nazi control by Yugoslav partisans under the leadership of Josip Broz Tito. After the war Stalin tried to impose his plans for economic development in Yugoslavia, i.e. to concentrate on heavy industry. Tito resisted this policy and took initiatives to form a customs union with Bulgaria and Hungary. Stalin could not allow this form of 'national communism' and withdrew his economic and military advisors from Yugoslavia. In June Yugoslavia was expelled from Comintern, the international communist organisation, accused of 'bourgeois nationalism'. The Eastern Bloc now announced an economic blockade and broke off their diplomatic relations. **Yugoslavia was expelled from the Eastern Bloc** but Tito and his regime had considerable support. The US also offered considerable financial assistance.

In Czechoslovakia the communist party had genuine support and governed the country in a coalition with non-communist parties. 'The ghost of Munich' – the betrayal by the Western democracies in 1938 – had not been forgotten. In 1947 the country suffered from an economic crisis and the communist party feared that it would affect its chances in the 1948 elections. After disputes within the government regarding nationalisation of industries, non-communist ministers resigned. The Prime Minister formed a new National Front government with only communists and reliable supporters. When elections eventually took place, the communists got 237 of 300 seats in the parliament and soon all other parties were dissolved. **The only country in the Eastern Bloc with a genuine multi-party system had now been transformed to a single party state.**

In the West and in the US this confirmed the view of the 'hard-liners'. The **coup in Czechoslovakia** helped the US government to pass the Marshall Aid Programme in Congress.

In accordance with the policy announced by Byrnes in his Stuttgart Speech in 1946, the Western occupation powers proceeded in their policy of a revival of Germany. The USSR feared and opposed this development. In January 1947, the US and the British zones had been merged into one zone, Bizonia. In June 1948 the US and some other European states recommended that an assembly should convene from the West German Länder to draft a constitution. The same month a currency reform in the three Western Zones was announced. A single Western currency required one national economic policy, which again was opposed by the USSR. It was an obvious step towards a pro-Western German state, according to the Russians. On 23 June the Russians cut off all land links to West Berlin. The city was a capitalist island surrounded by the Russian controlled Eastern zone. Two million West Berliners were now cut off from power, coal, and food. Western leaders, hypnotised by Russian strength, feared an attack on the Western zone of Berlin, and even on the rest of Germany. The Berliners were made a symbol of freedom and the Western powers now started an **airlift**, which supplied two million people with food and other necessities until the blockade was called off in May 1949.

1949

The Berlin Blockade made it clear that the 'two' Germanys established in the years prior could not co-operate.

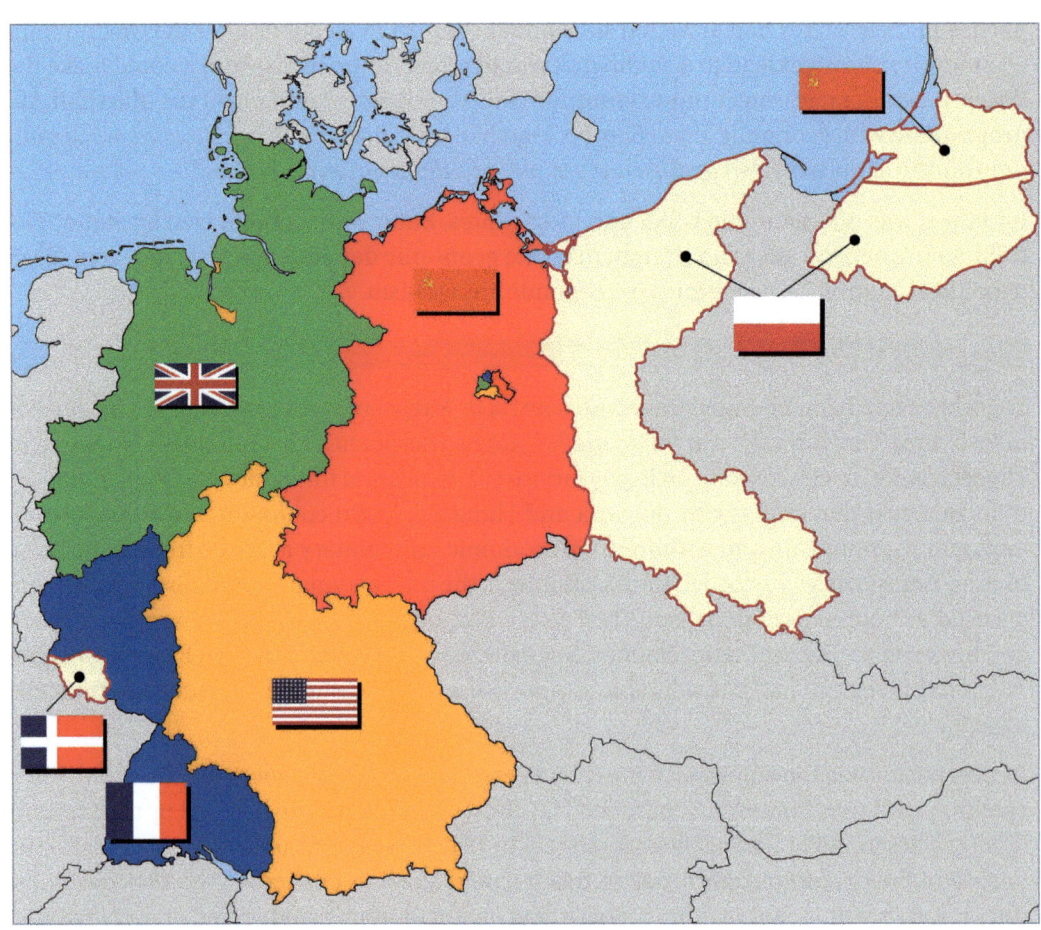

Figure 18.4: **Occupation zone borders in Germany, 1947.**
The territories east of the Oder-Neisse line, under Polish and Soviet administration/annexation, are shown as white as it is the likewise detached Saar Protectorate. Berlin is the multinational area within the Soviet zone.

18. THE ORIGINS OF THE COLD WAR 1945–49

The first West German parliament was elected in August 1949 and the government took office in September. **West Germany** was now an independent state. The Soviets answered by supporting the formation of an independent **East Germany** in October the same year.

The Berlin Blockade had also increased the military insecurity in the West. In April 1949 the North Atlantic Treaty Organization, **NATO**, was formed.

In August 1949 the **USSR** exploded their first **atomic bomb**. It came as a shock to the Americans who had expected it would be at least ten years before a Russian A-bomb was developed. In October, the **most populous state in the world, China**, fell to 'godless communism'. Truman's message about 'armed minorities' in his speech to Congress, when announcing his doctrine in 1947, can be questioned if we refer to China. Mao had mobilised millions of peasants in the struggle against the Nationalists. South of China, the Viêt Minh was fighting French forces and a re-unification of Korea had failed. The Cold War was expanding globally.

 1950

In early 1950, the National Security Council (NSC) delivered a classified report to the Truman administration known as the **NSC-68** report. It stated, *"Soviet efforts are now directed towards the domination of the Eurasian land mass"* and **recommended a massive US build-up of both conventional and nuclear arms**. It can be seen as a response to an expected increase in Russian aggression as a nuclear power and the 'loss' of China. A dominant economy was not enough, the US needed to be militarily superior to meet the challenge of communism: the US should develop a hydrogen bomb. The problem was that this policy would require higher taxes, causing domestic problems for Truman. **In June, North Korea suddenly attacked South Korea and this is considered a turning point in the Cold War.** It was assumed that Stalin had ordered Kim to attack and Soviet aggression would follow in other countries (the Domino Theory). The recommendations of NSC-68 were now implemented and **US defence spending went from $13 billion in 1950 to $50 billion** within a few years. The Cold War was now a global conflict. The Russian A-bomb, the 'loss' of China and the Korean War provided Senator Joseph McCarthy with ammunition for his witch-hunt in the US in the early 1950s.

37. To what extent was the Cold War a result of WWII?

(Structure: Write one part to show how the result of the war led to problems after the war and a second part claiming that even without these events, there would have been a Cold War anyway.)

The war caused problems between the US and the USSR because:

1. The war resulted in **two victorious superpowers** with opposing **ideologies**.
2. Nuclear bombs and rocket technology were a result of WWII and one of them had a **nuclear monopoly**.
3. **The USSR had suffered** enormously from WWII: 25 million people were killed, 1,700 cities and 70,000 villages were in ruins, 70% of its industries and 60% of its transportation facilities destroyed.
4. The US had experienced a wartime economic boom.
5. **Germany** did not exist politically and economically when the war ended. There was an enormous **power vacuum** in the centre of Europe.
6. The **Red Army had liberated and controlled most of Eastern Europe**.
7. In Asia, Japan had occupied **Korea, China and Indochina**. Both Korea and Vietnam should be temporarily divided and later unified. Would it work? Would the civil war in China continue? The outcome had a profound effect worldwide, i.e. also in Europe.

8. There had also been disputes during the war: The Molotov-Ribbentrop Pact and the question of a second front. It would affect the relations between the two superpowers after the war.

9. In general, it can be argued that the ideological differences were clear from 1917. There was tension after 1917 but not a global Cold War conflict, which started *after* 1945. So we need to ask what changes were produced by WWII.

There would have been some kind of Cold War even without WWII

1. These two systems were **so fundamentally different**, opposing each other in every vital aspect, that there would have been a conflict even without the war. Support your point by describing the differences in their ideologies. The ideological differences are important parts of the second part of the essay and try to make the most out of the differences.

2. You can support point one above by showing that there **had been major problems before WWII,** which we can clearly link to distrust. The Western Powers had intervened in the **Russian Civil War**, officially to re-open the Eastern front. When the war ended, and when there was no need for this second front, the Western powers continued to fight the Bolsheviks. There are even historians who argue that this was the beginning of the Cold War. The US did not recognise the USSR diplomatically until Roosevelt became President in 1932. The **Munich Agreement** from 1938 had clearly shown how Western capitalist states (but not the US) distrusted the USSR. The USSR also made several attempts to form some **co-operation with the Western powers against Germany**, but did not meet a positive attitude from the Western powers.

3. There were events after the war, which revealed how much distrust there was between these two systems, that were not a result of WWII. **The Civil War in China** had started in 1927 and continued after the war. It shows us that the conflict was not only a result of WWII. The decolonisation process where some states turned to communism, was not a direct result of WWII. One example is the Vietnam War. It can be argued that this war started due to post-war problems, but the underlying problem was deeper, i.e. the appeal of communism in poor agricultural countries and a will to maintain colonial empires.

4. **Development of nuclear weapons** would probably have taken longer without WWII.

Conclusion: It is clear that we can link many post-war conflicts to the war. But it can be argued that there would have been conflicts in the long run, even without the war due to the fact that these systems were so fundamentally different.

38. "The Cold War was a clash between two irreconcilable ideologies." To what extent do you agree with this statement?

(Structure: in the first part of the essay you show that you do believe that the Cold War was a result of two different ideologies and in the second part you show that it had nothing to do with ideology.)

Yes, ideology was important:

1. **Explain their ideologies**: a **Marxist** believes that the masses are exploited by a rich class of capitalists and that religion is a part of the superstructure, enabling this oppression. The ultimate aim of Marxism is to liberate the masses worldwide from this oppression. In the immediate aftermath of the revolution of the working class, a period of 'dictatorship of the proletariat' is necessary, i.e. the masses exercise a dictatorship against the few, until they realise the benefit of socialism. During this period, freedom of press etc. must be restricted.

2. If you believe in a **market economy and a western style of democracy** there must be free elections with more than one alternative, freedom of speech, worship, and assembly.

18. THE ORIGINS OF THE COLD WAR 1945-49

You are also positive to private ownership and private companies and want free trade between states i.e. an 'open-door policy'. We can conclude that these two systems opposed each other in every vital aspect.

3. To a **Marxist** or a representative of the Soviet system the US primary aim was to make the world open for trade, i.e. economic imperialism. By making other areas economically dependent, they would later be politically controlled. The capitalists also needed new markets for expansion. This was prevented by the socialist camp with hostility being expected. American attempts to rebuild Germany was a policy directed against the USSR. Germany was a bulwark against communism in Europe. **The Truman Doctrine** was a doctrine aiming at securing territories for the capitalists and to prevent the spread of communism. The communist camp prevented the imperialists from expanding. **The Marshall Aid Programme** was of course a policy to make other states economically dependent on the US and then later politically controlled. The struggle between the two camps during the Cold War, in Germany, Greece, Eastern Europe, Korea or China, must be seen in this light.

4. To an American who genuinely believed in civil rights and privately-owned companies etc., the development in Soviet-controlled areas was of course unacceptable. The state controlled the press, persecuted the church and nationalised the economy. It is easy to find support for this: in Poland the Peasants' Party and Prime Minister Mikolajczyk were subjected to harassment, coercion and terror, and the elections in 1947 were manipulated by the communists. In Hungary the KGB arrested deputies from the Smallholders' Party. The Prime Minister was blackmailed into resigning and the country was soon a single party state. In both Bulgaria and Romania elections were rigged. It was a clear **violation of the Declaration on Liberated Europe from Yalta**.

These were two fundamentally different systems and both wanted to expand. This explains the Cold War.

No, it was not due to ideology:

1. The '**Realpolitik school**' argues that politicians may act out of other reasons than ideology. If a state gains from co-operation with the 'enemy', and coexists with this enemy, both states may benefit from it. Was Stalin driven by ideology or were there other reasons behind his policy? His pact with Germany in 1939 and his lack of support for the communists in Greece may indicate this. The Americans also gave substantial support to the USSR during the war indicating that ideology perhaps was not the main driving force.

2. It is also possible to bring in arguments from the **post-revisionist school**. The main element in explaining the Cold War is mutual misunderstanding due to fear. The 'fear' is perhaps possible to link to strong ideological beliefs; but it was also fear of nuclear weapons. This fear linked to nuclear weapons was 'the driving force' behind the Cold War, and consequently ideology was less important.

Conclusion: It may be argued that there were other reasons for the Cold War than just ideology and if it had been mainly an ideological dispute, the Cold War should have started in 1917 and not in 1945–47. But ideological differences are important in explaining the origins of the Cold War.

39. By referring to events from the period 1945–49, discuss how historians have explained who was responsible for the Cold War.

(Use a historiographical approach. Account for, or list, the orthodox school, the revisionist school, the post revisionist school, and support each school with different events.)

The Orthodox Western school

1. **The Orthodox Western view**: Stalin and communism was responsible for the Cold War. To Americans it was in the nature of communist ideology to make attempts to spread the ideal of communism. Marxist-Leninism was an expansionist, aggressive force in its desire to 'liberate the masses' from capitalism. Stalin had also, throughout his career, clearly shown that he tolerated no rivals. His policy in Eastern Europe after the war is a very good example. At Yalta he had signed the Declaration on Liberated Europe promising free elections in Eastern Europe. In Poland the Peasants' Party and Prime Minister Mikolajczyk were subjected to harassment, coercion and terror and the elections in 1947 were manipulated by the communists. In Hungary the KGB arrested deputies from the Smallholders' Party. The Prime Minister was blackmailed to resign and the country was soon a single-party state. In both Bulgaria and Romania, elections were rigged.

   His desire to control other areas could also be seen in Czechoslovakia in 1948, The Berlin Airlift, the support for Kim Il Sun in attacking South Korea in 1950.

   Kennan, who knew the Russians better than most Americans, was right when he described the USSR as *"more dangerous and insidious than ever before"*.

2. **The Revisionist view** emerged mainly from American historians in the late 60s. The US didn't realise how weak the Soviet Union was after WW II and how much stronger the Americans were. Russia had suffered enormously during WW II. 25 million people were killed, 1,700 cities and 70,000 villages were in ruins, 70% of its industries and 60% of its transportation facilities were destroyed. The Americans not only experienced an economic boom; they also had a nuclear monopoly. Stalin realised Russia's weaknesses and his desire to control Eastern Europe was a defensive move to protect the USSR. How did the Americans use their superiority? They issued the Truman Doctrine giving them a right to intervene everywhere. With Marshall Aid and their economic 'open door policy' they tried to control countries by economic dependence. This aggressive policy by the US is the main explanation to the Cold War.

3. **The Post-revisionist view**: with access to new archives a new school of post-revisionist historians emerged in the late 1970s. The Cold War was a result of mutual misunderstanding and overreaction due to fear. The Americans didn't really understand the USSR's need for security against the West and its need for buffer-states and how their strength and 'open-door policy' affected the USSR. The Russians were not aware of how their policy in Eastern Europe affected opinions in the West. It is clear that the development of nuclear weapons and their different ideologies resulted in a lot of mutual fear. Defensive measures by one power were often seen as offensive by the other power. It was met by further measures and a dangerous cycle of action and reaction came into being. The net outcome, especially if we take into account the development of nuclear weapons, was less security for both. This is called the **security dilemma**. So the post-revisionist view argues that it was more miscalculations by both than aggression from one that led to The Cold War.

   (The Realpolitik school does not provide us with an explanation to the Cold War. It is more a rejection of using ideology as an explanation to conflicts.)

Conclusion: Summarise the main points of these three schools. The question does not ask for your opinion.

Chapter 19: Khrushchev

Issues

How shall we describe his foreign policy? It combined both confrontation and détente. What judgement shall we make about his domestic policy?

19.1 The transition from Stalin to Khrushchev

When Stalin died in 1953 there was no clear successor and a **collective leadership** emerged with Malenkov and Khrushchev as the most prominent leaders. In 1955 Malenkov was ousted by his rival Khrushchev. The new leadership opened up for new opportunities in the Cold War during the years 1953–56.

- An armistice was signed in **Korea** in 1953.
- In 1954 a peace conference was arranged at **Geneva** to deal with the **Indo-China** War, under the chairmanship of the USSR and Britain.
- In 1955 there was a Great Power summit in Geneva between the USSR, the US, Britain, and France. The leaders met for the first time since Potsdam 1945. The new and positive atmosphere was referred to as **'the spirit of Geneva'**.
- In 1955 the occupational forces of **Austria** decided to end the occupation and re-establish full independence of the country. This had not been possible in countries like Germany and Korea. Soviet troops were also withdrawn from Finland.
- Khrushchev started to **reduce the size of the Red Army** unilaterally (without the other side doing it). Khrushchev continued this reduction in the late 1950s and reduced the size of the Red Army from 3.6 to 2.4 million men.
- Khrushchev went to **Yugoslavia** in 1955 to heal the rift between the two states and to show that the USSR could accept the existence of a communist regime not totally controlled by Moscow, a clear break with Stalin's policies.

19.2 Khrushchev's Secret Speech

In 1956, it was time for Khrushchev to take a new and very dramatic step at the 20th Party Congress. In a speech, which became known as the **Secret Speech**, he revealed all the crimes committed by Stalin and denounced him as a leader. The speech, which took a weekend to deliver, focused on four main areas:

1. The truth about the **terror** in the 1930s was revealed and Stalin's personal responsibility was shown.
2. Stalin's capacity as a **wartime** leader was ridiculed.
3. Stalin's **failures in foreign policy** especially in Eastern Europe were outlined.

4. Khrushchev also declared that he believed in **peaceful co-existence** with the capitalist West. To an orthodox Marxist, and to Lenin and Stalin, this would have been an unacceptable departure from Marx's ideas of the inevitability of a clash between capitalist and socialist countries. The reason for Khrushchev's new policy was the existence of nuclear weapons, which made a war unthinkable.

It was an amazing and a very dramatic speech especially if we take into account that most delegates had been involved in the purges themselves and made a career in dead man's shoes. Khrushchev himself had definitely been very active in the purges in Moscow and the Ukraine.

Why did Khrushchev make an unexpected move?

1. It was probably a way to **absolve himself** and other leaders from the crimes committed in the past. One day the truth would be exposed anyway, and it would be dangerous politically. He said to the other leaders before the speech: *"If we don't tell the truth at the Congress, we'll be forced to tell the truth some time in the future. And then we shan't be the speech-makers; no, then we'll be the people under investigation"* – so he wasn't motivated on moral grounds.

2. It was a way to re-establish the **authority of the Communist Party** which had been eroded by Stalin's reign of terror (one example is that 98 out of 139 members of the Central Committee which had been elected in 1934, were later executed)

3. By making a clear break with the Stalin era, it was easier **to justify a new policy**. Khrushchev wanted to introduce a new economic policy and the idea of peaceful co-existence with the capitalist West was a total break with orthodox Marxist/Bolshevik policies.

Consequences:

1. Mao saw the denunciation of the great leader in the USSR as an indirect attack on China's 'great leader': **Mao** himself. Some argue that this made Mao introduce the Hundred Flowers Campaign in China and as a result, Mao developed a negative attitude to Khrushchev which would lead to the Sino-Soviet split.

2. When Khrushchev talked about Yugoslavia he said *"we have found a new proper solution"* to the relation between the two states (Yugoslavia was not controlled by Moscow). This encouraged **Poland** to seek independence from the USSR but after pressure from the Soviets they remained within the Eastern Bloc. In Hungary the new leader Imre Nagy announced that free elections soon should be allowed and that the country was planning to leave the Warsaw Pact. This made Khrushchev order the Red Army to crush the **Hungarian Uprising** with military power in 1956. Nagy was executed. This development brought an end to the '**Spirit of Geneva**'.

3. In 1957 there was an attempted **coup** by orthodox party leaders who had never accepted Khrushchev's attack on Stalin in 1956 and who blamed Khrushchev for the development especially in Hungary. The image of the USSR suffered from the violence in Hungary and many blamed Khrushchev for this.

4. We must not forget the psychological dimension of the Secret speech. The Soviet historian Dmitri Volkogonov would later estimate the number of victims due to Stalin's policies to 21 million. To speak openly about these crimes and the responsibility for it, must have had enormous consequences in all aspect of the Soviet society. De-Stalinisation brought an end of terror to the USSR, which of course totally changed this country. **This is the most important legacy of Khrushchev's rule**.

Another thing worth emphasising with the new leadership was the **Khrushchev Thaw**. Censorship in the Soviet Union was relaxed, and millions of Soviet political prisoners were released from Gulag labour camps. In nine months, after the Party Congress in 1956, 617,000 prisoners in the Gulag system were allowed to leave the prison camp system.

19.3 Economic policies

Khrushchev made real attempts to reform **agriculture**. The state now started to pay higher prices on grains to the farms and taxes were reduced. The machine tractor stations, which had supported the collective farms with machinery, were abolished. Between 1952 and 1958, farm workers' incomes more than doubled, but they were still paid less than industrial workers.

Khrushchev has, however, been most remembered for his **Virgin Land Policy**, introduced in 1954. Previously unused farmland in southern Siberia and Kazakhstan was used and 250,000 volunteers were mobilised together with 120,000 tractors, when six million acres were ploughed. It developed into a fiasco. The reasons included:

- crops were sown in **unsuitable soil**;
- the **climate** was not optimal;
- not enough **fertilisers** were available;
- **poor planning and management**.

In 1963 poor weather conditions in combination with the land being exhausted and under-fertilised, led to a dramatic **harvest failure**. The USSR, once the leading export nation of grains in the world (early 20th century), had to buy large quantities of grains from Australia and the US, to avoid a famine. This damaged Khrushchev's reputation and it is not a coincidence that he was overthrown the following year.

The industry should use more light engineering and produce more consumer goods, and chemicals. While Stalin had used coercions, **Khrushchev offered incentives**. Khrushchev realised that bureaucracy, the planners and decision makers, had grown far too much. Decisions had to be **decentralised and bureaucracy streamlined**. Economically this was a correct policy but by cutting down bureaucracy at central level and moving the nomenklatura (party officials) to the regions, he provoked powerful interests within the party. It must also be noted that the USSR took a lead in space technology and when the first **satellite was sent into space in 1957** and the first manned space flight in 1961, it not only shocked the US, it also represents the absolute high point in the history of the USSR.

Many production results from this period, except for agriculture, are very impressive:

- industrial production increased by 96% between 1958 and 1965;
- Gross National Income rose by 58% during the same period.

Another way of looking at the Khrushchev era is to study the growth rate of the GNP annually over four decades. The GNP growth was around 10% annually in the 1950s. It was 7% in the 1960s and fell to 5% in the 1970s. In the early 1980s, the growth was around 3%.

19.4 Trouble spots in foreign policy

It was not only Hungary that was problematic for Khrushchev to deal with. He had also inherited the **Berlin problem**. The Western zones in Berlin were a capitalist island within the Eastern zone. The US was pumping money into their Western zone and in Berlin the disparity in terms of economic conditions was problematic. In eight years, after 1949, two million refugees fled from East Germany to the West. It was a drainage which East Germany could not survive in the long run.

In 1958, Khrushchev gave the United States, the United Kingdom and France six months to conclude a peace treaty with the two German states and the Soviet Union. If no such agreement was signed the Soviet Union would conclude a peace treaty with East Germany. This would leave East Germany in control of the routes to the city. It would force the US to deal with a state they refused to recognise. Khrushchev's ultimatum was a method to put pressure on the US to solve the Berlin problem. The ultimatum created an international crisis but Khrushchev repeatedly extended the deadline, which resulted in this **Second Berlin**

Crisis dying out. In 1961, he again announced that the Berlin problem must be solved and the Western powers should leave. This only increased the flight of refugees until the regime ordered the erection of the **Berlin Wall**. While the wall in the West became a symbol of communist policies it was described in the East as the Anti-Fascist Wall – a protection. The practical outcome of the wall was in many ways that the tension actually decreased, i.e. the refugee situation was less acute.

In 1959, Khrushchev went on a much-publicised trip to the US. The relationship with the other superpower was never without problems, but Khrushchev realised that the cost of the army must be reduced and concluded that the trip to the US made détente possible. In January 1960 Khrushchev ordered a **reduction of one-third in the size of Soviet armed forces**, arguing that advanced weapons would make up for the lost troops. This further alienated key groups in the Soviet nomenklatura and gave Khrushchev powerful enemies.

In April 1959 a **US U-2 spy aircraft** was shot down over the USSR. It put Khrushchev in a dilemma. In May, a summit meeting was planned in Paris and the US claimed that it was a weather plane, but the Soviets had captured the pilot alive and had the wreckage. To not react would provoke the Soviet army. When Khrushchev made it public and the US president refused to apologise, Khrushchev left the summit meeting in anger.

Another trouble spot was China. In 1960 when Soviet technicians were withdrawn from China, the split became official. Khrushchev did his best from the beginning and substantial aid was given to China from 1953. The historian William Kirby describes it as *"the largest transfer of technology in world history"* but it didn't help. There were many reasons for the Sino-Soviet split.

1. To some extent it probably had to do with the question of **world leadership** of the communist movement. With the Great Leap Forward, China was trying to find its own path to communism, which challenged Moscow.
2. On a **personal level** Mao and Khrushchev didn't get along very well.
3. Mao had expected much better terms when he signed the **Sino-Soviet treaty** with Stalin in 1950.
4. Mao disliked Khrushchev's **de-Stalinisation** policies and especially the Secret Speech was seen as an indirect attack on Mao.
5. Mao strongly disliked Khrushchev's talk about **peaceful co-existence and détente** with the capitalist enemy.
6. The critical question in the relation was Mao's request to get access to the **A-bomb**. Khrushchev was prepared to give such assistance provided that the A-bombs were controlled by the USSR.

Khrushchev's worst problem was, however, Cuba; Fidel Castro had seized power in a revolution in 1959. In 1961, the US tried to overthrow the regime in the Bay of Pigs invasion. The same year Castro declared himself a Marxist-Leninist. The following year Khrushchev made a drastic move and started **secretly to place nuclear missiles in** Cuba. Why?

1. He wanted to **protect the Cuban revolution.**
2. He would gain prestige in the **Third World** by protecting a small nation against an aggressive superpower. Khrushchev talked about creating *"many Vietnams"*. There were many countries in **Latin America** where a communist revolution could be spread.
3. He would **reduce the Soviets inferiority in terms of nuclear weapons**. The US had 100 intercontinental ballistic missiles (ICBM) and 1,700 intercontinental bombers at the time. The USSR had only 50 ICBMs and 150 bombers. An intermediate range missile in Cuba would reach major cities in the US and compensate for the lack of ICBMs.
4. It could give the USSR a **bargaining position**, which could be used in Berlin or elsewhere.

19. KHRUSHCHEV

After a 13-day crisis in autumn 1962 the issue was resolved. The USSR promised to **withdraw the missiles** if the US promised:

- **not to invade Cuba**;
- to remove missiles from **Turkey**. This part of the deal was secret because the US could not openly admit that NATO missiles aimed at protecting Turkey had been part of a deal to secure US protection.

In the USSR, and especially in the Red Army, it was seen as a humiliation to withdraw the missiles and bow to US demands. In reality, however, it can be argued that Khrushchev made a very good deal: Cuba would be protected from a US invasion, which was probably Khrushchev's main goal. Consequences of the crisis:

1. The US was forced to tolerate a **communist state in the Caribbean**.
2. The time had come for a **more constructive dialogue**. The crisis had a profound sobering effect on the nuclear powers.
3. A **Test Ban Treaty** was signed in 1963 forbidding nuclear testing in the atmosphere.
4. A **Hotline** – a direct telephone line – was established between the White House and the Kremlin.
5. **Khrushchev** was criticised not only by Mao in China but also in Moscow. In 1964 he was forced to resign. The Cuban crisis was one important factor behind his **dismissal**.
6. With a longer perspective it led to renewed **Soviet efforts to close the missile gap**. The consequence was an extensive and very expensive Soviet nuclear build-up as shown in the following table, which would have far-reaching consequences for the Soviet economy.

		1964	1966	1968	1970	1972
US	ICBM	834	904	1054	1054	1054
	SLBM	416	592	656	656	656
	ICB	630	630	545	550	455
USSR	ICBM	200	300	800	1300	1527
	SLBM	120	125	130	280	560
	ICB	190	200	150	150	140

ICBM = intercontinental ballistic missile
SLBM = submarine-launched ballistic missile
ICB = intercontinental bombers

When Khrushchev was forced to resign in 1964 the Central Committee used its power to depose the leader. The reasons for his resignation were:

1. The policy of **streamlining the bureaucracy and cutting down the size of the Red Army** had given him many enemies within the nomenklatura.
2. His **de-Stalinisation** policies and especially the Secret Speech can also be seen in this light. It provoked party hard-liners.
3. **Peaceful co-existence** was a departure from orthodox Marxism and this also provoked party hard-liners and Mao in China.
4. The Secret Speech led to the crisis in **Hungary**, which damaged the image of the USSR internationally. This eroded Khrushchev's position.
5. The failure of the **Virgin Land Policy**, especially in 1963, was critical.
6. The final step was the missile crisis in **Cuba** in 1962. The Red Army and party hard-liners found it extremely humiliating to remove the missiles from Cuba.

In 1964, when Khrushchev was forced to resign, *Pravda* criticised him for being 'hare-brained' and for "*wild schemes, half-baked conclusions and hasty decisions.*"

40. "With the possible exceptions of Khrushchev and Gorbachev, no Russian ruler brought so much relief to so many of his people as did Alexander II, autocratic and conservative." To what extent do you agree with this statement concerning Khrushchev made by the historian J N Westwood?

(Show arguments supporting the view that he brought relief and arguments against.)

Yes, he brought relief:

1. The initial policies 1953–55 during the collective leadership: **Korea, Austria, Geneva**.
2. **The thaw** from 1955; in nine months, after the Party Congress in 1956, 617,000 prisoners in the Gulag system were allowed to leave the prison camp system.
3. **The Secret Speech**. When Volkogonov concludes that Stalin was responsible for the killing of 21 million of his subjects, the effects of this speech on the victims must have been enormous, and difficult to explain in all aspects. Stalin's crimes were revealed and someone was held accountable. Stalin's responsibility cannot be denied. The very fact that the terror ended with Stalin's death in 1953 supports this view. The Secret Speech also gave hope of more independence to the satellites (a hope which proved to be unfulfilled).
4. The idea of **peaceful co-existence** was an important signal in an era when hydrogen bombs had been produced.
5. **Industrial growth** was impressive during Khrushchev's rule. The impact of sending the first man into space cannot be ignored. This was the high point of the USSR.
6. It must be emphasised that with Khrushchev, Stalinism was brought to an end. When Beria, former head of the NKVD and partly responsible for the terror during the purges, was executed just after Stalin had passed away, it marks and end and a new era in the history of the USSR. Politicians and others were no longer executed without reason. Khrushchev was a hard-liner in many aspects but **he brought the terror to an end**.

No, he did not bring relief:

1. Khrushchev was responsible for crushing the **Hungarian revolt**, which killed thousands. Imre Nagy was even executed. He made it very clear to the satellites in Eastern Europe that no real independence was expected.
2. Even though he was talking about peaceful co-existence, he was expanding Soviet interests in **the Middle East and Latin America**. Khrushchev was the first leader to arm allies that were not bordering the Soviet Union.
3. Agricultural production did not improve during his rule. The failure of the **Virgin Land Project** forced the USSR to import grains to avoid famine.
4. With the **Berlin Wall**, Germany was divided and families were prevented from seeing each other.
5. **The Cuban Missile Crisis** is normally considered the most dangerous nuclear crisis that the world has ever seen. Khrushchev was definitely responsible for part of this. It was his idea to secretly deploy nuclear weapons close to Florida, which put the American president in a very difficult situation. Even though he finally agreed to withdraw the missiles, he must be seen as partly responsible for creating the crisis.

Conclusion: It is very easy to find pros and cons here, but taking into account Stalin's policies, it must be concluded that with Khrushchev the USSR entered into a new era. (But if you read about Khrushchev's career, before the war, during the war, and after, it is clear that this man was personally responsible for the killing of hundreds of thousands of people.)

19. KHRUSHCHEV

41. "It is unjustified to see Khrushchev as a 'Cold Warrior'." To what extent do you agree with this statement?

(Write one part where you argue that it was unjustified and a second part showing that he deserves to be called a 'Cold Warrior'.)

Yes, it is unjustified:

1. He took many initiatives like accepting the independence of **Austria in 1955, the armistice in Korea, the visit to Yugoslavia in 1955 accepting 'national communism', withdrawal of troops from Finland in 1955, dissolving Cominform in 1956**, showing signs of détente.
2. In the **Secret Speech** from 1956 Khrushchev showed political braveness by challenging orthodox Stalinism in several ways. He indicated that there could be a liberalisation of policies towards the satellites. He also showed that he believed in **peaceful co-existence** with the capitalist West, which was a clear rejection of orthodox Marxist-Leninism.
3. He accepted a form of liberalisation in **Poland** in 1956.
4. Hungary will be the main point in the 'no' part below, but you can argue that the Hungarians went too far demanding a multi-party system and to leave the Warsaw Pact. It would lead to a 'domino effect' in Eastern Europe and leave Khrushchev with no alternative if he wanted to survive politically. One can understand why he acted but not to justify all the violence.
5. He never really pressed his point over Berlin. After all, the erection of the Berlin Wall did not lead to a war over Berlin.
6. **The Cuban Missile Crisis** is probably the second point against him. He can be defended by arguing that he wanted to defend the Cuban revolution, by doing only the same thing that the Americans had done in Turkey. It was Khrushchev who gave in and accepted a portrayal as a 'loser', to preserve peace.
7. It is worth emphasising that he didn't allow the transfer of Soviet **nuclear technology to Mao** in China. The reason was probably that he didn't trust Mao to handle these weapons with care. Khrushchev had to pay a high political price for this refusal as it is one of the main reasons for the Sino-Soviet split.
8. He made substantial **reductions to the Russian Red Army** for which he paid a high political price
9. After the missiles crisis in 1962 the USSR signed both the **Test Ban Treaty** and accepted setting up a **Hotline**, to improve communications.

No, he deserves the reputation as a Cold Warrior:

1. We cannot ignore the fact that he was responsible for crushing the **Hungarian uprising** which led to the killing of 30,000 Hungarians. Nagy was also executed. If we compare him to Gorbachev, the latter allowed a peaceful transformation of the satellites and respected the will of the populations in the satellites. Khrushchev did not.
2. Khrushchev was adventurous. In 1955 the Czechs made an **arms deal with Egypt.** This couldn't be done without an approval from Moscow. Khrushchev was the first leader to arm allies that were not bordering the Soviet Union.
3. In the late 1950s, Khrushchev announced that he believed that the ultimate victory of communism would be achieved through '**national-liberation wars**' in the Third World and that he would support such wars wholeheartedly and without reservation. It was a dangerous escalation of the Cold War. It would lead to engagements in Vietnam and Cuba.

4. Khrushchev was the aggressor over **Berlin** in 1958 with his first ultimatum. He issued a second ultimatum in Vienna 1961, and was behind the erection of the Berlin Wall later in 1961.

5. The world has never been closer to a nuclear war as during the **Cuban Missile Crisis** in 1962. He should have been aware of the danger by secretly placing missiles in Cuba and he must therefore be held partly responsible for this crisis.

Conclusion: It is possible to argue the he was a typical representative for this time: He played both the détente and confrontation games.

Chapter 20: The fall of communism in the USSR

Issues

How shall we explain the fall of communism in the USSR? Was it due to internal or external factors? And how important was Mikhail Gorbachev in this process?

20.1 Soviet problems in the early 1980s

The situation in the USSR in the early 1980s was complicated due to many internal problems. In 1982, the ageing leader **Leonid Brezhnev** died and was succeeded by **Yuriy Andropov**. Brezhnev had not realised the need for reforms and of reducing defence spending. Andropov had serious health problems and was under medical treatment for most of his time in power. When Andropov passed away after only two years he was succeeded by another veteran, **Konstantin Chernenko**, a man known for being without qualities. Chernenko passed away after only one year in power in March 1985. When Gorbachev was elected General Secretary in 1985 there were many problems to solve:

- The economic growth of the Soviet economy had been slowing down since the late 1950s.
- Soviet authorities had indicated that the military spending was around 20%. In the spring of 1987 it was announced that the real cost was 40% of the state budget. The US spent 4–6%.
- The gap between the GNP of USSR and the US was growing steadily and had been doing so since 1958.
- Infant mortality was rising, the birth rate was declining and average male life expectancy had gone down from 66 years in the 1960s, to only 60 in 1986.
- Revenues from the oil industry were going down.
- In Poland the situation was tense with the challenge from a trade union called Solidarity.
- The war in Afghanistan did not go well and discredited the USSR in the Third World and in the Middle East.
- China was still challenging the USSR as an alternative leader of the socialist camp.
- Reagan was following a policy of 'systematic challenge' towards the 'evil empire' and his 'Star Wars' project worried leaders in the Kremlin.

GNP growth had been around **10% annually in the 1950s**. It was **7% in the 1960s** and fell to **5% in the 1970s**. In the **early 1980s the growth was around 3%**. It was **negative during the later Gorbachev era** (−15% in 1991).

20.2 Gorbachev and the fall of communism

Mikhail Gorbachev was elected General Secretary at the age of 54 after Chernenko passed away in March 1985. He was the youngest member of the politburo and the first Soviet leader to be born in the Soviet Union and not in Tsarist Russia. Old hard-liners and former Stalinists like Brezhnev, Andropov, and Chernenko had now been replaced by an open-minded optimist and reformer.

Gorbachev introduced a number of breathtaking reforms both domestically and internationally. He described it as *"a complete renewal of all aspects of Soviet life, economic, social, political and moral"*. It must be noticed that Gorbachev initially was a Leninist who made attempts to reform the system in order that it should survive.

Gorbachev's plan for reconstruction comprised two main points:

1. co-operation with the west to end the Cold War in order to reduce the costs of the arms race;
2. a reconstruction of the Soviet empire. The key words were:
   - *glasnost* ('openness'),
   - *perestroika* ('restructuring'), and
   - *demokratizatsiya* ('democratisation').

THE GORBACHEV ERA: MAIN EVENTS

1985 Gorbachev made his first visit to the West – France – as Soviet leader. He proposed that the superpowers should reduce their strategic weapons by 50%. Gorbachev and Reagan met annually in four different summits. The first took place in **Geneva** in 1985. No major agreements were made except for the fact that they agreed to meet again. There had been no summits for five years so the meeting was important in establishing personal relations.

In 1985, Saudi Arabia increased their oil production fourfold, and as a result **oil prices collapsed**. The USSR lost $20 billion per year. According to Yegor Gaidar, Prime Minister of Russia, after the collapse of the USSR, Gorbachev disregarded the problem and started to **borrow money from abroad**. In 1989 when the economy stalled completely, the USSR had to negotiate with Western powers to get new money. It is also worth noting that in 1985 Gorbachev introduced an anti-alcohol campaign, which was wise perhaps from a health perspective, but this together with the collapse of the oil prices, **eroded the tax base** of the country.

1986 Gorbachev announced at the 27th Party Congress that he believed that far-reaching economic reforms were needed and that the war in Afghanistan was a 'bleeding wound'. The price control system in this planned economy should be relaxed and decision-making should be decentralised. A nuclear reactor in **Chernobyl** exploded during that year. It not only resulted in enormous costs for the government, it also revealed many of the weaknesses in the Soviet system. The government first denied the accident and denounced it as a creation of Western media. It convinced Gorbachev that far-reaching reforms were needed. There had been no serious debate over the danger of nuclear power and Gorbachev saw it as a symptom of the stagnation in Soviet society.

After six years of internal exile in Gorky, the famous scientist and dissident Andrei **Sakharov** was invited to return to Moscow by Gorbachev in December 1986. It signalled a new era.

The second summit meeting between Gorbachev and Reagan in **Reykjavik**, Iceland, was an astonishing conference. Gorbachev announced that he was prepared to **withdraw** his **SS-20 missiles** from Europe if the US withdrew their Pershing and cruise missiles – an acceptance of Reagan's 'zero-option' solution. This had until now been rejected by the USSR.

20. THE FALL OF COMMUNISM IN THE USSR

He also proposed a **50% reduction of all long-range missiles**. In return Gorbachev wanted the Americans to call off the Star Wars Project (**SDI**) but Reagan refused to abandon his project. Gorbachev then shocked the Americans by proposing **the abolition of all nuclear weapons** within ten years. Reagan's commitment to the SDI resulted in no agreement being made.

1987   The Washington Treaty (or **INF Treaty**) was signed. All land-based missiles in Europe and Asia, with a range of between 500 to 5500 kilometres were to be destroyed within three years.

1988   In May 1988 the **Law on Co-operatives** was enacted. It was perhaps the most radical reform of the Gorbachev era in terms of the economy. For the first time since **Lenin's New Economic Policy**, the law permitted private ownership of businesses in the service, manufacturing, and foreign-trade sectors.

The same year, an agreement on ending the war in Afghanistan between the superpowers was made in Geneva. Later this year Gorbachev announced that Soviet armed forces should be **reduced by 500,000 soldiers**, without any demands on US reductions (a unilateral reduction). He also announced a gradual withdrawal of troops from the GDR (East Germany), Czechoslovakia and Hungary. Gorbachev announced that the USSR would no longer interfere in the internal affairs of the satellites, i.e. the **Brezhnev Doctrine was dead**.

1989   Elections in the USSR to a new supreme legislative body called the Congress of People's Deputies. Contested elections were introduced resulting in **non-communists being able to be elected**. The majority was, however, still in the hands of the Communist Party. The dissident **Andrei Sakharov** was elected and he criticised the Communist Party when meetings in the Congress were broadcast on television. It had an enormous impact in the USSR.

In early 1989 round-table talks in Poland led to free elections being scheduled to June the same year. In May, Hungary announced that the Iron Curtain would be opened. It was a test of Gorbachev's willingness to abandon the Brezhnev Doctrine. This year communist rule was brought to an end in the satellites Poland, Hungary, GDR, Bulgaria and Romania, without the USSR intervening. The withdrawal of Soviet troops from Afghanistan was completed. The Cold War had been brought to an end.

'Gorbymania', enthusiasm for Gorbachev, swept around the world but in the USSR communist hard-liners saw it as a betrayal of the Soviet Union and the sacrifices its people had made during WWII.

1990   Gorbachev was elected to a new office: president of the USSR. To Gorbachev this was a way of creating his own political platform independent of the Communist Party. In March, the Congress had removed article 6 in the constitution i.e. the Communist Party no longer had a political monopoly. The economy was now in a critical situation. The GNP went down by 4% in 1990 and 15% in 1991. There were severe shortages of basic food supplies such as meat and sugar. Communist hard-liners were criticising Gorbachev *and* nationalism in the Baltic States and Georgia posed an enormous problem to Gorbachev who had committed himself to democratic solutions. In the Congress of People's Deputies, Yeltsin had been offered a new platform criticising the president. Gorbachev's solution to the mounting nationalist problems was a new Union Treaty giving the republics within the Soviet Union far more autonomy. But it didn't seem to satisfy some republics and by the end of the year many hard-liners were given key positions in the Soviet government. Due to this the foreign minister **Eduard Shevardnadze** resigned dramatically in December claiming that 'Dictatorship is coming'.

1991   January: local branches of the **KGB** and armed forces worked together to seize the TV tower in Vilnius in Lithuania, most likely without Gorbachev knowing. 14 civilians were killed. This disastrous clash made a new Union Treaty even more important to Gorbachev.

It is important to realise the *significance of these reforms* or policies in a country, which had gone through a 70-year single party communist dictatorship. It should also be noted that it is somewhere here that Gorbachev's reforms are beginning to spin out of control. The economy, in particular with an eroded tax base, led to enormous problems. Salaries that cannot be paid or lack of commodities will deprive any leader of popular support.

HISTORY HL: EUROPE

Boris Yeltsin was elected president of Russia in June 1991 and the question of Russia's willingness to sign a new Union Treaty became a key question. Without Russian membership in the union, the Soviet Union was dead.

In August, just before a new Union Treaty was to be signed, communist hard-liners made an attempted coup. Yeltsin took the leadership in Moscow against the coup, and it collapsed.

The coup was seen as a collapse of the old system and Gorbachev, to some extent, was perceived as a part of it. Yeltsin's authority gained from the coup, while Gorbachev was more or less in the hands of the Russian president.

In December the leaders from Russia, Ukraine and Belarus declared that the **USSR no longer existed** and founded the **Commonwealth of Independent States** (CIS). Later the same month it was extended and eleven former republics joined the CIS.

On **25 December, Gorbachev had to resign**. Without a Soviet Union, Gorbachev had no political platform. On 31 December the USSR formally ceased to exist. Yeltsin was the new leader in Russia.

20.3 Why did Soviet communism collapse?

A. External pressure:

1. **Military reasons**

- It is interesting to notice that the stagnation of the Soviet economy goes back to the 1960s. In 1958, the difference between the US and Soviet GNP was at its narrowest and after that the gap constantly grew wider. This was the time when the 'space race' and the development of intercontinental ballistic missiles started. As a result of the Cuban Missile Crisis, the Soviets decided to **close the missile gap**. The costs were astronomical: Soviet authorities had indicated that military spending was around 20%. In the spring of 1987 Gorbachev announced that the real cost was **40% of the state budget**. The US spent 4–6%.

- The critical question to be asked is if we shall see this cost as a result of external pressure, i.e. an adequate response to pressure from the US, *or* as an inadequate response to a situation where communist leaders (raised in a system preaching the message of an inevitable clash with the capitalist world) ignored all sense of reality. If the latter, it's not external pressure.

- In the 1970s, the USSR had to keep 44 army divisions on the Chinese border, due to the Sino-Soviet split, and they only had 31 divisions in Europe.

- The annual cost for supporting Cuba, Vietnam, Ethiopia, and Afghanistan alone was estimated to be USD 40 billion. The USSR suffered from a 'global over-stretching'. The war in **Afghanistan** was of major importance. Eduard Shevardnadze, Gorbachev's foreign minister, said: *"The decision to leave Afghanistan was the first and most difficult step. Everything else flowed from that"*. The war in Afghanistan also made it impossible to take action against Solidarity in Poland.

- But it is important to emphasise that during the Gorbachev years, we cannot find evidence for a substantial military build-up as a response to Reagan's policies, i.e. military spending did not cause a sudden collapse.

Martin McCauley writes: *"It [the USSR] had to devote about two-thirds of its scientists and about one-third of its economy to its military efforts"*. It is not likely that any state can afford this.

20. THE FALL OF COMMUNISM IN THE USSR

2. **Nationalism**

   Glasnost (openness) soon led to the abolition of censorship. It became evident that the republics within the **Soviet Union and the satellites in Eastern Europe** were not satisfied with decentralised power and democracy without independence. They wanted real independence. Freedom of speech released decades of bitterness over Stalin's repression and terror. In 1988, Gorbachev abandoned the **Brezhnev Doctrine** and allowed the satellites to determine their own internal affairs. Nationalist feelings led to Soviet control of Eastern Europe coming to an end in the autumn of 1989. It also led to a number of republics within the Soviet Union becoming independent states.

3. **Influences from the outside world weakening the Soviet system**

   The Soviet empire was influenced from the outside in different ways.

   - The Russian population was attracted by Western habits and **consumer goods** which contrasted with the shortages and the queues in the Soviet Union. The Soviet system in the 1980s was eroded by Western influence and consumer goods just as the Tsarist system had once been eroded by liberal and socialist ideas.
   - There were spiritual influences like **Pope John Paul II** among Catholics in Eastern Europe and especially in Poland. When he visited Krakow in 1979, 2-3 million Poles were there to welcome him. John Lewis Gaddis writes that *"he began a process by which communism...would come to an end"*.
   - The influence of **Islam** became important in Soviet republics in Central Asia especially when the conflict in Afghanistan started. The Iranian revolution brought Khomeini to power in 1978-79 and even though there were different schools of thought in Islam, both the revolution in Iran and the war in Afghanistan were fertile grounds for radical Islamist groups, gaining more support in Central Asia.

4. **The price of oil collapsed**

   In December 1985, Saudi Arabia decided to alter its oil policy drastically. In six months, oil production in Saudi Arabia increased fourfold which led to a collapse of oil prices. The Soviet Union lost $20 billion per year. The reason for the new policy was that the Saudis feared that the Soviet invasion of Afghanistan was a first step in gaining control of the oil fields in the Middle East. The historian Richard Pipes, an advisor to President Reagan in the 1980s, has claimed that the US did what they could to keep oil prices low as a part of their policy of weakening the Soviet Union. The leaders in the USSR now faced a difficult problem because oil money was needed to pay for imports of grain to the USSR.

5. **Solidarity in Poland**

   In 1980, the Polish regime recognised that a union, not controlled by the government, could exist as a legal entity. Ten million Poles joined this union, **Solidarity**. It soon led to Solidarity challenging the regime politically and in December 1981 the Polish government decided to introduce martial laws and ban Solidarity. An independent union organising millions of workers was sensational and posed a major challenge to the whole Eastern Bloc. The war in Afghanistan made it impossible for the Soviet army to intervene. Suslov, a leading member in the politburo, said *"We simply cannot afford another Afghanistan"*. When Gorbachev introduced his reforms it affected the satellites in Eastern Europe. In 1988, there were massive strikes in Poland and the government made an agreement with Solidarity to end the strikes and to sit down in round-table talks. In February 1989, a decision was made to allow free elections in Poland. In the elections in June, Solidarity won 99 out of 100 seats in the Senate and Poland got a non-communist Prime Minister. Solidarity played a major role in breaking down communist control in the Eastern Bloc.

HISTORY HL: EUROPE

6. **Growing economies in the developing world undermined Lenin's ideas about imperialism**

Developments in the Third World further eroded support for the Soviet system. Countries that accepted Western investments and market economy had the fastest growing economies while countries with a socialist orientation were facing serious economic problems. Lenin's ideas about colonialism and imperialism were abandoned by economists even in the USSR.

B. Was the collapse of the Soviet system due to internal reasons?

1. **Planned economy did not generate growth**

Was the collapse due to the economic system of the USSR, i.e. a **planned economy**? A planned economy means that a large proportion of the economy is owned and controlled by the state. Thousands of state planners or bureaucrats decided what to produce, when it should be produced, and at what price. It has been described as a rigid command economy. In 1990, the USSR had one of its greatest grain harvests ever, but 40% of the harvest rotted or was eaten by insects. The same problems existed within the industrial sector. The *nomenklatura*, **the old elite**, obstructed systematic reforms and new initiatives. Richard Crockatt writes: *"a rigidity inherent in its ideology and institutions rendered it incapable of adaptability to change"*. McCauley concludes that *"only a market economy generates rising prosperity over decades"*.

2. **Gorbachev made mistakes**

Most historians agree that the reforms opened a floodgate, especially *glasnost*, which led to a collapse. Did he reform this iron-system too much too soon? Crockatt writes: *"Once given rein, the direction of the newly released force of public opinion could not necessarily be controlled"*.

(a) The economy was transformed

The **Law on Co-operatives** in 1987 permitted private ownership of businesses in the service, manufacturing and foreign trade sectors. Workers were allowed to leave collective farms. Between 1985 and 1988 13,000 producing co-operatives were formed and 300,000 family-owned businesses. 50% of the service sector was suddenly in private hands.

The **Enterprise Law** transferred decision making from the central ministries to the enterprises. Managers in state owned companies were now given much more power.

The **Law on Joint Ventures** allowed foreign ownership of companies and Crockatt describes the effects as 'explosive'.

Goldman argues *"shock therapy might have worked in a country where there were producers ready and waiting for the optimum market conditions"*. When Gorbachev now reformed from above; there was no effective system for capital investment, credit, fiscal, and monetary controls, i.e. institutions and administration necessary to organise a market economy.

(b) Political changes

In 1988, Gorbachev announced in the UN that every nation had the right to choose its own government, i.e. a **rejection of the Brezhnev Doctrine**. It didn't take long until both republics within the USSR, like the Baltic States, and the satellites in Eastern Europe demanded real independence: Crockatt writes: *"Nationalism within the Soviet republics could hardly have been given voice had it not been for glasnost"*. There were 15 republics and more than 120 ethnic groups within the USSR and Gorbachev assumed that they would remain loyal if they were offered democracy. In late 1989, communism collapsed in Eastern Europe and the impression was that it had Gorbachev's tacit support.

20. THE FALL OF COMMUNISM IN THE USSR

(c) Poor timing

The liberalisation coincided with an economic crisis where state incomes from reducing production of alcohol went down due, to Gorbachev's policies and, even more important, there was a fall in world **oil prices**. So the political reform programme was introduced in a severe economic crisis. If Lenin had once 'timed' the October Revolution, Gorbachev did not time the right moment for this drastic transformation.

	1986	1987	1988	1989	1990	1991
Soviet economic growth (%)	2.3	1.6	4.4	2.4	−4.0	−15.0

Gorbachev writes in his memoirs: *"I thought we had a system that could be improved. Instead I learned that we had a system that needed to be replaced"*. It is, however, possible to argue that the collapse of the Soviet system, and thus the end of the Cold War, was due to both external and internal factors.

(d) The conflict with Yeltsin

Yeltsin and Gorbachev were enemies ever since Yeltsin had been dismissed from the politburo in 1987. **The Congress of People's Deputies offered him an unexpected opportunity to come back**. In 1991 when he was elected **president** of Russia, he became a driving force in the process of **keeping Russia out of the union**. Without Russia there could be no Soviet Union. When finally the CIS was formed, the USSR ceased to exist and this deprived Gorbachev his platform. Is it possible to argue that animosity between two leaders might cause the fall of an empire? Margaret Thatcher writes: *"If the two of them had been able to sink their differences [...] the reforms might have been renewed"*. Yeltsin writes: *"But why hide it – the motivations for many of my actions were embedded in our conflict, which had arisen in earnest just prior to the central committee plenum in 1987 that led to my being ousted from the politburo"*.

Historiography and analysis

Many historians emphasise that the collapse of the Soviet system was due to an **internal collapse**. P M H Bell writes *"The essential point still seems to be that they contributed to a drama which started **within** the Soviet Union"*. Dobrynin, the Soviet Ambassador in Washington, concludes: *"The fate of the Soviet Union was decided inside our country"*. Shevardnadze, the Foreign Minister, agrees and points out that Soviet Russia had once survived WW II. *"Neither Hitler or Reagan could do it,"* he said, talking about breaking up the Soviet Union from the outside.

The *key* issue is to determine to what extent this internal collapse was affected by **external factors**. You will find a wide range of explanations. Kennan, the father of Truman's containment policy in 1947, writes: *"The suggestion that any Administration had the power to influence decisively the course of a tremendous domestic political upheaval in another great country on the other side of the globe is **simply childish**"* and that the *"Republican Party leadership won the Cold War is intrinsically silly"*. The historian Richard Pipes, also an adviser to Reagan, found the statement astonishing and quoted Kennan's famous 'Mr. X' article from *Foreign Affairs*, July 1947: *"it is entirely possible for the US to influence by its actions the international development, both within Russia, and throughout the international Communist movement"*. The idea behind Kennan's containment policy had once been based on the assumption that containment would *"encourage an internal implosion in the Soviet Union"*. Those supporting the view of the importance of external pressure, emphasise the importance of Reagan's 'systematic challenge'. But there are few historians who explicitly claim that it was Reagan who made the Soviet system collapse. Gaddis writes: *"hanging tough paid off"*.

Crockatt writes: *"The Soviet economy was not on the point of collapse when Gorbachev came to power. The catastrophic decline in the late 1980s was a direct result of Gorbachev's policies"*. But he makes a further distinction between 'failures of the system' and Gorbachev's policies.

Hence, he is making a distinction between the two main points if we want to discuss 'internal reasons': "[…] *the collapse* [as a result of Gorbachev's policies] *would not have taken place had not serious structural weaknesses existed"*. Gorbachev wanted to save socialism but would not use force to do so. Gaddis concludes that he could not achieve one without abandoning the other and that his goals were incompatible, hence Gorbachev made important mistakes.

It is, however, possible to find a **combination** of these two interpretations. External pressure affected the USSR but there were also problems within the empire, which led to the collapse. McCauley concludes that *"monocausal answers are no longer acceptable"*. Bell believes that internal factors were more important than external factors, but he accepts that both are of importance: *"…the Soviet Union collapsed primarily through **internal failures**, exacerbated but not created by **external pressure**"*.

42. To what extent did external pressure lead to the collapse of the Soviet system?

(Compare the importance of external and internal factors. This is a key issue among historians.)

Yes, external pressure made the Soviet Union collapse:

1. Write about the Soviet attempts to close the missile gap from the early 1960s and link it to the stagnation of the Soviet economy.
2. Write about the size of the GNP in the Soviet Union compared to the GNP of the US and its allies.
3. Write that a large proportion of GNP was used for military reasons. It is a strong argument to claim that this must have affected the Soviet economy in a negative way. (But we must really ask if the 40% from the state budget that was used on military spending was due to a real external threat or if it in fact reflected mentalities of the Soviet leadership?)
4. Write about Reagan's systematic challenge and his SDI project which put additional strains on the Soviet economy. But it is important to emphasise that from a short-term perspective, i.e. the Gorbachev years, we cannot find evidence for a substantial military build-up as a response to Reagan's policies, so military spending did not cause a sudden collapse.
5. The Sino-Soviet split forced the Soviet Union to use a large proportion of its army to guard the border with China.
6. The war in Afghanistan was a military, political, and economic disaster.
7. The impact of Western consumption, and spiritual influences from the new Polish Pope and Islam in Central Asia, eroded support for the Soviet regime.
8. Strong nationalist feelings in the satellites challenged Soviet authority. In Poland the Solidarity movement challenged Soviet authority.

No, internal reasons led to the collapse:

1. Write about the Soviet command economy which didn't generate growth comparable to the growth of the market economies. The *nomenklatura* also obstructed a modernisation of the Soviet system.
2. Brezhnev ignored the need for reforms in the 1970s.
3. Repressive policies from the regime had alienated a large proportion of the population. This was especially important in the Baltic Republics where many people wanted independence.
4. Gorbachev reformed too much too soon. It was difficult, if not impossible, to allow freedom of speech, market economy and free elections in a society without any

20. THE FALL OF COMMUNISM IN THE USSR

democratic tradition. He opened a floodgate of reforms in a situation where there was strong external pressure and where oil prices had more or less collapsed. He was tested in many areas. Let's look at one to exemplify his problems: how do you combine *glasnost* (openness), Baltic nationalism and Gorbachev's desire to strengthen the Soviet system? Gorbachev's détente also led to the USSR being deprived of its 'outside enemy'. This outside enemy had partly united the country and justified economic hardship. The enemy had now disappeared but the economy collapsed. Few understood this.

5. There was a lot of nationalism in Soviet republics.

Conclusion: There is no definite answer but it is possible to support a combination between internal and external factors. Gorbachev's policies were probably very important.

43. Examine whether Gorbachev was responsible for the collapse of the Soviet system?

(Show the mistakes made by Gorbachev and all other causes and try to write a balanced argument discussing the issue.)

Yes, Gorbachev was responsible:

In 1985, Gorbachev became General Secretary of the Communist Party, the leader of the USSR. For seventy years the Communist Party had organised a rigid system where freedom of speech, the right to organise political parties, etc. had not existed. It was also a planned economy so private enterprise was not allowed. Within a couple of years he had made several fundamental changes:

- In 1986, foreign policy versus the capitalists was fundamentally changed. Genuine co-operation and **coexistence** with the capitalist states was desirable. For years the 'outside enemy' had been a justification for economic hardship.
- In 1988, **censorship** and the **Brezhnev Doctrine** were abolished. In the same year **private enterprises** were allowed.
- In 1989 there were elections to the **Congress of People's Deputies** where voters were allowed to cross out names of candidates. 20% of the delegates were not elected. It was a significant step towards free elections in the USSR. Non-communists were elected like the dissident Andrei Sakharov and he criticised the Communist Party when meetings in the Congress were broadcast on television. It had an enormous impact in the USSR. In Eastern Europe, the communist regimes collapsed with tacit support from Gorbachev. **Hungary and Poland were the first to allow free elections**, which gave power to non-communist parties.
- In 1990, the directing role of the Communist Party was brought to an end by a change in the constitution.
- Far reaching **economic reforms** were introduced in 1987 and 1988 which contributed to the collapse.
- Glasnost opened a floodgate – mistakes made by the party in the past were exposed.

Gorbachev allowed free debate, private companies, ended the Communist Party's monopoly of power, the satellites to choose their own governments and made peace with the outside enemy – after 70 years of iron rule. It was probably almost beyond imagination to most Soviet citizens. The difficulties were expected: the *nomenklatura* didn't want to co-operate in the destruction of their power. Nationalism was strong in many republics and in the satellites. It can be argued that it was too much too soon and that Gorbachev must bear responsibility for the collapse.

Crockatt writes that the Soviet economy was not on the point of collapse when Gorbachev came to power and that the decline in the late 1980s was a direct result of Gorbachev's policies.

No, it was not Gorbachev who caused the collapse:

- The Soviet system was doomed even without Gorbachev. Evidence for this is the stagnation of the economy which can be traced back to the 1960s.
- No genuine attempts to reform the economy were made during the Brezhnev years.
- The basic problem was that the planned economy didn't generate sufficient growth over a longer period.
- This internal weakness was exacerbated by external pressure (military expenditure, nationalism, the war in Afghanistan, Solidarity in Poland and Reagan's systematic challenge).
- Repressive policies had alienated large proportions of the population. Support for the regime had also been eroded by the impact of Western consumption and spiritual influences from the Catholic Pope and Islam. This was a long process for which we can't blame Gorbachev.
- Oil prices collapsed in 1985 resulting in export incomes going down drastically.

Conclusion: The problems which Gorbachev faced were to some extent caused by long-term events and the fact that the system had been suffering from internal weaknesses for a long time. Gorbachev's attempts to reform this system resulted in additional problems and contributed to the collapse because he had unleashed forces he couldn't control.

Essay title to a 'to what extent', i.e. 'either/or question':
Introductory points:
First main part:
Second main part:
Conclusion:

Essay title to a 'list' question:
Introductory points:
Main part:
Conclusion: